Sexuality in the Middle East and North Africa

Gender, Culture, and Politics in the Middle East
miriam cooke, Simona Sharoni, and Suad Joseph, *Series Editors*

Select Titles in Gender, Culture, and Politics in the Middle East

The Best of Hard Times: Palestinian Refugee Masculinities in Lebanon
Gustavo Barbosa

The Funambulists: Women Poets of the Arab Diaspora
Lisa Marchi

The Hammam through Time and Space
Julie Peteet

Iranian Women and Gender in the Iran-Iraq War
Mateo Mohammad Farzaneh

Istanbul Appearances: Beauty and the Making of Middle-Class Femininities in Urban Turkey
Claudia Liebelt

Quest for Love in Central Morocco: Young Women and the Dynamics of Intimate Lives
Laura Menin

Sumud: Birth, Oral History, and Persisting in Palestine
Livia Wick

Unveiling Men: Modern Masculinities in Twentieth-Century Iran
Wendy DeSouza

For a full list of titles in this series, visit https://press.syr.edu/supressbook-series/gender-culture-and-politics-in-the-middle-east/.

SEXUALITY

in the Middle East and North Africa

Contemporary Issues and Challenges

Edited by J. Michael Ryan and Helen Rizzo

Syracuse University Press

This book will be made open access within three years of publication thanks to Path to Open, a program developed in partnership between JSTOR, the American Council of Learned Societies (ACLS), University of Michigan Press, and The University of North Carolina Press to bring about equitable access and impact for the entire scholarly community, including authors, researchers, libraries, and university presses around the world. Learn more at https://about.jstor.org/path-to-open/.

First Edition 2024

24 25 26 27 28 29 6 5 4 3 2 1

∞ The paper used in this publication meets the minimum requirements of the American National Standard for Information Sciences—Permanence of Paper for Printed Library Materials, ANSI Z39.48-1992.

For a listing of books published and distributed by Syracuse University Press, visit https://press.syr.edu.

ISBN: 9780815604860 (hardcover)
9780815604907 (paperback)
9780815657248 (e-book)

Library of Congress Cataloging-in-Publication Data

Names: Ryan, J. Michael, editor. | Rizzo, Helen Mary, editor.
Title: Sexuality in the Middle East and North Africa : contemporary issues and challenges / edited by J. Michael Ryan & Helen Rizzo.
Description: First edition. | Syracuse, New York : Syracuse University Press, 2024. | Series: Gender, culture, and politics in the Middle East | Includes bibliographical references and index.
Identifiers: LCCN 2024016068 (print) | LCCN 2024016069 (ebook) | ISBN 9780815604907 (paperback) | ISBN 9780815604860 (hardback) | ISBN 9780815657248 (ebook)
Subjects: LCSH: Sex—Middle East. | Sex—Africa, North. | Sexual orientation—Middle East. | Sexual orientation—Africa, North.
Classification: LCC HQ16 .S4739 2024 (print) | LCC HQ16 (ebook) | DDC 306.70956—dc23/eng/20240716
LC record available at https://lccn.loc.gov/2024016068
LC ebook record available at https://lccn.loc.gov/2024016069

Manufactured in the United States of America

Contents

Sexuality in the Middle East and North Africa

Sexuality in the Middle East and North Africa

Contemporary Issues and Challenges

J. Michael Ryan and Helen Rizzo

The region of the Middle East and North Africa (MENA) has been a growing field of interest for many in the fields of sociology, anthropology, political science, international relations, and many others as well as in the general public.[1] The near-constant military incursions, the challenges to democratization, the threat of regional extremist groups (al-Qaeda, ISIS), the rise of regional cities to a level of global prominence (Dubai, Abu Dhabi, Doha), the increased funding for international projects coming from the region (most notably from Qatar and the Emirates), and the increasing presence/"concern" over Muslims in the rest of the world are just a few of the reasons why interest in this region has been growing in recent years.

Part of this growing interest in the region has been in the field of sexuality studies. As globalization, oil dependency, international tourism, political turmoil, and military conflict continue to make the MENA region increasingly interconnected with the rest of the world, changes to

1. For the purposes of this volume, we define the Middle East and North Africa as including the countries of Algeria, Bahrain, Djibouti, Egypt, Israel, Iran, Iraq, Jordan, Kuwait, Lebanon, Libya, Morocco, Oman, Palestine, Qatar, Saudi Arabia, Syria, Tunisia, Turkey, United Arab Emirates, and Yemen. All the contributions in this volume deal with some subset of these countries depending on the relevance of the countries to their topics.

how sexuality is understood in the region seem to be happening at accelerated rates, which makes continuing critical inquiries into this subject of increasing importance. That said, there are currently still no academic journals that focus exclusively on the issue of sexuality in the MENA region, despite a growing number of journals that include sexuality-related articles (e.g., *Journal of Middle East Women's Studies, British Journal of Middle Eastern Studies*) and other collected volumes that have addressed the topic (e.g., *Deconstructing Sexuality in the Middle East* [Ilkkaracan 2008a] and *Gender in the Middle East and North Africa: Contemporary Issues and Challenges* [Ryan and Rizzo 2020]). There are also other soft signs that scholarship related to sexualities in the MENA region is growing. For example, a simple Google scholar search including the terms *sexuality* and *Middle East* returned 1,570 results for the period 1980–90, 7,330 results for the period 1991–2000, 21,800 results for the period 2001–10, 27,700 results for the period 2011–20, and 18,100 results just for the three-year period of 2021–23.

Issues of sexuality in the region have long served as a lightning rod for international discussions, including those related to sexual harassment, sexual and reproductive health, same-sex relations and identities, the battle between states to control information and the disruptive power of the internet in doing so, and global human rights, among others. Expanding the realm of sexuality studies to include the MENA region more thoroughly is an important—nay, necessary—undertaking. As increasing attention has been paid to nonhegemonic gender and sexual identities around the world, not only academic output but also academic inquiry about the MENA region has lagged behind. Our own troubles in putting together this volume have been reflective of many of the broader problems associated with the initiative to reverse these deficiencies—a relative lack of scholarly output on the subject, a dearth of data from which to draw, and, perhaps most important, a justifiable fear of undertaking such an endeavor. For the moment, sexuality studies in the MENA region remains a dangerous, sometimes deadly, undertaking.

But why is this the case? As the world has witnessed an increasing global shift toward greater acceptance of female sexuality, public discussions and displays of sexuality, and gender and sexual minorities, there has been a simultaneous backlash against extending fundamental human equality toward many of the world's most disadvantaged populations, gender and sexual minorities included. This backlash has arguably been especially pronounced in the MENA region. As a growing number of countries have moved to extend civil equality in various ways—for example, by extending abortion rights, recognizing same-sex marriages, allowing LGBTQ+-identified individuals to openly serve in the armed forces (Yerke 2020), and extending gender recognition beyond the simple male/female binary (Ryan 2018)—other countries have responded by hardening their laws and, more importantly, the enforcement of those laws in criminalizing, imprisoning, and even executing those seen in violation of the local sexuality-related cultural mores. Even raising questions of gender and sexual equality is now increasingly seen as a punishable offense in many countries.

One of the principal issues impeding a more thorough understanding of sexualities in the MENA region is that researchers are often left dealing with social taboos rather than gaining reliable scientific data that reflect lived realities. Sociolegal analysis remains largely possible (though the ambiguity of laws in relation to sexuality should be acknowledged), but survey, ethnographic, and other forms of qualitative data collection are often extremely difficult and can be dangerous. This means that researchers are often forced to rely on individual accounts or to theorize based only on assumptions of what alleged cultural taboos might reflect. The kind of hard data that would normally be considered prudent for scholarship often has to be replaced by armchair speculation, particularly when dealing with issues not recorded in official registers and criminal prosecutions.

Despite these impediments, interest in issues pertaining to sexuality in the MENA region has been increasing in recent years. And much of the more recent research on sexualities is challenging previous Orientalist and exceptionalist views of the region, as evidenced in this volume. Moreover, the Arab Spring arguably awakened a call to justice for many in the region, and the region has since seen an increase in those willing to risk their lives in the pursuit of academic knowledge and political justice. Rather than declare a victor, the Arab Spring in particular seems to have renewed vigor in the battle between those seeking to expand fundamental human rights and those seeking to repress "alternative" identities. As Shereen El Feki has noted, "In recent decades, attitudes in many parts of the Arab region have hardened towards non-conforming sexualities and gender roles, a shift fueled in part by a rise in Islamic conservatism and exploited by authoritarian regimes. While political cultures have proved slow to change in the wake of the 'Arab Spring,' a growing freedom of expression, and increasing activity by civil society, [are] opening space for discreet challenges to sexual taboos in a number of countries, part of wider debates over human rights and personal liberties in the emerging political and social order" (2015, 38).

The objective of this volume is not to advocate for one position or another (although our personal allegiances should be transparent enough, if only given the fact that we have undertaken this endeavor). Rather, its goal is to bring together a collection of scholarship that tackles a variety of issues at the heart of understanding sexuality in the Middle East and North Africa and to do so on a more regional level rather than simply on the level of individual countries. This is not to say that some issues do not lend themselves to a focus on a particular country or set of countries but that the volume's goal is to provide a regional analysis of the topics presented to the greatest extent possible. Simply put, our goal is to add to the growing literature surrounding sexualities in the MENA region and, we hope, to inspire further research. Lives are quite literally on the line, as are religious ideologies, political empowerments, global support networks, and fundamental issues of human rights. For all of these reasons, this volume matters.

What Is Sexuality?

Although the answer to the question of what the term *sexuality* means might seem obvious to many who ask it, we want to take the time to address exactly what we mean when using it. To begin with, *sexuality* (singular) is probably better conceptualized as *sexualities* (plural). The latter more fully captures the idea that sexuality is a complex, multifaceted concept that seeks to do more intellectual labor than perhaps any single term should. Sexuality can address any number of conceptual and practical dimensions—sexual behaviors (physical, bodily acts), sexual attraction (intangible psychic desires), sexual identities (social and political proclamations with far-reaching interactional and legal consequences), and all of the cultural associations and political ramifications of all these dimensions. In short, we can conceive of sexuality as a social system whereby certain social, cultural, political, economic, legal, and other rights, responsibilities, roles, and identities are created, conferred, and enforced. It is a critical organizing principle in many societies. One's sexuality can bar one from gainful employment, housing, and social acceptance; it can dramatically increase the likelihood of becoming a victim of social or state-sponsored violence; and it can cause serious psychological trauma and lack of social integration and acceptance. Sexuality is, in short, one of the fundamental notions of how we live our lives, organize our societies, and exist in the world today.

It is important to emphasize several other aspects about the way we are using the term *sexuality*. First, it is not code for either *sex* or *gender*. Whereas sex has a more biological basis (one has a penis or clitoris, XX or XY chromosomes, ovaries or testicles, or something somewhere in between or beyond any of these characteristics) and gender has a more social aspect (how we dress, the public and private roles we play, and how we are empowered or policed by a series of ever-changing social regulations), sexuality rests somewhere in between the two. One's sexuality (as measured by behavior or attraction or identity) is not determined by one's sex and, despite many common cultural beliefs to the contrary, has no necessary fundamental association with one's gender. Sexuality is a stand-alone entity—albeit one intimately connected with a variety of other social demographics, including sex, gender, race, age, religion, and so on—and must be understood as such.

It is also important to note that we are not using *sexuality* in reference only to gays and lesbians or other sexual minorities. Sexuality is an attribute inherent to all of us (even asexuality is a form of sexuality). It is a critical component of our identities, albeit one that is often overlooked as a taken-for-granted aspect of who we are, particularly by members of the sexual majority. As noted earlier, sexuality is a social system that relies not just on understanding sexual minorities but also on understanding sexual majorities and the various complex dimensions of what the broader concept of sexuality entails.

Moreover, sexuality is regulated by societal institutions. As Michel Foucault (1984) pointed out, regulation of sexuality is often not through repression but rather through continuous discussion and disclosures, which then are controlled by various institutions. In everyday life and through legal and medical institutions specifically, sexuality is controlled by delineating what is seen as "normal" and "pleasurable." Regulations then define and put limits on what is sexually pleasurable and sexually normal in a particular society. State institutions, citizenship, and nationalism also enforce sexual respectability by drawing the line between what is "normal" sexuality and what is "abnormal" sexuality. Depending on the context, respectable sexuality (i.e., "normal") has been limited to heterosexual practices leading to reproduction by promoting marriage, children, and family values, especially for women. "Abnormal" sexuality, again depending on the context, has included premarital sex, extramarital sex, interfaith relationships, interracial/ethnic relationships, relationships between those of different nationalities, masturbation, sex work, and homosexuality. Laws, institutions, nationalist ideologies, and citizenship practices uphold respectability politics (Mikdashi 2014; Puri 2004).

Thus, it should also be noted that using sexuality as a singular framework can be a bit misleading because no single demographic should be considered without an intersectional perspective. One must consider not only sexuality but also race, class, gender, religion, citizenship, geography, family status, age, able-bodiedness, and a variety of other factors in tandem because no single dimension alone can give us any meaningful answers. Thus, although chapters in this volume foreground sexuality, none has done so at the expense of considering other important demographics as well.

Same-Sex Behaviors, Attractions, and Identities in the MENA Region

The terminology we use matters, not only as an issue of semantics but also, more importantly, as an issue of conceptual clarity (Ryan 2019). Many of the terms used to describe sexuality in the MENA region are imported from Western and largely English-based constructs of a particular phenomenon, and so they do not always hold the same clarity in different contexts. The need to use terms familiar to a particular audience combined with the limitations imposed by maintaining conceptual clarity after translation is oftentimes in stark contrast with the kind of specificity needed to more accurately understand what a given phenomenon is and how it operates in a particular context. We must be careful with our language, especially when language is understood as a conveyer of critical social and cultural concepts.

It is important to remember that sexuality can be understood as an issue of attraction, behavior, and/or identity and that how one bases one's understanding of it will greatly affect the ways in which it is tolerated, condemned, accepted, or penalized. Afsaneh Najmabadi has noted that "some scholars have emphasized the utility of the concept of homosexuality. Others have argued that we would be in better tune with the Islamicate cultures' own sensibilities if we focused on sexual practices (2008, 276). Serena Tolino has further argued that "in the Middle East two representations of homosexuality currently coexist: one representation, which is more traditional, approaches homosexuality as an issue of homosexual acts, while the other defines homosexuality as a sexual identity that stresses emotional components" (2014, 86). Tolino goes on to argue that the former understanding, based on homosexual acts, is more in line with conservative, religious approaches, whereas the latter, based on homosexuality as sexual identity, is more in line with activist LGBTQ+ approaches. These competing discourses highlight the need to be cautious when undertaking any reading of sexual minorities in the MENA region and in particular to pay attention to the nuances of representation.

The MENA region is also one where "alternative" genders and sexualities and those who violate their prescribed gender and sexual roles are very often heavily frowned upon and in some cases criminalized. Thus, what qualifies as "alternative" in terms of sexuality is an issue that must be taken as culturally relative but one that still has powerful and almost always negative effects on those who violate the "norm." Homosexuality is a contentious, sometimes even deadly topic in the MENA region. Although a few countries have legalized same-sex activity between consenting adults—including Bahrain, Israel, Jordan, and Turkey—most others punish, often quite harshly, even suspicions of homosexuality. For example, male homosexual activity is punishable by death in Saudi Arabia, the United Arab Emirates, Iran, Iraq, and Qatar, and it is punishable by imprisonment in Egypt, Kuwait, Oman, Morocco, and Syria. Although the laws are enforced to varying degrees, homosexuality remains illegal in most parts of the MENA region.

On May 11, 2001, a tourist boat moored along the Nile in an upscale district of Cairo was raided by the police. The Queen Boat had become a well-known hangout for the local and foreign gay community and had, according to most accounts, been widely overlooked by local authorities until that day. The names and addresses of the fifty-two men who were arrested (since then popularly monikered "the Cairo 52") were later released in the public media. Also notable is that all of the women and foreigners who were present on the boat were let go without charge. The subsequent trials would become international-media fanfare and serve as a lightning rod for calling global attention to the place of sexual minorities in societies across the MENA region.

So why the sudden crackdown on gays in Egypt after decades of turning a blind eye to the issue? Hossam Bahgat (2001) argues that one reason was an attempt by the Egyptian government to distract attention from larger sociopolitical failings, including an economic recession and a liquidity crisis. The crackdown also gave cover for the government to quietly introduce an additional sales tax and impose additional economic actions not favorable to the general population. Nicola Pratt has argued that "the case itself was constituted through a set of assumptions about the essential difference between Egypt and the West with regards to the nature of gender and sexual roles, relations and identities" (2007, 143). In short, it was used as a mechanism to shore up nationalistic ideologies of state security and sovereignty. In both explanations, the theme is that (homo)sexuality as an act or identity was not really at issue but rather that (homo)sexuality was a convenient means by which to start a witch hunt, attempt to impose a common enemy, and distract from the larger sociopolitical motivations of a state that was, by most accounts, failing.

In 2007, President Mahmoud Ahmadinejad of Iran told an audience at Columbia University, "In Iran we don't have homosexuals like in your country. In Iran we don't have this phenomenon." Although Ahmadinejad's media adviser later explained that the president meant Iran has fewer homosexuals compared to the United States, the statement was already made, and the media damage already done. As Pinar Ilkkaracan has noted, Ahmadinejad's statement "was not a statement of personal conviction or manipulation but a political one, reflecting the stand of the majority of Middle Eastern governments on sexual freedoms and rights." Moreover, she argues that in various Middle Eastern as well as some African and Asian countries "homosexuality has increasingly been constructed as a 'Western' practice that is 'imported' from the West, which threatens the social and moral order, although there is extensive evidence of sexual relations between people of the same sex, and of transgender cultures, throughout these countries, even if the way these practices and cultures are labeled and understood varies from place to place, and may well differ from Western lesbian, gay, bisexual and transgender (LGBT) identities and cultures" (2008b, 1). Just as those without power have often been used as pawns in the games of the elite, marginal identities have also often found themselves being used as tactical weapons in battles that have nothing to do with them.

The politics of fighting against the extension of equal rights and protections for nonhegemonic gender and sexual identities has extended well beyond the level of the state. On a global level, the most ardent stand against this kind of equality has often resulted in an alliance among the Vatican, conservative Catholic states, the majority of countries on the African continent, and the majority of countries in the MENA region. For example, in 2016 Egypt submitted a letter to the United Nations (UN) General Assembly on behalf of the Organization of Islamic Cooperation to block the involvement of eleven LGBTQ+ organizations in an upcoming high-level meeting on ending HIV/AIDS. Similar oppositions had previously taken place. In 2014, fifty-four states, including Egypt, Saudi Arabia, Syria, and Iran, protested the recognition of same-sex marriages among UN staff. Egypt and Qatar, in cooperation with Belarus, even led an initiative in 2016 to protest the UN issuance of six new stamps promoting LGBTQ+ equality. The opposition goes beyond the extension of rights to the mere recognition of such identities.

Discrimination against LGBTQ+ individuals is not just happening at the international level. Andrew Flores, in a report for the Williams Institute regarding the social acceptance of LGBTQ+ people, found that "the most accepting countries have experienced increased levels of acceptance," while "the least accepting countries have experienced decreased levels of acceptance" (2021, 3). Of the 175 countries included in Flores's study, MENA region countries tended to rank near the bottom in terms of social acceptance, including Egypt (159), Iran (164), South Sudan (150), Saudi Arabia (108), Sudan (137), Iraq (94), and Qatar (111). In fact, the only three countries in the region to rank in the top half were Bahrain (43), Israel (44), and Syria (57) (2021, 33–34).

Moreover, as in the trials of the Cairo 52, some in this region argue that homosexuality and other "deviant" gender and sexual identities originated in the West and were later spread to the Middle East. Interestingly, the so-called West used to make the same accusations against the "Orient," claiming that homosexuality had originated there and had infected Western explorers and missionaries. One must question, however, if these claims are based in a desire to seek out the origins of homosexuality (which is arguably not an achievable goal) or are being used as a political weapon to present "us" as pure and innocent and the "other" as vile and immoral. If one accepts the latter use, then it seems homosexuality is perhaps the innocent bystander in a larger political and cultural war.

Interestingly, there are strong arguments to be made that it is not the acceptance of homosexuality but rather the condemnation of it that originated in the West. At varying times, every country in the MENA region has been under either British or French rule, and at the time of colonization both colonizers had strict laws against homosexuality. These harsh penal codes were imposed on territories, and even after liberation many of the countries in the region continued to retain an element of various British and French legal codes. Thus, although the popular argument is that homosexuality came from the West, it is far more likely that opposition to homosexuality is what was left behind after French and British colonialism.

Sexual Activism in the MENA Region

A growing number of nongovernmental organizations (NGOs) and social activist initiatives have gained prominence in the region as not only bulwarks against the onslaught of antiequality laws and prosecutions but also as beacons of hope for those seeking justice for people penalized as being outside the bounds of what is considered "acceptable" sexuality. Often working with significant risk to themselves, these individual activists and organizations have been gaining increasing regional and international attention as awareness of sexual and sexuality-based injustices in the region have continued to enter the global consciousness. Prominent examples of NGOs working toward greater equality in the region are Himaya Lubnaniya lil Mithliyeen wal Mithliyat (Helem, Lebanese Protection for Gays and Lesbians), the Arab Foundation for Freedoms and Equality (AFE), and the Coalition for Sexual and Bodily Rights in Muslim Societies (CSBR).

Helem, an acronym that means "dream," was founded in Beirut in 2004 as the first LGBTQ+ rights organization in the Arab world. Although initially focused on overturning Article 534 of the Lebanese Penal Code, which punishes "unnatural sexual activity," the group has since become one of the leading LGBTQ+ rights organizations in the broader MENA region, engaging in advocacy and activism, providing a wide range of services, acting as a key referral system for those suffering from prosecution and discrimination, and empowering leaders to stand for LGBTQ+ equality. The organization has also engaged in broader civil and social rights issues, including antiwar movements, anti–Israeli aggression in the region, and antiracist and antixenophobic initiatives (Makarem 2011).

In 2009, the AFE was founded with the mission "to encourage and support sexual health, sexuality, gender, and bodily rights movements in the Middle East and North Africa through capacity building, knowledge production, protection and advocacy" (AFE n.d.). The organization has quickly become one of the leading LGBTQ+ rights organizations in the

MENA region and works with local organizations across the Arab states in the region on issues of sexual health, gender and sexual equality, and broader human rights initiatives. Through a series of programs, publications, and reports, AFE is one of the leading advocates for gender and sexual equality in the region, working to provide capacity building to local entities, build knowledge capacity within and beyond the region, and even assist activists and others with personal legal and safety issues.

The CSBR was founded in 2001 by a group of NGO representatives and academics from across the MENA region. CSBR has since expanded to work with organizations in South, Southeast, and Central Asia. With an extensive membership that now includes more than thirty-member organizations, it aims to "act as a resource hub to strengthen capacity and increase solidarity across regions, themes and constituencies, so that our movements succeed in accessing and transforming power structures and decision-making processes to ensure sexual & reproductive autonomy, bodily integrity, and gender-justice for all" (CSBR n.d.). The group has successfully challenged conservative politics and taboos around sexuality—including on the issues of marital rape, honor killings, virginity tests, and forced/early marriages, among others—from the level of grassroots movements up to the level of the UN.

These organizations, and there are certainly others, highlight the fact that sexuality is not a "dead issue" in the region. In fact, quite the contrary, it seems that interest in, concern about, and activism for bodily integrity, reproductive health and autonomy, sexual equality, and larger issues of human rights have only been growing in the MENA region in recent years, particularly since the rights-bearing awakening of the Arab Spring. And although there has indeed been backlash against these progressive movements, resistance to subjugation, including at the level of sexualities, appears to be undergoing a type of cultural awakening in recent decades and social reinvigoration in recent years.

Introduction to Chapters

In our earlier volume on gender in the Middle East and North Africa (Ryan and Rizzo 2020), we tackled issues related to men, masculinities, and gender relations (El Feki and Barker 2020), marriage and divorce (Sonneveld

2020), sexual- and gender-based violence (Abdelmonem 2020), female circumcision (Ryan 2020), and new media activism (Gheytanchi and Moghadam 2020), among others. Many of those issues overlap with prominent themes that appear in this volume. In fact, deciding in which volume to place particular chapters was a critical organizational issue that we faced as editors, and we would strongly recommend that this volume be read in tandem with our companion volume on gender. That said, this volume tackles issues that might be appropriately placed under the subheading "sexualities." We divided the volume into the three major parts: "Sexual Politics, Rights, and Movements"; "Gender and Sexual Minorities"; and "Sexual Health and Identity." Within these broad categories, the chapters tackle the similarities and differences in the contemporary challenges that countries in the MENA region face in terms of sexualities, addressing such critical issues as sexual rights movements, Islam and homosexuality, sexual citizenship and homonationalism, sexual and reproductive health, and sexualities and the internet. The contributors come from a variety of disciplines, such as anthropology (Zeina Zaatari and Maryam Hisham Fouad), political science (Grant Walsh-Haines), geography (Gilly Hartal), sociology (Orna Sasson-Levy, Ana Cristina Marques, J. Michael Ryan, and Helen Rizzo), psychology (Rusi Jaspal), epidemiology (Ismaël Maatouk and Moubadda Assi), public health (Inas Abdelwahed), and law (Salma Talaat). Moreover, the chapters rely on diverse methods and methodological approaches, such as ethnography, including observations and in-depth interviews (chapters 1 and 3), reviews of social psychological studies based on surveys and interviews (chapters 4 and 7), and reviews of the relevant literature, statistics, and demographic data (chapters 2, 5, and 6) to base their conclusions on rich empirical evidence. Drawing from different disciplines, methods, and methodologies enables this volume to provide a comprehensive overview of the important issues in sexuality studies in the MENA region now.

Part one focuses on sexual rights activism in the MENA region, which arguably did not begin to take formative political shape until the late 1990s and early 2000s. In chapter 1, Zeina Zaatari examines the sexual rights movement(s) occurring in the MENA region primarily through the actions and discourses of the movements' activists and the social transformations they have engendered over the past twenty to thirty years. Zaatari argues that "there have been three waves of the [sexual rights movements] in the MENA region. The first wave of public engagement on sexual rights from the late 1990s to the early 2000s focused on personal freedoms and choices. The second wave in the 2000s took further steps to organize around sexual and gender diversity, with intersectional politics grounding itself politically in anti-imperialist and decolonial struggles. The third wave grew exponentially after the 'Arab Spring' and became more deeply entrenched in sexual-orientation and gender-identity (SOGI) discourses utilizing international frameworks and mechanisms." Zaatari further argues that "the more the origins of the [sexual rights movements] and their activists are grounded in 'progressive' (leftist and/or feminist) activism, the more the movements display intersectional politics and practices, but the more the actors are initiated through an internal process of discovery of their sexuality, the more likely the movements and actions will be insular and focused on single-issue organizing, namely LGBTQIA+ identities."

Chapter 2 focuses on the influence of the internet on sexualities in the MENA region. Middle Eastern internet users are heavily censored, with most states in the MENA region engaging in some form of internet surveillance, monitoring, or restriction. That said, the internet offers an increasingly available tool for personal and professional use in the region, including for issues related to sexuality, such as viewing porn, creating online profiles for hooking up, and participating in LGBTQ+ activism. Grant Walsh-Haines and Maryam Hisham Fouad argue that the internet activism in the Middle East "is one site of resistance against oppressive state structures and often goes hand in hand with disseminating health and safety information." Access to the internet, they show, is ultimately "a key mechanism for expressions of sexuality [and] must be conceptualized in the human rights and human capabilities debate," essentially tackling the question of whether "access to the internet is a human right or should . . . be considered a mechanism for increasing human capabilities."

In chapter 3, Gilly Hartal and Orna Sasson-Levy critically examine the issues of sexual citizenship and homonationalism. Drawing on their extensive fieldwork in Tel Aviv and Jerusalem, they offer critical observations with the power to inform broader discussions of sexual citizenship and homonationalism in the broader MENA region. Citing the portrayal of Tel Aviv "as the westernized, secular, and liberal economic center of Israel" versus Jerusalem "as a local city oriented toward a religious and national past," they highlight the nuanced politics and distinct mechanisms by which sexual belonging is forged in each of these urban spaces. However, rather than drawing on an exclusive "West versus the Rest" or "global versus local" perspective, they show that both cities more critically "relate to their Middle Eastern location, albeit by merging East and West differently." The thrust of their argument focuses on "the way sexual politics, nationalism, and neoliberal economics play distinct roles . . . in the contexts of Tel Aviv and Jerusalem" and "how homonationalism and sexual citizenship interact in different urban spaces."

In part two, the volume discusses the issues that gender and sexual minorities are facing in the MENA region. It begins with addressing the widespread perception that Islam is fundamentally opposed to homosexuality, which can present social and psychological challenges to well-being among gay Muslims. In chapter 4, Rusi Jaspal "focuses on the relations between religion and sexuality—two facets of identity that are often interconnected—among Muslim gay men." He argues that Muslim gay men, given their awareness and acceptance of the negative social representation of homosexuality, may experience threats to identity, self-esteem, belonging, and psychological coherence as they struggle to reconcile their internalized homophobia with the reality that they cannot change their sexual orientation and "become straight." Jaspal looks at some of the possible challenges to the promotion of sexual health among Muslim gay men in light of these threats to identity. He concludes with a persuasive argument that it is essential to engage with existing social representations of homosexuality and "to challenge [those] representations that potentially threaten the identities of Muslim gay men" for the development of "a more accepting and affirmative context in which Muslim gay men can construct their identities and take steps to enhance their sexual well-being."

To complement Jaspal's chapter, in chapter 5 Ana Cristina Marques, Salma Talaat, and J. Michael Ryan tackle problems faced by trans communities in the MENA region. They begin their chapter by giving an overview of the legal, social, and cultural context of being trans in the region. They then problematize "the victimization of trans people in the MENA region as part of the 'West/East' opposition." They conclude their chapter "by underscoring the importance of going beyond regional dichotomies that associate the 'West' with freedom and the 'East' with oppression; having a better understanding of the influence (or lack thereof) of local, national, and inter/transnational (post)colonial agendas on trans people's rights and their actual experiences; and producing possible pluralities, spaces of resistances, and subterranean discourses . . . of trans people and issues in this region."

The final section of the volume focuses on sexual health and identity. Sexual and reproductive health (SRH) is a crucial part of the health status of populations and a precondition for human development. In chapter 6, Inas Abdelwahed examines how these issues have become of critical importance in the MENA region, particularly since the International Conference on Population and Development in Cairo in 1994. "Despite the remarkable global progress toward improved SRH," Abdelwahed argues, "there are still significant gaps between high-income countries (HICs) and low/middle-income countries (LMICs)." She also shows how humanitarian crises exacerbate inequities in access to SRH education and care across the MENA region. She pays particular attention to the ways SRH has been constructed, examined, and responded to in the cultural, social, and political context of the MENA region by "focusing primarily on youth and sexuality, maternal health, [sexually transmitted infections], infertility, and men's reproductive health."

Rusi Jaspal, Ismaël Maatouk, and Moubadda Assi focus in chapter 7 on aspects of identity and health outcomes in sexual minorities in the Middle East and North Africa. First, they outline tenets of minority stress theory and identity process theory from social psychology. Second, they briefly explore the social, cultural, religious, and political aspects of countries in the MENA region (in particular Lebanon). Third, they discuss their recent empirical research into sexual identity and mental health in sexual minorities in the MENA. Their research demonstrates that "sexual minorities in the region face multifaceted stressors, such as stigma on the basis of their sexual identity and internalized homonegativity," which may result in threats to their mental health and coping abilities. They point out that "in the MENA region, religiosity and self-identification with religious (and ethnic) groups appear to constitute key sources of social support and thus reflect a prime coping strategy. Yet sexual minorities may have decreased access to these support networks, potentially leading to a reliance on alternative, less adaptive forms of coping," such as substance misuse and sexual risk-taking. "The implications for mental health and well-being may be significant," they state. Through the lens of social psychological theory, these authors present a way forward for research and practice in enhancing social and psychological outcomes among sexual minorities in the MENA region.

Brought together, these chapters help to provide critical insights into the various issues, challenges, and opportunities that the role of sexuality(-ies) is bringing to the MENA region. Drawing on contemporary scholarship, ethnographic fieldwork, and modern reconciliations of interactions among the local, state, regional, and international networks of scholars, activists, and political powers, the contributors to this volume help to shed light on the ways in which sexualities have been a foundational element of national and regional discourses, serve as political tools for demarcating categories of an "us versus them" mentality, and have the possibility to enlighten, restrict, liberate, or oppress millions of individuals living in the region. We hope that this volume and the chapters within it will further add to the important conversation on the role of sexuality(-ies) in the MENA region, highlight the ongoing issues, challenges, and opportunities, and serve the search for reform.

References

Abdelmonem, Angie. 2020. "Sexual and Gender-Based Violence." In *Gender in the Middle East and North Africa: Contemporary Issues and Challenges*, edited by J. Michael Ryan and Helen Rizzo, 73–92. Boulder, CO: Lynne-Rienner.

Arab Foundation for Freedoms and Equality (AFE). n.d. "About." At https://www.afemena.org/about/.

Bahgat, Hossam. 2001. "Explaining Egypt's Targeting of Gays." *Middle East Report Online*, July 23. At https://merip.org/2001/07/explaining-egypts-targeting-of-gays/.

Coalition for Sexual and Bodily Rights in Muslim Societies. n.d. "About CSBR." At https://csbronline.org/.

El Feki, Shereen. 2015. "The Arab Bed Spring? Sexual Rights in Troubled Times across the Middle East and North Africa." *Reproductive Health Matters* 23, no. 46: 38–44.

El Feki, Shereen, and Gary Barker. 2020. "Men, Masculinities, and Gender Relations." In *Gender in the Middle East and North Africa: Contemporary Issues and Challenges*, edited by J. Michael Ryan and Helen Rizzo, 13–30. Boulder, CO: Lynne-Rienner.

Flores, Andrew R. 2021. *Social Acceptance of LGBT People in 174 Countries, 1981 to 2017.* Los Angeles: Williams Institute.

Foucault, Michel. 1984. "Selections from *The History of Sexuality*, Volume 1: *An Introduction.*" In *The Foucault Reader*, edited by Paul Rabinow, 292–329. New York: Pantheon.

Gheytanchi, Elham, and Valentine M. Moghadam. 2020. "The New Media Activism." In *Gender in the Middle East and North Africa: Contemporary Issues and Challenges*, edited by J. Michael Ryan and Helen Rizzo, 213–34. Boulder, CO: Lynne-Rienner.

Ilkkaracan, Pinar, ed. 2008a. *Deconstructing Sexuality in the Middle East: Challenges and Discourses.* London: Ashgate.

———. 2008b. "Introduction: Sexuality as a Contested Political Domain in the Middle East." In *Deconstructing Sexuality in the Middle East: Challenges and Discourses*, edited by Pinar Ilkkaracan, 1–16. London: Ashgate.

Makarem, Ghassan. 2011. "The Story of HELEM." *Journal of Middle East Women's Studies* 7, no. 3: 98–112.

Mikdashi, Maya. 2014. "Sex and Sectarianism: The Legal Architecture of Lebanese Citizenship." *Comparative Studies of South Asia, Africa and the Middle East* 34, no. 2: 279–93.

Najmabadi, Afsaneh. 2008. "Types, Acts or What? Regulation of Sexuality in Nineteenth-Century Iran." In *Islamicate Sexualities: Translations across Temporal Geographies of Desire*, edited by Kathryn Babayan and Afsaneh Najmabadi, 275–96. Cambridge: Center for Middle Eastern Studies.

Pratt, Nicola. 2007. "The Queen Boat Case in Egypt: Sexuality, National Security, and State Sovereignty." *Review of International Studies* 33: 129–44.

Puri, Jyoti. 2004. *Encountering Nationalism*. Malden, MA: Blackwell.

Ryan, J. Michael. 2018. "Gender Identity Laws: The Legal Status of Global Sex/Gender Identity Recognition." *LGBTQ Policy Journal* 8: 3–16.

———. 2019. "Communicating Trans Identity: Toward an Understanding of the Selection and Significance of Gender Identity–Based Terminology." *Journal of Language and Sexuality* 8, no. 2: 221–41.

———. 2020. "Female Circumcision." In *Gender in the Middle East and North Africa: Contemporary Issues and Challenges*, edited by J. Michael Ryan and Helen Rizzo, 93–112. Boulder, CO: Lynne-Rienner.

Ryan, J. Michael, and Helen Rizzo, eds. 2020. *Gender in the Middle East and North Africa: Contemporary Issues and Challenges*. Boulder, CO: Lynne Rienner.

Sonneveld, Nadia. 2020. "Marriage and Divorce." In *Gender in the Middle East and North Africa: Contemporary Issues and Challenges*, edited by J. Michael Ryan and Helen Rizzo, 51–72. Boulder, CO: Lynne-Rienner.

Tolino, Serena. 2014. "Homosexuality in the Middle East: An Analysis of Dominant and Competitive Discourses." *Deportate, esule, profughe* 25: 72–91.

Yerke, Adam. 2020. "Stronger Together: The Global Shift to Transgender-Inclusive Armed Forces." In *Trans Lives in a Global(izing) World: Rights, Identities, and Politics*, edited by J. Michael Ryan, 147–64. London: Routledge.

Part One. Sexual Politics, Rights, and Movements

1

Sexual Rights Movement(s)

Problematics of Visibility

Zeina Zaatari

Sexual rights activism in the MENA region began to take shape in the late 1990s and early 2000s. This chapter focuses on sexual rights movements (SRMs) primarily through the actions and discourses of their activists and the social transformations they have engendered over the past twenty-five years. The chapter understands a social movement as a project that aims to redefine culture rather than only political structures (Touraine 1985, 1988; Zaatari 2015), thus articulating a struggle over hegemony (narratives, cultures, and identities) (Tugal 2009). Social movements organize constituents to pursue a common political agenda through performing certain collective actions (Batliwala 2008; Tilly 1993–94). As such, over the past twenty-five years or so SRMs have been leaving their mark on the society of many Middle Eastern and North African (MENA) countries, slowly but surely.

In the first section of the chapter, I delineate my methodology and positionality vis-à-vis this research project. Then I offer a brief discussion of sexual rights as understood globally and locally within MENA, which is followed by a quick historical framing of sexual rights, advocacy, and feminism in the MENA region. In the second section, I historicize the SRMs

This chapter is dedicated to the memory of my friend, the queer activist and scholar Tarek Moustafa Mohamed (Titi), who left this world too soon in August 2023.

in the MENA region and activism around sexual and bodily autonomy by highlighting early developments, major milestones, and shifts and transformations. I utilize the framework of waves to discuss these transformations in organizing and their connections to larger sociopolitical contexts as it allows for ebbs and flows and revisions rather than rigid boundaries. I argue that there have been three waves of the SRMs in the MENA region. The first wave of public engagement on sexual rights from the late 1990s to the early 2000s focused on personal freedoms and choices. The second wave in the 2000s took further steps to organize around sexual and gender diversity, with intersectional politics grounding itself in anti-imperialist and decolonial struggles. The third wave grew exponentially starting after the "Arab Spring" and became more deeply entrenched in sexual-orientation and gender-identity (SOGI) discourses utilizing international frameworks and mechanisms. Since the initial writing of this chapter in 2017, the region has been experiencing some significant backlash against political and civic activism in general and a particular targeting of LGBTQIA+ activists and individuals. It raises the question whether we are entering a period of foreclosure (Naber and Zaatari 2014) that may (or may not) create openings and transformation in the near future.[1]

The third section looks at issues and debates that have been central to the SRMs around questions of social change, including the politics of visibility and intersectional politics and practice. I argue that the more the origins of the SRMs and their activists are grounded in "progressive" (leftist and/or feminist) activism, the more the movements display intersectional politics and practices, but the more the actors are initiated through an internal process of discovery of their sexuality, the more likely the movements and actions will be insular and focused on single-issue organizing, namely LGBTQIA+ identities. These arguments apply generally across the region, with notable differences based on the particularities and political transformations in each country. The final section unpacks some of the core strategies utilized by activists in the SRMs, which include creation

1. Nadine Naber and I showed how periods of intense crisis and political upheavals, such as the invasion of Lebanon by Israel in 2006, lead to foreclosures and openings that could in turn lead to major transformations or at least expansion of spaces of possibility.

of safe spaces, advocacy and awareness raising, support and services, and knowledge production.

Positionality and Methodology

My contribution is grounded in years of working alongside and within the SRMs. As a trained anthropologist, I have used participant-observation methodology to enrich my arguments through the in-depth knowledge gained from years of collaboration and engagement. For a period, I was also in the position of a feminist funder who set a funding strategy devised through conversations with activists and advisers that prioritized, among other things, sexual and bodily rights/integrity.[2] As such, I was in a position to fund and support some of the earliest organizing by lesbian, bisexual, and queer women and trans folks in the region as well as work by feminist organizing that looked at bodily integrity, body image, legal reforms in penal and family codes, masculinity, and violence against women.[3] I like to think that the feminist political grant-making strategies and decisions we made at the time supported local efforts to build a stronger and accountable movement that is not beholden to donor-driven agendas or a predetermined set of global terminologies, strategies, or outcomes.[4] In addition, I worked to open spaces for the inclusion of "queer" activists in the larger feminist movement. In 2015, I worked with many activists to establish the Women Human Rights Defenders–MENA Coalition, on whose board I have served as adviser and/or treasurer since its inception.

2. Between July 2004 and November 2012, I worked as the program director for the MENA program at the Global Fund for Women, a grant-making foundation that supports women's and trans folks' rights by providing core funding to women-led organizations. My job there included work on violence against women in its entire array (domestic, public, and within conditions of war) as well as on sexual and reproductive health.

3. During my tenure at the Global Fund for Women, we supported some of the groups highlighted throughout this chapter.

4. These strategies included accepting proposals in local languages and in any form or shape, providing support to registered or nonregistered collectives, foregrounding trust and building relationships with organizations and advisers from the region as an accountability strategy, providing core support without restrictions, requiring simple and minimalist reporting documents, and setting strategies in conversation with activists.

The coalition has been vocal on addressing the concerns of LGBTQIA+ activists over the years. As such, I situate myself and this research as an insider/outsider in contributing to this movement, a position that has afforded me critical distance to assess and analyze and at the same time invest in understanding transformations and producing knowledge that can support social change project(s).

In addition to participant observation, I also conducted in 2017 in-depth open-ended interviews with twelve activists from Lebanon, Palestine, Tunisia, Algeria, Morocco, and Egypt/Sudan, including seasoned activists such as Senda Ben Jebara, Najma Kousri Labidi, Ghassan Makarem, Haneen Maikey, Nadine Moawad, Rauda Morocos, Azza Nubi, Yahia Zaidi, Zakaria, and three others who preferred to stay anonymous. In addition, I reviewed research and writing produced in scholarly journals and nonacademic outfits. Finally, I did extensive review of primary sources, writings by sexual rights activists, including publications—blogs, essays, and books—by the different groups.

What Are Sexual Rights Movements?

Sexual Rights: Sexual Orientations and Gender Diversity? Freedom? Choice? Bodily Integrity?

Defining sexual rights has been a complicated process as social concepts are often fluid and have a genealogy of their own that is constantly shifting and changing. However, precisely because activists have had to fight for these specific rights, they have also had to name them and categorize them. Thus, although the social or scholarly project may be suspicious of clear definitions, the social justice or political project that aims to create change is often intent on clear definitions. Not only academics but also right-wing and religious groups (e.g., Family Watch International) have been critical of the term *sexual rights* and its use. Sexual rights are fundamental rights entrenched by international human rights law that includes several areas pertaining to one's body and sexuality. They include the right to control and decide freely on matters related to one's sexuality; to be free from violence, coercion, or intimidation in one's sexual life; to have access to sexual and reproductive health-care information, education, and services; and to be protected from discrimination based on the exercise of one's sexuality.

Activists worked to include specific language around sexual rights in the various United Nations (UN) treaties and conventions to ensure protections from discrimination and access to rights. The notion of sexual rights as such first appeared on the global scene in the preparation for the UN International Conference on Population and Development, held in Cairo in 1994. Sexual rights were alluded to but never spelled out in the final document (Ilkkaracan 2008). A year later at the UN Fourth World Conference on Women in Beijing, "an alliance of conservative Muslim and Catholic delegations strongly objected to . . . use [of the term *sexual rights*]" (Ilkkaracan 2008, 5).[5] Debates on women's control of their bodies and sexuality were heated. Despite the tremendous objections, a global alliance of women succeeded in including in paragraph 96 of the Beijing Platform for Action language about women's control over their bodies and sexuality (Ilkkaracan 2008, 6; Sheill 2008, 45).

In 2006, a group of activists, scholars, judges, and UN experts came together in Yogyakarta, Indonesia, to discuss and clarify the "nature, scope and implementation of States' human rights obligations in relation to sexual orientation and gender identity." The meeting resulted in the creation of the Yogyakarta Principles "on the application of international human rights law in relation to sexual orientation and gender identity."[6] The debate around these issues at the UN level continues as certain states attempt to pass clear language that protects and promotes the rights of everyone regardless of sexual orientation and gender identity (Ilkkaracan 2008), while other states, including the Vatican, oppose such legislation and instead aim to pass language on protections for the family (as in one kind of family) and for religious and cultural rights and traditional values.[7]

5. For more on the role of the Vatican in the UN, see Catholics for Choice 2013.

6. Yogyakarta Principles, 2006, at https://www.yogyakartaprinciples.org.

7. For UN Human Rights Council (UNHRC) resolutions that promote the principles, see "Resolution 17/19. Human Rights, Sexual Orientation and Gender Identity," 2011; "Resolution 27/32 Human Rights, Sexual Orientation and Gender Identity," 2014;

Most activists I interviewed emphasized freedom, autonomy, and choice as important elements of how they understood sexual rights. They were critical of the instrumentalization of a human rights framework and its ongoing co-optation by governments and the private sector. Nonetheless, they found that having a language in common helps in building bridges across national and international spaces. Najma, a rights activist from Tunisia, said: "It is all about freedom of choice."[8] Ghassan, one of the founders of Helem also stressed the notion of freedom: "Basically the freedom to choose partners and have the kinds of sexual relations one wants to have as an adult."[9] Several of the activists expressed their discomfort with the term *rights*, given what it has come to embody in terms of adopting the international human rights framework and the appeal to some authority that is expected to bestow rights or withhold them. Haneen, the founder of alQaws in Palestine, indicated that instead of rights she thinks of "a space to reflect on our sexualities in general and to reflect on which part of the oppression systems are we complicit with and where we are oppressed (no matter who we are), what are the links between these oppressions." Azza, one of the founders of Bedayaa in Egypt, emphasized an expansive view of sexual rights: "In general, we talk about anything that has to do with a person's body, to have the right to do what you want with your body, to have bodily integrity . . . to be active sexually or not, the nature of the sexual relations one wants to be part of, all the things that have to do with one's body or one's sexual life and freedom." The Coalition for Sexual and Bodily Rights in Muslim Societies (CSBR) indicates

---

"Resolution 32/2. Protection against Violence and Discrimination Based on Sexual Orientation and Gender Identity," 2016. See also Human Rights Watch 2016. For a UNHRC resolution that opposes the principles, see "Resolution 21/3. Promoting Human Rights and Fundamental Freedoms through a Better Understanding of Traditional Values of Humankind: Best Practices," 2012. For an analysis of Resolution 21/3 from a human rights framework, see Reid 2012.

8. Interviews were conducted in Arabic and English, and my translations are given throughout the chapter where needed.

9. The name "Helem," the abbreviation for Himaya Lubnaniya lil Mithliyeen wal Mithliyat (Lebanese Protection for Gays and Lesbians), means "dream."

that it is "founded on the fundamental principle that all people, regardless of their gender, citizenship, class, age, religion, marital status, ethnic identity, sexual orientation, mental and physical ability, have the right to bodily and sexual integrity and autonomy and the right to freely decide on all matters concerning their sexuality and fertility."[10] CSBR's core values articulate a clarity of the embeddedness of sexual and bodily rights within the universality of human rights and their essentiality to achieving women's rights, gender equality, and democracy. Although the language of rights has its genealogy in international frameworks, it also carries cultural and humanistic meanings colloquially. Sexual and bodily rights are important signifiers of autonomy, access to choice and resources, and self-determination.

Women's Rights: Bodily Rights Camouflaged

Gender and sexuality have been a politicized issue in the MENA region since at least the period of modernization of the nineteenth century (Ilkkaracan 2008). Tremendous political and economic transformations affected gender relations and family life. This was also the period of public debates on gender roles and women's issues, as evidenced by the literature and research on the role of women (and men) in building the region's nations. The process of modernization varied across the region, with some countries adopting staunchly secular and westernized interpretations of law and customs, such as Turkey, but others pushing for technological and economic advances but adhering to earlier and often conservative interpretations of Islamic law for matters related to the family and women.

The various phases of the women's movements since the late nineteenth century tended to accompany other social movements and political upheavals (Badran 1993; Kamal 2016; Zaatari 2023). Women took part in nationalist activism against colonization and brought to the fore issues affecting their lives. The women's movements often focused on the right to education, the right to work, the right to vote and to run for political office, and rights within marriage (access to divorce, custody, and treatment as

10. See the coalition's website at https://csbronline.org/.

an adult, not a minor). Efforts were made to address reproductive and maternal health, although this issue was rarely framed as reproductive rights. The women's movements in the early stages did not bring up issues of sexual freedom or desire directly as demands or program for change (Ilkkaracan and Ronge 2008). Instead, women talked about the importance of choice in marriage, an increase in the age at which it was legal for them to marry, the right to decide how many children they would have and when to have them, and other family-planning concerns. Malak Hifni Nassif, for example, campaigned in Egypt for reform in the educational system and marriage laws, particularly denouncing polygamy, men's unhindered access to divorce, early marriage of girls, and marriages with major age differences (Ahmed 1993; Kamal 2016).

Feminists from the 1950s to the 1980s organized a lively and dynamic feminism that worked on the social and cultural as well as the legal arenas (Ahmed 1993; Badran 1993). "Women began to make visible the covert, unofficial aggressions and manipulations, both psychological and physical, to which they were subject and to address themselves and organize around taboo issues, such as contraception and clitoridectomy" (Ahmed 1993, 214). Among these feminists was Andre Chedid, the Egyptian novelist, who wrote about child marriage and so-called honor killings in her novels. Nawal El Saadawi is credited with discussing sex and sexuality more directly (Amireh 2000; Badran 1993). Her book *Al-mar'a wa-l-jins* (Women and Sex, 1971) drew on her observations as a medical doctor in different parts of Egypt to discuss how women's bodies were treated. Leila Ahmed (1993) argues that this was the generation that linked the personal and the political and uncovered the exploitation of women in both the private sphere and the public sphere, their personal lives within their families and their lives as members of society.

Second Beginnings: Sexual Rights in the Middle East and North Africa

Identifying a Movement

Most scholars (e.g., Amer 2015; Ilkkaracan 2008; Kamal 2016; Zaatari 2016, 2023) and activists I interviewed argue that the SRMs began to take shape in the late 1990s and early 2000s. Pinar Ilkkaracan (2008) argues that in the past twenty-five years there has been an increased level of politicization of gender and sexuality across the region. She emphasizes that in the 1990s more organizations in the region began speaking about sexual and bodily rights, often including issues around violence, such as honor killings, female genital mutilations, and forced virginity tests. Groups demanded penal code reforms to guarantee women's rights as full human beings and began gently defending the human rights of LGBT peoples. Hala Kamal (2016) argues that feminist groups in Egypt began including sexuality rights on their agenda in the 1990s. Although conversations initially focused on personal freedom and sexual health, issues around sexual freedom, sexual and gender identities, and the human rights of LGBTQIA+ individuals started intensifying around 2004–5 with the formation of organizations working on such issues directly. Enough momentum had been built locally around personal freedoms that individuals felt ready to be more public and to organize particularly on issues important to them.

The Political Stage

In the 1990s and early 2000s, growing economic inequalities, Islamist movements with religious-right ideologies, and militarization and wars, including the US invasion of Iraq, meant a decrease in spaces for organizing and possible reforms. "On the other hand, the rise of new feminist and civil movements, globalization, the increasing influence of a global human rights discourse, and changing socio-economic conditions affecting population patterns have led to the emergence of new discourse, demands and patterns regarding sexual behavior and a growing push for change from below" (Ilkkaracan 2008, 3).

In addition, new communication technologies played a very important role in effecting change. Jared McCormick's (2006) research with men who have sex with men (MSM) in Lebanon identifies the internet as an important avenue of exploration for many. This finding was supported by numerous stories I heard in Lebanon, Palestine, Egypt, and Sudan. However, beyond enabling a reaffirming of identity, internet technology made it possible to create public forums, including blogs, where issues of personal freedoms and choices could be discussed and debated. It also created possibilities for online listservs, which in many instances were the first attempt at organizing. Groups such as Aswat, Helem, Meem, and Abu-Nawwas began as online listservs. The technology also made it feasible for ideas and information to be shared across the region in a way that fostered the building blocks of a movement.

The political transformations that began with the Tunisian Revolution in 2010–11 also created a sense of the possibility of social change, although in certain contexts this opening was followed a few years later by a further shrinking of democratic space and possible foreclosure of those possibilities given the increased militarized and religious-autocratic rules and ongoing wars in several countries. Yet global transformations had local reverberations: the internationalization of wars (such as with/against ISIS, the refugee crisis, the wars in Yemen and Syria), the increased advocacy by SOGI activists in various international structures, and the solidifying of homonationalism (Puar 2007) as a normalized vision of the world, particularly with Hillary Clinton's term as US secretary of state (equivalent of minister of foreign affairs) and Israel use of pinkwashing strategies.

Thus, globalization enabled a space for activists to network on such issues as sexual rights and bodily autonomy. But it also brought the fruits of a post-9/11 world and antiterrorism policies. Thus, activists and groups often felt they had to walk a fine line in organizing around the various oppressive structures and systems affecting their lives, around the link between local patriarchy and heteronormativity that was producing strict policing of bodies/sexualities, and around the link between imperialist patriarchy and heteronormativity that was contributing to oppressive structures and generating new restrictive realities (Naber and Zaatari 2014).

Three Waves of the Sexual Rights Movement

The *initial wave* of organizing in the late 1990s to the early 2000s had three sometimes overlapping roots or trajectories. The first stemmed from the health sector, in particular work on HIV/AIDS prevention. In Algeria, the main organization working on AIDS was not initially comfortable opening up its workshops to the MSM community in 2003. A small group of men invested in doing this work managed to establish a program for MSM. The second root evolved from lesbian women's concerns about their own oppression but was grounded in the ideas of women's autonomy over their bodies. Nadine, a longtime feminist and LGBTQIA+ rights activist from Lebanon, argued that whereas many heterosexual women could make compromises or bargain as such with patriarchy (Kandiyoti 1988), many lesbian women felt they had no choice. "Lesbians in particular push the envelope because they cannot but push it, because they cannot exist otherwise," Nadine explained. The third root stemmed from political organizing on citizenship and governance and was invested in expanding the realm of the private space and personal freedom, a space supposedly away from the state, family, and religious establishment's control and power.

The *second wave* (roughly 2004–9) started a clearer articulation of sexual and gender diversity with the forming of organizations specifically to address such issues publicly and internally. This wave benefited from various political movements, particularly in Lebanon and Palestine, that allowed it to further ground its work in an intersectional politics that looked at imperialism, class, settler colonialism, race, ethnicity, and gender as co-constitutive elements of the oppressive structures individuals must deal with (AlQaisiya 2018; Shapiro 2022).

The *third wave* resulted from the opening of new spaces for organizing when governments were toppled, which created civil society spaces and potential regional and global interactions. This opening led to a mushrooming of organizations in many countries in the MENA region. While in Tunisia this wave was a direct result of the revolution and the transformation of civil society, it also had to do with increased support (funding) and networking regionally and globally. In Lebanon, the wave was connected also to internal issues or divisions within the local movements based on contrasting visions of organizing (an intersectional versus identity-based or strictly SOGI framework), which caused groups to break up or disappear (Rizk and Makarem 2015). The shifts of the third wave are also connected to transformations in the discourse and spaces: younger generations are growing up in a different world that takes for granted the global terminologies of sexuality because these terminologies are readily accessed through television programs, online sites, and political discussions. I highlight some of these transformations in a few of the countries in the region to demonstrate the local shifts and trends.

In Lebanon in the 1990s, online sites began emerging, some purely focused on dating and others on discussion, along with an underground club and pub scene that catered to a growing "gay" clientele engaged in drag shows and *shakhir* (Meem 2009, 122–24; Qubaiova 2019).[11] However, more public presence began with Club Free and the group Hurriyyat Khassa in the early 2000s, where discussions of *hurriyat khassa* (personal freedom) and sexuality began to take shape initially among a small circle of people and then slowly moved onto a more public stage. Club Free organized an exhibition titled *I Exist* toward the end of 2000 (Makarem 2011, 102). Khat Mubashir, a radical leftist group, organized a radical film festival on sexual liberation at the end of 2001 (Makarem 2011, 102). Hurriyyat Khassa initiated a successful campaign against a proposed draft of a new Lebanese Penal Code in 2002 that was to expand the meaning of Article 534, which criminalizes copulation "against nature" (Makarem 2011; Scalenghe 2004). Helem was born in 2004 out of these initiatives as a public organization to work on legal reform and societal change (Makarem 2009). Meem, the lesbian collective, came out of Helem in 2006, when some of its female members (Helem Girls) addressed their invisibility inside Helem and other spaces. Almost parallel to Meem or out of Meem, Nasawiya was born in 2009 as a specifically radical feminist space interested in questions of feminism, the body, sexuality, and power. These were the first-generation groups and activists. Today, there are many groups in Lebanon working directly on issues related to sexual rights and bodily integrity, including some of the older generation, such as Helem; others that work on the regional level, such as Mosaic, M-Coalition, and the Arab Foundation for Freedoms and Equality; and still others that are locally based, such as the A Project, Marsa: Sexual Health Center, LebMASH, Dameh, Proud Lebanon, and Qorras and Tajassod (trans focused).[12]

11. According to the anonymous author of "How It All Started" in Meem's book *Bareed Mista3jil* (2009), in *shakhir* contests, similar to "radi7" in Egypt, "a man takes on the role of a housewife, screaming comically at someone. They would do impressions of a housewife hanging out the laundry, cutting up vegetables, cleaning the stairs, all while making fun of her neighbor or complaining about her husband" (122–23).

12. Within the movement, Proud Lebanon has been seen as deeply controversial and problematic.

In Algeria, the men working on HIV/AIDS with the MSM community in 2003 weren't able to implement their workshop until 2006. Soon after that and almost independently in 2007, three people (two men—one later to identify as trans—and one woman) formed Abu-Nawwas, which faltered when one of its founding members had to flee to Lebanon and later to Sweden. In 2009, Yahia recalled trying to restart Abu-Nawwas with the older members and other active bloggers, but the group eventually split into several new groups, including Association Alouen, Akham, Mahaba, Trans Homo DZ, and an independent women's group in Constantine.

Similarly, in Palestine, women's rights and feminist movements worked on issues related to the body, including violence, honor killings, and reproductive health, but outright discussions about sexual rights were not common. Muntada: The Arab Forum for Sexuality, Education, and Health, formed in 2003, began providing education and resources on sexuality and sexual health, including in schools. Aswat: Palestinian Gay Women came out of feminist activism and a desire to emphasize the multiplicity of identities.[13] It was started online in 2000 by two women until members dared an in-person meeting in 2001 at someone's house. Individuals were looking for a "place to speak our language and not have to translate our emotions," clarified Rauda, one of the founders of Aswat from Palestine. AlQaws for Sexual & Gender Diversity in Palestinian Society was founded officially in 2007 to build a future Palestinian society that celebrates diverse sexualities and genders.[14]

In Tunisia, both Najma and Senda reinforced the narrative of earlier feminists focusing largely on reproductive rights.[15] Directly speaking up about and working on sexual rights, including SOGI, began with the formation of new groups initiated by mostly younger-generation activists after the revolution in 2010–11. "Now we talk about sexual rights and

13. Aswat recently changed its name to "Aswat: The Palestinian Feminist Center for Gender and Sexual Freedoms."

14. AlQaws had been operating as an independent project inside the Open House, an Israeli LGBTQ group, since 2001.

15. In Tunisia, abortion is available to women within the first three months without restrictions and can be performed at public clinics, which also provide free contraception. At five months, abortion is possible only when the mother's life is in danger.

bodily rights . . . enabled by this democratic transition and freedom of speech," Najma stressed. These new groups, such as Chouf (which identifies as a feminist organization), Mawjoudin, Damj, Shams, and Kelmty, are working with some of the older more established organizations, such as the Association tunisienne de femmes démocrates (Tunisian Association of Democratic Women), building collaborative work, creating new coalitions such as the Tunisian Coalition for the Rights of LGBTQI, producing reports (e.g., Tunisian Coalition 2017), and addressing violations. Divisions over strategy and framework for organizing continue to be negotiated.[16]

In Morocco, efforts began with work on access to reproductive health and the right to abortion. However, open discussions could be grounds for persecution under Hassan II (r. 1961–99), and such persecution continues today. Kif Kif was one of the earliest formations predominantly focused on gay men; Menna wa Fena was formed in 2010 as an entity within Kif Kif addressing lesbian, trans, and queer concerns; the Mali Movement began in 2015 to focus on freedom of expression and religion; Aswat Mag and the Collective arose after the demonstrations of February 20, 2011; and the Aqaliyat Group and Magazine campaigned to eradicate discriminatory laws. Although some of these groups are no longer active in Morocco, a few have formed active organizing collectives in Spain and Holland. After two years of organizing and advocacy to register, L'Union feministe libre (Free Feminist Union) became the first nongovernmental organization (NGO) registered and recognized for working on gender and sexuality in June 2018. Nasawiyat is another organization that addresses LGBTQI issues. Several trans groups were also established, such as Transat, Kasbah Tal'Fin, and Talay'an.

The first-generation regional coalition was CSBR, but Mantaqitna began to take shape in 2007, even though the idea started much earlier for Rauda when she suggested a meeting between Aswat and Helem Girls

16. For instance, as of 2018 Shams is not a member of the Tunisian Coalition. A press statement by the coalition in April 2018 criticized Shams for its "outing" strategy to address homophobia and stressed that the coalition does not support such practices and that Shams is not a member of the coalition.

in 2005. Those early exchanges had tremendous impact on the activists. Yahia, one of the founders of Mantaqitna, remembered a Euro-Med summer institute on sexuality where several activists from different countries "identified a need to meet in our region. We were fed up with the instrumentalization and each time trying to change the discourse and provide a different picture of what we are facing; one that was not all dark, or black and white, but had gray nuances to it, so we decided to have our own space for our own region." Rauda worked on getting the funding and brought the group together with nine cofounders from the region. The group decided on the name "Mantaqitna," which simply means "Our Region," in a conscious effort to be inclusive of various ethnic and linguistic diversities within the region. Casting a broad net, the network organized trainings for individuals working on sexual rights. It graduated future activists and helped create new groups (including, for example, the Bedayaa Organization for LGBTQI of the Nile Valley Area), actively linking the Machreq and the Maghreb and ensuring an inclusive space. Mantaqitna was grounded in intersectional politics and responded to the growing unease felt by activists regarding the status quo in the region, the oppression of sexual and gender "minorities," and increased Islamophobia and homonationalism—the background for many international engagements in the region.[17]

The third wave is represented in the growing number of organizations, collectives, and initiatives focusing directly on sexual orientation and gender identity and engaging with international actors and entities, while sometimes also working locally to push for transformation. There are also a growing number of organizations in the diaspora, such as the ANKH Association (Arab Network for Knowledge about Human Rights), established in 2018 in France by an Egyptian who had to flee their country. Initiatives also include publications and forms of information sharing. In addition to groups mentioned earlier, some of the newer formations include IraQueer (Iraqi Kurdistan), *Mawaleh* (an online magazine, Syria), Quzah (Libya), Mesahat for Sexual and Gender Diversity (Egypt and

17. For more on this background, refer to Joseph Massad's work on the "gay international" (Massad 2007) and the critique by activists in books such as *Bareed Mista3jil* (Meem 2009) and in online sites.

Sudan), Cairo 52 (Egypt), the North African Center for Strategic Partnerships, and MyKali (Jordan). A longer list of unnamed efforts across countries with even more limited space for organizing and public discourse on sexuality has also been growing over the years.[18]

At the same time, several feminist initiatives have been working on issues related to sexuality and the body, producing publications, and organizing campaigns. They include Ikhtyar (Egypt), Sawt el Niswa (Lebanon), L'Union feminist libre (Morocco), the Knowledge Workshop (Lebanon), Nasawiyat (Morocco), Nour Sarah, Jeem, and a number of new initiatives addressing sexual harassment in Egypt and elsewhere (Hassan 2016; Roushdy 2016).[19]

Issues and Debates: Movement Trajectories

Politics of Visibility

Is the practice of visibility an inevitability in organizing around sexual and gender diversities (invisibility as only ever a temporary practice/strategy), or is invisibility a necessary strategy of resistance to imperialist sexuality (invisibility as the "authentic" expression of sexual and gender diversity)? Does a certain discourse around invisibility mask and possibly foster other oppressive structures and systems of oppression, or is visibility in its essence an "incitement to discourse" that leads to further horrors? These questions have been debated by SRM activists in the MENA.

Yahia stressed that visibility has always had a unique interpretation for the MENA region. It was "about being visible without being 'visible'"—or, in other words, "visibilize the work but not the people." There were often debates as to whether "the visibly queer women would advance or change some of the taboos around being queer," Nadine added. Haneen explained: "We used to say we will make our strategies and discourse visible and people less visible." However, the newer generation is more intent on visibility by way of making links to people's actual lives and experiences.

18. See the interview notes on organizing in Oman, Jordan, Libya, Bahrain, and Kuwait in, for example, the Human Rights Watch report *Audacity in Adversity* (Ghoshal 2018).

19. Sawt was originally a Nasawiya project but eventually became independent.

Nadine stressed that she does not believe that queer women wanted to be "out and proud," so to speak. The almost essential strategy of being out as a first step toward liberation, ascribed to in the United States, Israel, and western Europe (Gaudio 2009; Ritchie 2010), is not a strategy that has particularly appealed to queer women in the MENA region; in fact, they have often been critical of such practices (Darwich 2010; Darwich and Maikey 2011; Hamdan 2015; Hochberg, Maikey, and Saraya 2010). Nadine said: "It [out and proud] does not fit in our lives. There are more important things. One is for your family to respect your choices, which is different than accepting your sexuality. Lots of the women's struggles is about accepting their choices to not marry, to live abroad, to work or live somewhere else, not so much their choice to be lesbian. . . . There is a need for legitimacy, [a] need to be a legitimate member of society, of the family, but not the legitimate gay son or daughter." In a roundtable discussion in 2010, Haneen Maikey said that "the coming-out narrative has become oppressive in and of itself as it functions as a standard by which to tag people: those who are out (healthy, strong, mature) and those who are not (weak, immature, backward)" (in Hochberg, Maikey, and Saraya 2010, 605).

Families are particularly significant as sources of support, love, and survival for sexual-minority individuals. It is not really feasible to forgo one's family, move to a different location, and start a new life. Nadine argued that "there is so much kindness from someone who may not understand you but loves you. . . . There is a place of uncertainty, of not-said things, that you can sit comfortably with." She talked about numerous other occasions where families do a lot of work, a lot of cover-up, so to speak, a lot of denial, in order to survive. Silences and taboos around sexuality allow for maneuverability, "a space of negotiability," Bruce Dunne argues (1998, 9). However, these silences leave normativity unchallenged and unchanged, which in turn can legitimize patterns of violence (Dunne 1998, 9). Haneen, reflecting on this issue, raised questions about the possible oppressions that may underlie such structures. She indicated, "All the people that are 'out' to their families, so they can do this work, they kind of entered into an agreement to get their whole family so to speak into the closet." She wondered if as "we criticized visibility at all cost, we became complicit in new forms of gender and sexual oppression in certain reproductions of these systems, and we have to find new ways to break that." The question is then raised regarding what gets obfuscated in a process of ensuring invisibility as a strategy to protect families and individuals. Lama Abu-Odeh wonders what relations of power and oppression the practice of invisibility leaves untouched or unchallenged. Masculine women and effeminate men as well as trans-identified individuals, for example, do not have the privilege of invisibility. "What [Joseph] Massad calls invisibility associated with same sex identification is nothing but a capacity to 'pass' by some," writes Abu-Odeh. "Their bodies and affects do not bear the signification *khawal* because they have mastered masculine performance to the teeth, and their insistence on same sex identification is in fact a dissociation from and avoidance of the derogatory delineation *khawal*" (Abu-Odeh 2013).[20]

Critical activists expressed their challenge to invisibility with the push in SRMs to address oppressions openly or make them visible and intelligible for the explicit purpose of creating change; they pointed to the limitations of language and engagement that often made them feel co-opted by international machinery. Nadine explained that as women met, it "became obvious that our problem is not homophobia per say but the oppression of women's sexualities." However, "it was very difficult to frame work around sexuality outside the international framing of SOGI or LGBT or sexual rights or what sexual rights means internationally." Meem adopted a strategy of relative or "ambiguous invisibility." "This ambiguity becomes anti-productive to our movements when we situate our politics within an international (Read 'Western') framework of coming out / visibility" (Darwich 2010). Haneen explained to me: "The feature that is positive but also challenging is the whole anti-imperial and the gay international space/discourse . . . how to describe our work and who we are without using ready-made language by the colonial other." AlQaws has been critical of the Western narrative of gay liberation and as such of the necessity of a politics of visibility. Similarly, Meem's "feminist approach challenged the division between outness/closetedness and visibility/invisibility that [is]

20. *Khawal* refers to men with a more feminine representation.

reinforced by Western LGBT discourse" (Hamdan 2015, 72). Sarah Hamdan argues that an engagement with the "problematic or the multiplicity of difference" would be more apt for the SRMs (2015, 74).

On the one hand, when a group such as alQaws issues a political statement, it gets criticized for not being grassroots or for being too intellectual even though it organizes "over 100 hours of training with many people, but you cannot write an article about it as you are committed to these people and their safety and security, so this work becomes invisible," Haneen explained. Activists thus continuously ask the question about what becomes invisible because they make only certain things visible. These responses from the public, Haneen reiterated, indicates that this other important work also needs to be more visible to explain the negotiations and discussions that take place on the ground and to do this explaining in the spoken language of everyday people about the issues they face in this domain rather than in the language of the so-called gay international. According to Haneen, "You cannot break these barriers and systems of oppression in society except through visibility, but it has to be done really responsibly." Not only the younger generation but also some of the activists who started this movement work also feel that it may be time to practice more visibility. One activist from Lebanon indicated that visibility—through engaging the media, for example—has contributed to a shift of perception and engagement with issues of sexual and gender diversity.

In the context of new internet technologies and social media, it has become almost impossible to aim, even if only strategically, at a politics of invisibility. Nadine explained that it was possible to advance work between 2007 and 2013 in a more contained framework, to address things such as creating safe spaces, and to work internally to build strengths, tools, and languages. Today, the terrain has changed dramatically. Nadine stated: "The liminal space between private and public is shrinking. This is the space that we used to play within a lot; we would open a bit and then close; now if we open, we cannot close." The algorithm models that entities such as Facebook and Instagram are using and the tremendous increase in usership and accessibility have meant a huge implosion in connections and spaces. This visible cyberspace, Nadine argued, could be very advantageous for certain groups, but it also makes folks much more exposed and thus vulnerable. Limiting or containing the conversation becomes impossible, and so invisibility as an active strategy is also no longer possible. The plans for IDAHO in Lebanon in 2017 and the backlash from religious authorities and the state are but one example of such challenges (Chamas 2021; El Khazen 2017).[21]

Intersectional Politics and Practice

Almost all the activists I interviewed understand their organizing as intersectional (as defined in Crenshaw 1989, 1991; Lorde [1984] 2007), given their daily lived realities and the systems perpetuating their oppression. They experience their lives intersectionally and have thus felt that it is impossible for them to organize on single-issue agendas or one identity because addressing one "closet" may only force them into another "closet."

Intersectional lives. From the time of its founding, Aswat insisted on the intersectionality of identities. In its founding documents, it indicates that its members came together to "address our personal, social and political struggles as a national indigenous minority living inside Israel; as women in a patriarchal society; and as LBTQI women in a wider hetero-normative culture" (Amireh 2020, 46). In the introduction to its first book, *Home and Exile in Queer Experience* (2007), published in Arabic, Rauda Morcos writes:

> Our strength as women, as lesbians, as Palestinians does not reside in the choosing of a single identity and privileging it over others, but in the insistence that there is a way to create a space for all of them. I am these identities combined—we are lesbians, we are women, we are Palestinians, and these three identities cannot be separated from one another. And through outlining the multilayered discourse among the

21. IDAHO, the International Day against Homophobia, was established in 2004 by a group of activists to raise awareness of acts that discriminate against LGBT folks. It was later transformed to IDAHOBIT, the International Day against Homophobia, Biphobia, and Transphobia, and is acknowledged on May 17. On IDAHO 2017, see Fleming-Farrell 2017 and Meuse 2017. For a critique, see hashtagbeirut 2017 and Socialist Feminist Committee of the Socialist Platform 2017.

> nationalist, sexual, and gender struggles, we will continue our awareness work around the inseparable link between these three and carry this message to the international community of lesbians, bisexual, transsexual, transgendered, intersex, and queer that our struggle as lesbians against oppression cannot be separated from our struggles for social justice and human rights for all. (Aswat Palestinian Gay Women 2007b, 21, my translation)

Haneen Maikey similarly asserted that the intersectionality of Palestinian LGBTQ identities necessitates an intersectional politics rather than a hierarchy of identities. She stated in 2010: "We argue that our struggle as LGBTQ Palestinians is a struggle against both the occupation and homophobia, or, more accurately, it is about the intersection among these and other struggles within the Palestinian societies" (in Hochberg, Maikey, and Saraya 2010, 602). Najma reiterated that the community in Tunisia is becoming more aware that the concerns and problems that lesbians or bisexual women face may be different than those experienced by gay men or trans folks and that it is important to understand these various structures of oppression and how they intersect. A coalition of groups organized an event in 2017 that highlighted solidarity with the trans community in particular.[22]

Intersectional discourse and practice: anti-imperialist, anticolonial, class conscious, antiracist, anti-Zionist. The SRMs, particularly in Lebanon and Palestine, developed an intersectional discourse and practice that stemmed not only from people's personal experiences of oppression in terms of their identity formation but also in terms of their political experience. The choice was often a conscious one arrived at as a result of political engagement on multiple issues. Azza explained that Mesahat learned that one cannot deal with LGBTQIA+ issues as distinct from other areas of intersection. Nadine emphasized the idea of working with heterosexual woman, given that patriarchy affects all women, even if in different ways. Queer activists in Nasawiya worked very hard on the issue of marital rape,

22. See the Facebook posts for "Journée internationale contre l'homophobie et la transphobie Idahot-Tunisie" at https://www.facebook.com/TunisiaIdahot2017/.

an area that may have little to do directly with their lives or their identities. Activists understood their sexuality as co-constitutive of different experiences. Ghassan Makarem writes about Helem: "Although HELEM was formed to focus on LGBT issues, its roots in Hurriyyat Khassa and the anti-imperialist movement led to the adoption of an anti-sectarian, anti-racist, and anti-xenophobia position from its inception and to a focus on social work, especially within marginalized communities" (2011, 105). Makarem situates the founding of Helem against the background of anti-imperialist mobilization in support of Palestine in 2002 and against the war in Iraq in 2003. Then in 2006, when Lebanon came under attack from Israel, Helem joined solidarity efforts. It became part of Samidoun, which was a large campaign that brought together different organizing sectors, from environmental organizations to antiwar, student, labor, and Palestinian refugee organizations. This campaign collected donations and provided direct support to refugees during the war (Makarem 2011).

Through engagement in international convenings, SRM activists quickly realized that their intersectional politics required explaining and perhaps necessitated advocacy and outreach. Makarem recalls that during the OutGames of 2006 in Montreal, Helem prepared a video address to express its concerns about the Israeli aggression and expected nothing but support and solidarity. Its members quickly realized that there is a need to intervene in international forums on LGBT rights to address the single-issue agenda and lack of political awareness. Makarem and others engaged in the SRMs believe that "the experiences in Lebanon, occupied Palestine, and numerous groups around the world have shown that LGBT liberation is part of a wider struggle for change and against imperialism and capitalist exploitation" (Makarem 2011, 110).

Nadine Naber and I have argued that "the 2006 Israeli invasion and its aftermath provided a heightened moment of political activism in which activists came to articulate a feminist and LGBTQ critique that insisted that concepts and practices of gender and sexuality in Lebanon were shaped within the broader contexts of US and Israeli imperial war and the interrelated Lebanese state structures of sectarianism, classism, and racism" (Naber and Zaatari 2014, 93). Activists' experiences during the Israeli invasion in 2006 highlighted the ways in which these imperialist intersections reinforced heteronormativity. Activists shared stories that spoke to the ways in which systems of oppression such as neoliberalism, classism, militarism, sectarianism, patriarchy, and homophobia intersect. Makarem (2011) argues that the work of Helem members in Samidoun was an important milestone that solidified the practice of intersectionality as it also politically opened up the organization and its members to other groups—beyond the human rights and health organizing. It necessitated shifts in practice and discourse that foregrounded the later split in Helem and its more recent turn toward SOGI discourse.

Pinkwashing and settler colonialism. Jasbir Puar's (2007, 2013) term *homonationalism* analyzes certain shifts in history that have led to specific state formation and specific articulations of modernity. It signifies "the historical convergence of state practices, transnational circuits of queer commodity culture and human rights paradigms, and broader global phenomena such as the increasing entrenchment of Islamophobia" (Puar 2013, 337). The coming together of these circumstances has made it possible for nation-states to be labeled as gay friendly rather than homophobic and for duplicitous state practices such as pinkwashing to exist. Israel launched a public-relations media campaign in October 2005 titled Brand Israel (AlQaisiya 2018; Atshan 2020; Elia 2013; Franke 2010; Hochberg 2010; Gross 2007; Schulman 2011)—a conglomerate of marketing firms funded by the Foreign Ministry, the Prime Minister's Office, and the Finance Ministry—a few months after the call for Boycott, Divestment, and Sanction was issued.[23] One aspect of this campaign is pinkwashing—"Israel's attempt to present itself as a gay haven, an oasis of gay freedom in an otherwise violently homophobic backwards region" (Elia 2013, 50). Settler-colonial states and ideologies have a long history of articulating violence through supposed protection for specific populations, such as women and children and more recently the homosexual. Amireh argues: "The positive rhetorical function of queerness for Zionism, however, goes beyond those internal culture wars (between secular

23. On the Boycott, Divestment, and Sanction movement, see its website at https://bdsmovement.net/.

Jews and religious Jews) into the wider culture wars between Israelis and Palestinians, where it functions to consolidate a fractured Zionist consensus by casting Palestinians as the ultimate 'Other' for their alleged essentialist homophobia" (2020, 46). The pinkwashing campaign distorted and obscured the reality of everyday violence against all Palestinians. Israel's presentation of itself as civilized and Palestinians as barbaric and homophobic "has manifold effects: it denies Israel's homophobic oppression of its own gays and lesbians, of which there is plenty, and it recruits, often unwittingly, gays and lesbians of other countries into a collusion with Israeli violence towards Palestine" (Puar 2010). It further "distracts from Israel's violence against queer Palestinians, reproduces an essential aspect of settler colonialist discourse: the erasure of the native experience of displacement, dispossession and disenfranchisement, by the so-called 'gay haven'" (Elia 2013, 59).

The Israeli machinery sought support, funding, and collaboration from queer Western audiences and organizations. Thus, the response to such campaigns had also to be global in perspective and reach. Various queer groups informed by the Palestinian and Palestinian diaspora perspective and vision came together in the United States and Europe and organized local events to contradict this dominant narrative.[24] "To insist on queering the Israeli-Palestinian conflict, then, is to engage in undermining this normalized and naturalized political hierarchy. It is to reject the heterosexist portrayal of sexual politics as a 'superfluous' (queer) preoccupation with sex" (Hochberg 2010, 505).

Activists are being challenged by the fact that not only their strategic allies (queer groups around the world) are being co-opted in service of a settler-colonial state under the guise of sexual freedom but also intellectuals and academics (Puar and Mikdashi 2012a, 2012b; Schotten and Maikey 2012) who originally come from Palestine and other "third-world"

24. The groups included Queers Undermining Israeli Terrorism, https://www.quitpalestine.org; Pinkwatching Israel, https://www.pinkwatchingisrael.com/; Israeli Laundry, https://www.israelilaundry.org/category/pinkwashing/; and Queers against Israeli Apartheid, https://queersagainstapartheid.org/.

countries but now reside in the United States or Europe.[25] Massad (2007) states that while same-sex sexuality has always existed in the Arab world, homosexual identity has not, but the latter is now being fostered or imposed by the "gay international" intent on homogenizing the world into its vision of the hetero-homo binary. Hochberg argues, however, that "Massad's view of 'authentic' Arab sexuality is limited to his understanding of *male sexuality*, . . . for in his account, Arab women are situated outside these authentic cultural formations and outside sexuality altogether" (2010, 506). Furthermore, Massad accuses activists in groups such as alQaws and Helem of being at best unwilling agents of empire and at worst self-interested conspiratorial agitators.[26] This reaffirms in public discourse the idea that same-sex sexuality, identity or otherwise, is a Western or white thing, a phrase repeated and rehashed by various media outlets and fundamentalist and nationalist groups. In the context of Palestine, this connection translates into accusations of cultural betrayal and spying for Israel, which can have devastating consequences for LGBTQIA+ folks. Sometimes they are blackmailed to become informants for Israel or different Palestinian factions, and if they are attacked or killed, this violence is hard to identify as being either about their sexuality or about their position as informants (Amireh 2010; AlQaisiya, Hilal, and Maikey 2016; Hochberg 2010).[27]

Haneen Maikey and Gaith Hilal argue that the image of the "homosexual" has been linked to the "other" in the Palestinian national context as a result of particular historical, political, and social transformations.

25. Such co-optation in service of the settler-colonial state Israel is relevant not just to European and US queer organizing in that Israel has invested tremendous energy and resources into supporting LGBT organizing in different parts of the world under this pinkwashing media strategy.

26. Massad's views are available mainly in his book *Desiring Arabs* (2007), but also see Abu-Odeh 2013; AlQaisiya, Hilal, and Maikey 2016; Ewanje-Epee and Magliani-Belkacem 2013; and *Reset DOC* 2009.

27. For an exploration of a similar theme yet one targeting women's sexuality, see Amel Amireh's article "Between Complicity and Subversion" (2003).

This "other" is "the informant collaborating with the forces of occupation against his people" in its worst manifestation or "someone influenced by the western/Israeli/imperialist culture and execut[ing] agendas foreign to our society without being conscious of it" in its best (2015, 22). The factors that have supported such an image include the policies of the Palestinian political organizations, which in their attempt to fight Israel's blackmailing of people into collaboration have adopted and promoted a "moral society" discourse. Instead of challenging oppressive structures within societies that generate fear and vulnerability in anyone engaged with nonconforming sexual practices, whether sex outside marriage or same-sex relations, these political organizations have reaffirmed such notions and thus increased the risks and the discourse of homophobia (AlQaisiya, Hilal, and Maikey 2016). With pinkwashing, the Palestinian "homosexual" is further imagined as someone outside their community, particularly as the campaign insists on the discourse of homophobia as a primary axis of oppression irrespective of or unconnected to other oppressive structures (AlQaisiya, Hilal, and Maikey 2016; Maikey and Hilal 2015). In contrast, Amireh argues that "the community Aswat and Al-Qaws create by being 'out'—in the political sense—is crucial for loosening the grip that the trope 'homosexuality as collaboration' has on Palestinian society" (2020, 47). In this framework, visibility could be a strategic tool to reclaim authenticity and refuse the western and Israeli narratives that only allows for queers to exist as victims in need of Israel's support.

Axes of Intervention

Creation of Safe Spaces

One important issue that affects LGBTQIA+ folks—depending on the country, the location within the country, the family's socioeconomic background, and age—is the need for safety and security. Gender nonconformity is a significant indicator/marker of potential rejection by family and society and possible risk to one's safety. As the introduction to this volume attests, the number of dangers potentially affecting nonnormative folks are numerous. In the stories compiled in *Bareed Mista3jil* (Meem 2009), many of the women talk about how the challenges they first faced had to do with how they looked and acted in ways deemed nonconforming to standards of femininity. In my current research on the lives of queer women in Lebanon, I have similarly identified that gender nonconformity rather than sexual nonconformity acts as the moment of contention and then realization of difference (Zaatari 2014). Women have more leeway in performing masculinity, but when men perform femininity, they generally are seen as threatening to masculinity as a whole. The different stories of Sudanese men in Mesahat's collection *LGBT Voices from Sudan* (2016) highlight the challenges that men confront when they display feminine qualities or are perceived as feminine. They are attacked by their families, beaten by strangers or colleagues at universities and in the streets, and attacked in police stations. In Lebanon, men can be targeted for looking feminine or "soft" (Frangieh 2014; Gazza 2012; Rizk and Makarem 2015; Saleh and Qubaia 2015). Sometimes people with nonconforming identities are disowned, and at other times they may find it unbearable to stay in their family home and so leave or are thrown out. Thus, the issue of safety becomes paramount for individuals, which is why for many organizations one of the main strategies is to create a safe space where people can bring their nonconforming identity and feel accepted and where questions about one's self, one's desires, one's preferences, and the world can be voiced and discussed. Many groups have struggled to find ways to provide secure spaces for individuals who have had to leave or were kicked out of their homes. Establishing such spaces has been a constant struggle given the lack of adequate resources to support needed long-term solutions.

Sometimes such spaces, once established, have unfortunately reproduced patriarchal and heteronormative practices and narratives and ended up creating further oppressions and borders. Groups talk about the need to create "our own" space to be able to address "our" concerns as lesbian women or trans folks because those positionalities may be different from that of the more mainstream gay male organizing. While such calls are not unique to the region, a closer look at practices and behaviors by some men in the movement (though certainly not exclusively) highlights the ways in which patriarchy and heteronormativity are embedded in behaviors, ideas, and norms that they end up reproducing within supposedly "safe" spaces.[28] Anthony Rizk and Ghassan Makarem argue that masculinity-under-threat has evolved "as a political response to both LGBT and women's activism" and has as such reinforced hegemonic masculinity even within "queer" spaces, where "'good' masculinity [is] constructed as respectable, middle-class, educated and professionalized homosexual masculinity" (2015, 106, 103).

Of increasing concern is not only the lack of safety that the digital world masks, given assumptions about its anonymity and safety, but also the ways in which surveillance technologies and the security state have developed strategies to target activists and nonconforming individuals. Stories abound of folks who have been lured into captivity and arrested by police officers posing as potential dates on internet dating apps (Bahgat 2004; Human Rights Watch 2023b; Long 2004). Various social media sites either have been targeted by governments or have voluntarily provided data on activists' activities and stated positions. In response, digital-security training has become very common among organizations in the past five to six years across the region. Mesahat, for example, has dedicated significant programming to digital-security training and provides information in Arabic on how individuals can take steps to protect themselves.

Advocacy and Awareness Raising

Many of the groups and the activists I interviewed focused on advocacy as an important avenue to create change. Their strategy includes not only traditional advocacy, meaning campaigns to change laws, but also visibility in different layers of society as an attempt to transform public opinion. Groups utilize an advocacy strategy on three levels: *civil society*, including traditional human rights organizations, development NGOs, and women's rights groups; *public opinion*, involving primarily various media outlets; and, finally, *governments*, involving politicians and various public institutions. A fourth and historically minor, though recently growing, level of advocacy intervention has been at the international

28. Read the debates and statements in Ghoulama 2012 and NFASHARTE 2012.

level—namely, international agencies and governing bodies, such as the UN Human Rights Council.

Civil society advocacy. Most of the first-generation SRM groups were invested in opening up spaces for conversation and understanding (even if not acceptance) within civil society organizations. Entities that have long fought for human rights, freedom, and self-determination were perceived to be natural allies. In many instances, sexual rights activists in the MENA region were already working within such organizations or engaging with them but had experienced silencing and exclusion in them. These organizations often worried about their already fragile image in MENA society. Women's rights organizations had suffered a long history of being accused of westernization and of attempts to dismantle family structures and societal harmony. Human rights organizations were under the microscope as opposition or potential dissidents. Development NGOs needed legitimacy from disenfranchised communities who increasingly seemed to be inclined to follow the lead of religious-based organizations, while NGOs were constantly being accused of following donor-driven agendas. For many of these groups, highlighting yet another deeply controversial or taboo topic as part of their work seemed insurmountable and risky. However, sexual rights activists believed there were additional layers to these civil society organizations' resistance to including SRM activists, including the reproduction of patriarchy and homophobia within these structures, even as such groups used the language and framework of human rights and expressed a belief in individual freedoms. Activists organized trainings and meetings to discuss how to push the envelope in established NGOs.

Media advocacy. Activists either actively decided to intervene in the public conversation by engaging media outlets or at times were forced to be part of the conversation. Initially, the most supportive media were predominantly online, independent bloggers and journalists already invested in freedom and equality. Activists themselves often had their own blogs. As the more traditional media began paying attention, their coverage either continued to reproduce derogatory discourse on the SRMs—borrowed from Western media under the guise of "liberal" engagement—or was outright antagonistic and worked to intensify the moral panic and paranoia around the issues raised by the SRMs (Bahgat 2004; Long 2004; Mikdashi 2014). Activists engaged with print media initially, seeking out journalists, including them in training sessions, and providing them with information and the appropriate terminologies. This work led to tremendous shifts in media representation and writing, particularly in the print media both online and offline in several countries, namely Lebanon, Palestine, Algeria, and Tunisia. Groups also utilized the online space by creating their own websites, blogs, and magazines to share stories and educate.

According to many of the activists I talked with, visual and audio media continue to be the most reactionary and unpredictable. In the era of twenty-four-hour television programming and talk shows, many programs have addressed these SOGI issues negatively, with a caricaturist representation, sensationalist overtones, and often an overemphasis on outdated medicalized explanations even in the attempt to be understanding.

State and legal advocacy. Advocacy at the state and legal level took different forms, including formalized campaigns targeting specific laws and informal ongoing conversations to change policy and practice on the ground.[29] Service work, such as HIV prevention among MSM communities in Algeria and Lebanon, involved collaboration with national committees and ministries. This on-the-ground work eventually led to the inclusion of these strategies at the national level and within the government's service-provision centers. Yahia discussed how the work of the HIV Prevention group in Algeria led to its full incorporation into the National Strategy Plan on AIDS in 2007–12.

Groups also organized formal campaigns to address current laws or proposed modifications. In Lebanon, Hurriyyat Khassa's campaign against the proposed penal code change did lead to the indefinite postponement of addressing the proposed draft. Soon thereafter, Helem began its campaign to abolish Article 534, which criminalizes copulation "against nature."[30]

29. For a quick review of the different laws in the region, see the Human Rights Watch report *Audacity in Adversity* (Ghoshal 2018).

30. The article was adopted from the French Penal Code in Lebanon and Syria. Syria uses the same wording.

Although the campaign itself was short-lived and did not result in direct legal change, Helem and the Legal Agenda have continued their efforts to address this law.[31] Engagement with judges through formal and informal dialogues, conferences, and model defense led to several important rulings that began to shake the article's legal foundation (Karame 2016). A recent ruling clearly stipulates that same-sex relations are not a crime and are not against nature (see Human Rights Watch 2018a). Another active campaign in Tunisia against Article 230, which criminalizes homosexuality (lesbian and gay), among other laws, has resulted in judges sometimes issuing reduced sentences. Senda and Najma explained that the law is seen as unconstitutional, particularly in terms of the new Constitution of 2014, and groups are hoping to be able to strike it down. In fact, the Commission on Individual Freedoms and Equality appointed by the president released its report in June 2018, recommending decriminalizing homosexuality and affirming gender equality, among other important legal reforms (Commission des libertes individuelles et de l'egalité 2018; see also Human Rights Watch 2018b, 2018c). In contrast, other countries, such as Egypt, have increased repression and introduced new legislation that criminalizes homosexuality (Hisham 2017; Ramzi 2017). In chapter 5 of this volume, Ana Cristina Marques, Salma Talaat, and J. Michael Ryan demonstrate the tremendous legal challenges facing trans individuals in the region. The backlash since 2019 has been significant as more countries are working or pushing for new legislation to criminalize same-sex relations and trans identities (see Human Rights Watch 2023a; Mroue and Chehayeb 2023; Noralla 2022, 2023a, 2023b).

International advocacy. While international advocacy among LGBTQIA+ activists is a growing field, feminists addressing women's sexual autonomy and bodily integrity have had a longer history and experience. Through the Turkish delegation to the UN, Turkish activists played an important role in the inclusion of marital rape, honor crimes, and forced marriages in the outcome document of the Commission on the Status of Women conference in 2000. This success was owed to the strong role of the women's

31. Hurriyyat Khassa was the predecessor to Legal Agenda.

movement in Turkey, which precipitated the feminists' invitation to join the official delegation. It was also the first time that "Turkey supported language on sexual orientation, that is the inclusion of sexual orientation in the list of barriers women encounter in enjoying their human rights" (Ilkkaracan 2008, 6). The Tunisian Coalition for the Rights of LGBTQI Individuals produced a Universal Periodic Review report, which was launched in Tunis in February 2017 (Tunisian Coalition 2017) and submitted to the UN Human Rights Council as Tunisia was under review in May 2017.[32] Although some groups have engaged in these various international efforts, activists themselves feel conflicted about the efforts' efficacy given larger political dynamics (i.e., neocolonization, imperial projects), even while also realizing that there is a need for complex and multiple strategies for social change.

Support and Services

Most groups and activists working on sexual rights agree on the important need for service provision for members of the community. What they disagree on is who is the best entity to provide such services. More accurately, most feel strongly that services should be the realm of the government. However, given the clear lack of such possibilities, some feel that groups or NGOs should take on such a task, while others feel strongly that the government should be held accountable and pushed to provide such services. Omar Fattal, Hossam Mahmoud, and Lama Bazzi (2018) argue that NGOs in Lebanon have primarily taken on the responsibility of supporting mental health and have done so really well. In certain contexts, government service-provision apparatuses are weak, inefficient, and rarely inclusive. They tend to target the poorest populations and rarely have a policy against discrimination. In other contexts, the entrenchment of neoliberal economic policies and structural-adjustment programs has meant the near disappearance of already weak and highly bureaucratic government services.

32. See coverage of the report in Ben Ali 2017.

Many of the early SRM initiatives began working on HIV/AIDS prevention and testing, particularly with MSM communities. When Helem started, it created such a program to provide support to the community. The program realized, however, that not only the MSM community needed such services around sexual health and that the community space was not a very confidential location. As such, Marsa was born, with leadership from Meem and Helem and infused with feminist politics; this center provides sexual health services, counseling, and a referral program. In addition to sexual health services, psychosocial support was seen as important and necessary, especially for a community that has been under tremendous familial and societal pressure to conform and that has had to live a life of secrecy. Meem initially established such a program in the womyn house. Other organizations have also created such programs, locating supportive counselors and therapists in them. Some have established hotlines that provide support to individuals in need of urgent assistance or direction.

Knowledge Production

In the introduction to *Bareed Mista3jil*, Meem states, "We have published this book in order to introduce Lebanese society to the real stories of real people whose voices have gone unheard for hundreds of years. They live among us, although invisible to us, in our families, our schools, our workplaces, and our neighborhoods" (Meem 2009, 1). Although the book is targeting Lebanese readers primarily and readers in other Arab-majority countries secondarily, it nonetheless also attempts to address the stereotyping of Arab women, lesbians, and others by Western writers and audiences. Meem claims that between the shrouding of sexuality in morality and the impact of colonization and Western Orientalist ideas about Arabs and their sexuality, "sexuality [in Arab countries] has . . . become silenced, governed by shame and misconceived myths" (5). Thus, the group hopes this book will work to "dispel these myths" (5). Meem decided not to use any names in the book to ensure the safety of those speaking up about these issues. The collection also does not aim to give a representative sample or a typical story because Meem felt it was more important to be inclusive. Instead, the group acknowledges that "the stories in this book represent many common fragments from the lives of many queer women in this country" (8).

In *Haqi an a'yysh, an Akhtar, an akun* (My Right to Live to Choose to Be, 2007), Aswat insists on the importance of documenting personal narratives and presenting them to the public. It believes that the embodiment of real-life experiences has a strong capacity to raise awareness in society and thus create change in perception and understanding (Aswat Palestinian Gay Women 2007a, 11). "We want to appeal to those who have tried to understand lesbians and gays, but were not able to understand our lives, our experiences, our choices. We hope that this contribution can help in shedding light onto this world where you would be able to see us like you [as] humans with feelings, emotions, and problems. Perhaps if we succeed then we can see you next to us, dear friends, our families, our colleagues, helping and supporting us to create a new world that accepts the other different from him and sees him as a partner" (12–13, my translation). The book also plays an important role in supporting and empowering Arab readers in understanding their own experiences of difference and in building connections, particularly in their own language (Abboud 2017). The group states: "We aim through these texts to tell you that you are not alone and that there are many others like you and that your desires are legitimate no matter how different they may be" (Aswat 2007a, 12, my translation).

In the initial issue of *Barra* magazine, Makarem (2005) explains that the magazine, although not claiming to rewrite history, constitutes an attempt to open a space for gay, lesbian, bisexual, transgender, and queer folks and their friends to contribute to the public discussion of various issues important to them. It stresses the invisibility of and misconceptions regarding members of the "queer" community and its issues among the media, organizing spaces, and legal practices. As such, *Barra* has become one space among others where these issues can be debated, where awareness can be generated, and where openings can be achieved through the acts of writing and reading.

In *LGBT Voices from Sudan: Recording a Past, Building a Future* (2016), the organization Mesahat explains the conditions under which the community lives in Sudan, which has led to them "remaining invisible, and their voices not heard" (7). The group hopes the oral-history documentation can "play an important role in raising awareness about sexual orientation and gender identity issues in Sudan" (7).

There is a much longer list of online and print publications that tell stories and personal experiences, highlighting voices of those who have long been excluded from the stories of community and "normality"; studies speaking to trends, challenges, and needs of the community; and explorations of identities and terminologies in native languages (Arabic, Tamazigh, Kurdish, etc.).

Conclusion

The history of the sexual rights movements in the MENA region and the debates and issues they historically have grappled with and currently challenge are as complex as those of any movement facing the attempt to create societal change. Space is always limited to be able to adequately represent all the layers of that complexity and all the vantage points of narrating that history. I have argued here that there are already three distinguishable waves of SRMs in the region, each affected by local, regional, and global transformations. I have also argued that first-generation activists were mostly already activists (feminists, socialists, leftists, etc.) battling normative practices and ideas in society and within organizing circles. They pushed the accepted boundaries, struggled to gain legitimacy, and worked to equip themselves and others with the necessary tools and language to speak of the unspeakable, to enable choices, and to materialize just visions. Others have since followed suit, and organizing continues to grow in various directions, even as the backlash intensifies with increased harassment, persecution, and attempts at criminalization.

References

Abboud, Rima. 2017. "Inclusion, Diversity, and Exclusion: Thoughts from within Aswat-Palestinian Gay Women." *Adult Education and Development* 84. At https://www.dvv-international.de/en/adult-education-and-development/editions/aed-842017-inclusion-and-diversity/section-1-identity/inclusion-diversity-and-exclusion-thoughts-from-within-aswat-palestinian-gay-women.

Abu-Odeh, Lama. 2013. "That Thing That You Do: Comment on Joseph Massad's 'Empire of Sexuality.'" *Al-Akhbar*, Mar. 25. At https://english.al-akhbar.com/content/thing-you-do-comment-joseph-massad%E2%80%99s-%E2%80%9Cempire-sexuality%E2%80%9D.

Ahmed, Leila. 1993. *Women and Gender in Islam: Historical Root of a Modern Debate*. New Haven, CT: Yale Univ. Press.

AlQaisiya, Walaa. 2018. "Decolonial Queering: The Politics of Being Queer in Palestine." *Journal of Palestine Studies* 47, no. 3: 29–44.

AlQaisiya, Walaa, Ghaith Hilal, and Haneen Maikey. 2016. "Dismantling the Image of the Palestinian Homosexual: Exploring the Role of alQaws." In *Decolonizing Sexualities: Transnational Perspectives, Critical Interventions*, edited by Sandeep Baskhi, Suhraiya Jivraj, and Silvia Posocco, 125–40. Oxford: Counterpress.

Amer, Sahar. 2015. "Political-Social Movements: Homosexuality and Queer Movements: Egypt." In *Encyclopedia of Women and Islamic Cultures Online*, edited by Suad Joseph. Leiden, Netherlands: Brill. At https://dx.doi.org/10.1163/1872-5309_ewic_COM_002012.

Amireh, Amal. 2000. "Framing Nawal El Saadawi: Arab Feminism in a Transnational World." *Signs* 26, no. 1: 215–49.

———. 2003. "Between Complicity and Subversion: Body Politics in Palestinian National Narrative." *South Atlantic Quarterly* 102, no. 4: 747–72.

———. 2010. Afterword to "Queer Politics: The Question of Palestine/Israel," edited by Gil Z. Hochberg. Special issue, *GLQ: A Journal of Lesbian and Gay Studies* 16, no. 4: 635–47.

———. 2020. "Palestinian Queerness and the Orientalist Paradigm." In *Women Rising: In and Beyond the Arab Spring*, edited by Rita Stephan and Mounira M. Charrad, 44–49. New York: New York Univ. Press.

Aswat Palestinian Gay Women. 2007a. *Haqi an a'yysh, an Akhtar, an akun: Majmu'at nusus adabiyya linisa' 'arabiyyat mithliyaat* [My right to live to choose to be: A collection of literal texts written by Arab lesbian women]. Haifa: Aswat Palestinian Gay Women.

———. 2007b. *Al-watan wa al-manfa fi tajribat al-mutaharirat jinsiyan* (Home and exile in queer experience: Collection of articles about lesbian and homosexual identity). Haifa: Aswat Palestinian Gay Women.

Atshan, Sa'ed. 2020. *Queer Palestine and the Empire of Critique*. Stanford, CA: Stanford Univ. Press.

Badran, Margot. 1993. "Independent Women: More Than a Century of Feminism in Egypt." In *Arab Women: Old Boundaries, New Frontiers*, edited by Judith Tucker, 129–48. Bloomington: Indiana Univ. Press.

Bahgat, Hossam. 2004. "Egypt's Virtual Protection of Morality." *Middle East Report* 34, no. 230: 22–25.

Batliwala, Srilatha, ed. 2008. *Changing Their World: Concepts and Practices of Women's Movements*. Toronto: Association for Women's Rights in Development.

Ben Ali, Faz. 2017. "Report sur la situation des personnes LBGTQI en Tunisie." Kapitalis, Feb. 23. At https://kapitalis.com/tunisie/2017/02/23/situation-des-personnes-lgbtqi-en-tunisie/.

Catholics for Choice. 2013. *The Catholic Church at the United Nations: Church or State?* Washington, DC: Catholics for Choice. At https://www.catholicsforchoice.org/wp-content/uploads/2013/08/CFC_See_Change_2013.pdf.

Chamas, Sophie. 2021. "*Lil Watan*: Queer Patriotism in Chauvinistic Lebanon." *Sexualities* 26, nos. 1–2: 230–51.

Commission des libertes individuelles et de l'egalité. 2018. "Taqrir Lajnat al-Huriyyat al-Fardiyya wa al-Musawat" (Report of the Personal Freedom and Equality Committee). June 1. At https://colibe.org/wp-content/uploads/2018/06/Rapport-COLIBE.pdf.

Crenshaw, Kimberle. 1989. "Demarginalizing the Intersection of Race and Sex: A Black Feminist Critique of Antidiscrimination Doctrine, Feminist Theory and Antiracist Politics." *University of Chicago Legal Forum* 140: 139–67.

———. 1991. "Mapping the Margins: Intersectionality, Identity Politics, and Violence against Women of Color." *Stanford Law Review* 43, no. 6: 1241–99.

Darwich, Lynn. 2010. "Framing Visibility: Coming Out and the International LGBT Spectrum of Progress." *Bekhsoos*, Dec. 12.

Darwich, Lynn, and Haneen Maikey. 2011. "From the Belly of Arab Queer Activism: Challenges and Opportunities." *Bekhsoos*, Oct. 12. At https://www.alqaws.org/articles/From-the-Belly-of-Arab-Queer-Activism-Challenges-and-Opportunities?category_id=0.

Dunne, Bruce. 1998. "Power and Sexuality in the Middle East." *Middle East Report* 206: 8–11, 37.

Elia, Nada. 2013. "Gay Rights with a Side of Apartheid." *Settler Colonial Studies* 2, no. 2: 49–68.

Ewanje-Epee, Felix Boggio, and Stella Magliani-Belkacem. 2013. "The Empire of Sexuality: An Interview with Joseph Massad." *Jadaliyya*, Mar. 5. At https://www.jadaliyya.com/pages/index/10461/the-empire-of-sexuality_an-interview-with-joseph-m.

Fattal, Omar, Hossam Mahmoud, and Lama Bazzi. 2018. "A Brief Overview of Advances in LGBT Mental Health Advocacy in Lebanon." *Harvard Review of Psychiatry* 26, no. 4: 237–40. At https://doi.org/10.1097/HRP.0000000000000169.

Fleming-Farrell, Niamh. 2017. "Beirut Pride Week Goes Ahead despite Islamist Threats." *Telegraph*, May 21. At https://www.telegraph.co.uk/news/2017/05/21/beirut-pride-week-goes-ahead-despite-islamist-threats/.

Frangieh, Ghida. 2014. "The Hammam al-Agha Raid: Collective Prosecution in Violation of Individual Rights." *The Legal Agenda*, Sept. 18. At https://legal-agenda.com/en/article.php?id=650&folder=articles&lang=en.

Franke, Katherine. 2010. "Sexual Rights and State Governance." *Proceedings of the Annual Meeting* (American Society for International Law) 104: 385–88.

Gaudio, Rudolf Pell. 2009. *Allah Made Us: Sexual Outlaws in an Islamic African City*. Hoboken, NJ: Wiley-Blackwell.

Gazza. 2012. "Fuhus al-'ar fi lubnan: 'Indama 'yughtasab' mawquf litathabut min mithliyatihi" [Shame tests in Lebanon: When a detainee is "raped" to prove his homosexuality]. *Duniya al-watan*, July 29. At https://www.alwatanvoice.com/arabic/news/2012/05/29/282495.html.

Ghoshal, Neela. 2018. *Audacity in Adversity: LGBT Activism in the Middle East and North Africa*. Washington, DC: Human Rights Watch.

Ghoulama. 2012. "Niqash fi 'aliyyat al-tanziym al-mithly wa qawunanat al-jinsaniyya fi lubnan" (A discussion about tactics of homosexuality organizing and regulating sexuality in Lebanon). *Bekhsoos*, June 26. At https://www.bekhsoos.com/2012/06/discussion-about-community-organizing-politicizing-sexuality-in-lebanon/.

Gross, Aeyal. 2007. "Queer Theory and International Human Rights Law: Does Each Person Have a Sexual Orientation?" *Proceedings of the Annual Meeting* (American Society for International Law) 101: 129–32.

Hamdan, Sarah. 2015. "Becoming-Queer-Arab-Activist: The Case of Meem." *Kohl: Journal for Body and Gender Research* 1, no. 2: 66–82. At https://kohljournal.press/becoming-queer-arab-activist.

hashtagbeirut. 2017. "So, This Is Your First Beirut Pride. Wonderful! Let's Talk." Tumblr, May 22. At https://hashtagbeirut.tumblr.com/post/160798887649/beirutpride.

Hassan, Maissan. 2016. "Political-Social Movements: Community-Based: Egypt: Post Revolution." In *Encyclopedia of Women and Islamic Cultures Online*, edited by Suad Joseph. Leiden, Netherlands: Brill. At https://dx.doi.org/10.1163/1872-5309_ewic_COM_002053.

Hisham, Jihad. 2017. "Al-balraman al-masry yatajih l'iqrar qanun ya'aqib al-mithliyyin bil-habsi 15 'aman" [The Egyptian Parliament leans toward passing a law that sentences homosexuals with 15 Years in jail]. *Erem News*, Oct. 5. At https://www.eremnews.com/news/arab-world/egypt/1015504.

Hochberg, Gil Z. 2010. "Introduction: Israeli, Palestinian, Queers: Points of Departure." *GLQ: A Journal of Lesbian and Gay Studies* 16, no. 4: 493–516.

Hochberg, Gil Z., Rima Haneen Maikey, and Samira Saraya. 2010. "No Pride in Occupation: A Roundtable Discussion." *GLQ: A Journal of Lesbian and Gay Studies* 16, no. 4: 599–610.

Human Rights Watch. 2016. "UN Makes History on Sexual Orientation, Gender Identity: Human Rights Body Establishes an Independent Expert." *Human Rights Watch*, June 30. At https://www.hrw.org/news/2016/06/30/un-makes-history-sexual-orientation-gender-identity.

———. 2018a. "Lebanon: Same-Sex Relations Not Illegal: Homosexuality Not an 'Unnatural Offense,' Appeals Court Rules." *Human Rights Watch*, July 19. At https://www.hrw.org/news/2018/07/19/lebanon-same-sex-relations-not-illegal.

———. 2018b. "Tunisia: Landmark Proposals on Gender Bias, Privacy." YouTube video in French. At https://www.youtube.com/watch?v=PwB6LUgWSHE&feature=youtu.be.

———. 2018c. "Tunisia: Landmark Proposals on Gender Bias, Privacy: Adopt Changes in Laws on Freedoms and Equality." *Human Rights Watch*, July 26. At https://www.hrw.org/news/2018/07/26/tunisia-landmark-proposals-gender-bias-privacy.

———. 2023a. "Iraq: Scrap Anti-LGBT Bill. Death Penalty for Same-Sex Conduct; Imprisonment for Transgender Expression." *Human Rights Watch*, Aug. 23. At https://www.hrw.org/news/2023/08/23/iraq-scrap-anti-lgbt-bill.

———. 2023b. "Middle East, North Africa: Digital Targeting of LGBT People: Arbitrary Arrests, Torture Follow Online Abuses, Illegal Phone Searches." *Human Rights Watch*, Feb. 21. At https://www.hrw.org/news/2023/02/21/middle-east-north-africa-digital-targeting-lgbt-people.

Ilkkaracan, Pinar. 2008. "Introduction: Sexuality as a Contested Political Domain in the Middle East." In *Deconstructing Sexuality in the Middle East:*

Challenges and Discourses, edited by Pinar Ilkkaracan, 1–16. London: Ashgate.

Ilkkaracan, Pinar, and Karin Ronge. 2008. "Integrating Sexuality into Gender and Human Rights Frameworks: A Case Study from Turkey." In *Development with a Body: Sexuality, Human Rights and Development*, edited by Andrea Cornwall, Sonia Correa, and Susie Jolly, 225–42. London: Zed.

Kamal, Hala. 2016. "A Century of Egyptian Women's Demands: The Four Waves of the Egyptian Feminist Movement." *Gender and Race Matter: Global Perspectives on Being a Woman* 21: 3–22.

Kandiyoti, Deniz. 1988. "Bargaining with Patriarchy." *Gender and Society* 2, no. 3: 274–90.

Karame, Lama. 2016. "Lebanese Article 534 Struck Down: Homosexuality No Longer 'Contrary to Nature.'" *The Legal Agenda*, July 11. At https://english.legal-agenda.com/lebanese-article-534-struck-down-homosexuality-no-longer-contrary-to-nature/.

El Khazen, Elia. 2017. "Monster Terrorist F(l)ag." *Salvage*, Oct. 13. At https://salvage.zone/monster-terrorist-flag/.

Long, Scott. 2004. "The Trials of Culture: Sex and Security in Egypt." *Middle East Report* 34, no. 230: 12–20.

Lorde, Audre. [1984] 2007. "Learning from the 60s." In *Sister Outsider: Essays and Speeches*, 134–44. Berkeley, CA: Crossing Press.

Maikey, Haneen, and Gaith Hilal. 2015. "'I'adat bina' surat al-mithli fi al-mujtama' al-falastini" [Reconstructing the image of the "homosexual" in Palestinian society]. *Jadal* 24: 22–25.

Makarem, Ghassan. 2005. "Introduction." *Barra* 0, no. 3. At https://www.7iber.com/society/reconstructing-the-image-of-homosexuals-in-palestine/.

———. 2009. "We Are Not Agents of the West: Ghassan Makarem Replies to Joseph Massad." *Reset DOC*, Dec. 14. At https://www.resetdoc.org/story/00000001542.

———. 2011. "The Story of HELEM." *Journal of Middle East Women's Studies* 7, no. 3: 98–112.

Marques, Ana Cristina, Salma Talaat, and J. Michael Ryan. 2024. "The (Im)Possibilities of Being Trans in the MENA Region." In *Sexuality in the Middle East and North Africa: Contemporary Issues and Challenges*, edited by J. Michael Ryan and Helen Rizzo, 161–94. Syracuse, NY: Syracuse Univ. Press.

Massad, Joseph. 2007. *Desiring Arabs*. Chicago: Univ. of Chicago Press.

McCormick, Jared. 2006. "Transition Beirut: Gay Identities, Lived Realities: The Balancing Act in the Middle East." In *Sexuality in the Arab World*, edited by Samir Khalaf and John Gagnon, 243–60. London: Saqi.

Meem. 2009. *Bareed Mista3jil: True Stories*. Beirut: Meem.

Mesahat. 2016. *LGBT Voices from Sudan: Recording a Past, Building a Future*. Cairo: Mesahat Foundation for Sexual and Gender Diversity.

Meuse, Alison. 2017. "At Beirut's First Pride Week, a Chance to Celebrate—and Take Stock of Challenges." NPR, May 26. At https://www.npr.org/sections/parallels/2017/05/26/529687842/at-beiruts-first-pride-week-a-chance-to-celebrate-and-take-stock-of-challenges.

Mikdashi, Maya. 2014. "Moral Panics, Sex Panics, and the Production of a Lebanese Nation." *Jadaliyya*, Feb. 22. At https://www.jadaliyya.com/pages/index/16570/moral-panics-sex-panics-and-the-production-of-a-le.

Mroue, Bassem, and Kareem Chehayeb. 2023. "Rainbows, Drag Shows, Movies: Lebanon's Leaders Go After Perceived Symbols of the LGBTQ+ Community." *ABC News*, Sept. 1. At https://abcnews.go.com/International/wireStory/rainbows-drag-shows-movies-lebanons-leaders-after-perceived-102853956.

Naber, Nadine, and Zeina Zaatari. 2014. "Reframing the War on Terror: Feminist and Lesbian, Gay, Bisexual, Transgender, and Queer (LGBTQ) Activism in the Context of the 2006 Israeli Invasion of Lebanon." *Cultural Dynamics* 26, no. 1: 91–111.

NFASHARTE. 2012. "Where Do We Stand?" Oct. 13. At https://nfasharte.wordpress.com/2012/10/.

Noralla, Nora. 2022. "The Middle East Has an Anti-transgender Bills Problem." *The New Arab*, July 22. At https://www.newarab.com/features/middle-east-has-anti-transgender-bills-problem.

———. 2023a. "The 'Chromosome Trap': Anti-trans Narratives and Policy in Egypt." Tahrir Institute for Middle East Policy, June 29. At https://timep.org/2023/06/29/chromosome-trap-anti-trans-narratives-and-policy-in-egypt/.

———. 2023b. "Transgender Discrimination Continues in Kuwait, despite a Court Ruling." *DAWN: Democracy for the Arab World Now*, Feb. 13. At https://dawnmena.org/transgender-discrimination-continues-in-kuwait-despite-a-court-ruling/.

Puar, Jasbir K. 2007. *Terrorist Assemblages: Homonationalism in Queer Times*. Durham, NC: Duke Univ. Press.

———. 2010. "Israel's Gay Propaganda War," *The Guardian*, July 1. At https://www.guardian.co.uk/commentisfree/2010/jul/01/israels-gay-propagandawar.

———. 2013. "Rethinking Homonationalism." *International Journal of Middle East Studies*, no. 45: 336–39.

Puar, Jasbir, and Maya Mikdashi. 2012a. "On Positionality and Not Naming Names: A Rejoinder to the Response by Maikey and Schotten." *Jadaliyya*, Oct. 10. At https://www.jadaliyya.com/pages/index/7792/on-positionality-and-not-naming-names_a-rejoinder-.

———. 2012b. "Pinkwatching and Pinkwashing: Interpenetration and Its Discontents." *Jadaliyya*, Aug. 9. At https://www.jadaliyya.com/pages/index/6774/pinkwatching-and-pinkwashing_interpenetration-and-.

Qubaiova, Adriana. 2019. "Cross-Bracing Sexualities: Hedging 'Queer'/Non-normativity in Beirut." PhD diss., Central European Univ.

Ramzi, Mahmoud. 2017. "Nanshur mashrou' qanun tajriym 'al-mithliyya al-jinsiyya' as-sijin min 3 'ila 5 sanwat" (We publish the criminalizing homosexuality law 3- to 5-year jail sentence." *Masrawy*, Oct. 25. At https://www.masrawy.com/news/news_egypt/details/2017/10/25/1178761/.

Reid, Graeme. 2012. "'Traditional Values' Code for Human Rights Abuse?" *Human Rights Watch*, Oct. 17. At https://www.hrw.org/news/2012/10/17/traditional-values-code-human-rights-abuse.

Reset DOC. 2009. "The West and the Orientalism of Sexuality: Joseph Massad Talks to Ernesto Pagano." Dec. 14. At https://www.resetdoc.org/story/1530.

Ritchie, Jason. 2010. "How Do You Say 'Come Out of the Closet' in Arabic? Queer Activism and the Politics of Visibility in Israel-Palestine." *GLQ: A Journal of Lesbian and Gay Studies* 16, no. 4: 557–75.

Rizk, Anthony, and Ghassan Makarem. 2015. "'Masculinity-under-Threat': Sexual Rights Organizations and the Masculinist State in Lebanon." *Civil Society Review* 1: 97–107.

Roushdy, Noha. 2016. "Sexual Harassment: Egypt." In *Encyclopedia of Women and Islamic Cultures Online*, edited by Suad Joseph. Leiden, Netherlands: Brill. At https://dx.doi.org/10.1163/1872-5309_ewic_COM_002085.

Ryan, J. Michael, and Helen Rizzo. 2024. "Sexuality in the Middle East and North Africa: Contemporary Issues and Challenges." Introduction to *Sexuality in the Middle East and North Africa: Contemporary Issues and Challenges*, edited by J. Michael Ryan and Helen Rizzo, 1–19. Syracuse, NY: Syracuse Univ. Press.

El Saadawi, Nawal. 1971. *Al-mar'a wa-l-jins* [Women and sex]. Cairo: Dar wa Matabi' al-Mustaqbal.

Saleh, Ahmad J., and Adriana A. Qubaia. 2015. "Transwomen's Navigation of Arrest and Detention in Beirut: A Case Study." *Civil Society Review* 1: 109–18.

Scalenghe, Sara. 2004. "We Invite People to Think the Unthinkable: An Interview with Nizar Saghieh." *Middle East Report* 230: 34–47.

Schotten, Heike, and Haneen Maikey. 2012. "Queers Resisting Zionism: On Authority and Accountability beyond Homonationalism." *Jadaliyya*, Oct. 10. At https://www.jadaliyya.com/pages/index/7738/queers-resisting-zionism_on-authority-and-accounta.

Schulman, Sarah. 2011. "A Documentary Guide to 'Brand Israel' and the Art of Pinkwashing." *Mondoweiss*, Nov. 30. At https://mondoweiss.net/2011/11/a-documentary-guide-to-brand-israel-and-the-art-of-pinkwashing.html.

Shapiro, Adam. 2022. "Activist Ghadir Shafie and Artist Bashar Murad on the Intersectional Struggle for Liberation in Palestine." *DAWN: Democracy for the Arab World Now*, Sept. 27. At https://dawnmena.org/activist-ghadir-shafie-and-artist-bashar-murad-on-the-intersectional-struggle-for-liberation-in-palestine/.

Sheill, Kate. 2008. "Sexual Rights Are Human Rights." In *Development with a Body: Sexuality, Human Rights and Development*, edited by Andrea Cornwall, Sonia Correa, and Susie Jolly, 45–53. London: Zed.

Socialist Feminist Committee of the Socialist Platform. 2017. "Bayrut pride wa al-nidhal min 'ajil al-huquq wa al-hurriyyat al-jinsiyya wa al-jandariyya" (Beirut pride and the struggle for gender and sexual rights and freedoms). *Al-Manshour*, June 1. At https://genderiyya.xyz/wiki/%D9%88%D8%AB%D9%8A%D9%82%D8%A9:%22%D8%A8%D9%8A%D8%B1%D9%88%D8%AA_%D8%A8%D8%B1%D8%A7%D9%8A%D8%AF%22_%D9%88%D8%A7%D9%84%D9%86%D8%B6%D8%A7%D9%84_%D9%85%D9%86_%D8%A3%D8%AC%D9%84_%D8%A7%D9%84%D8%AD%D9%82%D9%88%D9%82_%D9%88%D8%A7%D9%84%D8%AD%D8%B1%D9%8A%D8%A7%D8%AA_%D8%A7%D9%84%D8%AC%D9%86%D8%B3%D9%8A%D8%A9_%D9%88%D8%A7%D9%84%D8%AC%D9%86%D8%AF%D8%B1%D9%8A%D8%A9.

Tilly, Charles. 1993–94. "Social Movements as Historically Specific Clusters of Political Performances." *Berkeley Journal of Sociology* 38: 1–30.

Touraine, Alan. 1985. "An Introduction to the Study of Social Movements." *Social Research* 52, no. 4: 749–87.

———. 1988. *The Return of the Actor.* Minneapolis: Univ. of Minnesota Press.

Tugal, Cihan. 2009. "Transforming Everyday Life: Islamism and Social Movement Theory." *Theory and Society* 38, no. 5: 423–58.

Tunisian Coalition for the Rights of LGBTIQ People. 2017. *UPR Report.* Tunis: Tunisian Coalition for the Rights of LGBTIQ People. At https://tn.boell.org/en/2017/11/23/stakeholders-report-universal-periodic-review-tunisia.

Zaatari, Zeina. 2014. "Queer Subjectivities in Lebanon: Interrupted Heteronormativity?" Paper presented at the Arab Studies Conference "Subjectivity and Its Discontents," University of California, Davis, May.

———. 2015. "Social Movements and Revolution." In *A Companion to the Anthropology of the Middle East,* edited by Soraya Altorki, 338–60. Malden, MA: Wiley.

———. 2016. "A Fourth Wave of Feminism: The Body as Core, the Story as Voice." Paper presented at the "Feminism and Theory in the Arab World" workshop at the Asien Orient Institut, Univ. of Zurich, Zurich, Mar.

———. 2023. "Women's Movements in the Middle East: From Feminist Consciousness to Intersectional Feminism and Everything in Between." In *Routledge Handbook on Women in the Middle East,* edited by Suad Joseph and Zeina Zaatari, 221–51. New York: Routledge.

2

Sexualities and the Internet

The Rights and Capabilities of Online Access

Grant Walsh-Haines and Maryam Hisham Fouad

This chapter focuses on internet use among sexual-orientation minorities in the Middle East and North Africa (MENA) region. How and why do queers in the MENA region access the internet, and what are the limitations or constraints for doing so? The term *queer* as it appears in this chapter includes identities across the LGBTQ+ spectrum, including but not limited to gay men, lesbian women, bisexual men and women, trans individuals, and others. Although terminology varies, and much of the terminology is a Western convention, the terms *queer*, *LGBTQ+*, and *sexual-orientation minorities*, as used here, embody a spirit of inclusion. The role of heteronormativity, the need to marry for social survival, and adherence to moral strictures according to certain interpretations of religions in the region, such as Islam, Christianity, Judaism, and others, are all reasons for queers in the MENA region to go online to find opportunities for expression of sexuality that may otherwise be unavailable or penalized in real space. In the introduction of this book, J. Michael Ryan and Helen Rizzo make a very important remark regarding the queer community as those "penalized as being outside the bounds of what is considered 'acceptable' sexuality" (p. 11). Echoing this definition of the queer community, it is important to ask, What is considered "accepted sexuality" in the MENA region? And what happens to those who fall outside this categorization or understanding of accepted sexuality? For this chapter, it is central to understand that by falling outside of what is accepted sexuality, the queer community in the MENA region finds the internet to be a space in which sexualities can be expressed.

Online media facilitate expressions of sexuality. Internet access is an increasingly available tool for personal and professional use in the region, with consideration of class in the mix (because smartphones and internet subscriptions are usually expensive). Users might have any number of reasons for logging on, such as viewing porn, creating online profiles for hooking up, or participating in LGBTQ+ activism. Internet activism in the MENA region is one site of resistance against oppressive state structures and often goes hand in hand with disseminating health and safety information. Sites such as IraQueer and Ahwaa.org highlight the intersection of queer expressions of sexuality and grassroots movement against the state. IraQueer started operating from Sweden in 2015. A recent visit to Ahwaa.org, however, indicates that most chat rooms have moved from discussions of movements or social organizing to sharing sexual fantasies. This shift can be reflective of the overall lack of the activist spirit, which has diminished over time in the MENA region owing to the huge punitive backlash against any sort of movements. Both IraQueer and Ahwaa.org act as media where expressions of sexuality are available, but they also highlight the challenge in keeping up the grassroots movement within the MENA region. These organizations are also tasked with resisting the censorship, surveillance, homophobic violence, and entrapment that occur as real consequences for queers acting online in the region. Many online activities related to sexuality are heavily monitored and policed by state and religious authorities. Anonymity, which is provided, for example, on Ahwaa.org, is a central factor in the expression of online sexuality to avoid policing and other serious consequences, such as lashings, imprisonment, anal exams, and death. The backlashes from the state are homophobic and often violent, and they constitute human rights violations.

Class is another major theme that needs to be approached when looking at expressions of sexualities on the internet in the MENA region. Statistics from 2021 show that 77 percent of MENA region populations have access to the internet (World Bank 2021). Although this portion is higher than the global average, some countries have better access to the internet and a higher internet-penetration rate. Even within the same country, some wealthier cities and spaces allow for greater amount of time spent on the internet. The discrepancies are due to multiple and multilayered reasons, not only lack of infrastructure in remote areas but also mainly socioeconomic factors such as poverty and income inequality, which make the cost of purchasing a smartphone or a laptop or a computer and having an internet subscription quite challenging for many. In the MENA region and with the challenge of "coming out of the closet" (which is arguably a Western concept that does not really fit the complexity of expressing one's sexuality freely), "Who has access to the internet?" is an important question, but we also have to ask about those with the privilege of internet access, Who has the access and the knowledge to download dating applications? These dating applications are usually reserved for the upper social class and are usually in English, both of which create an extra barrier to "the digital coming out of the closet." In her article "*Lil Watan*: Queer Patriotism in Chauvinistic Lebanon" (2023), Sophie Chamas argues that "the ability to survive and/or thrive as an LGBT subject in Lebanon is contingent on privileges related to race, class, gender and citizenship, as a number of scholars have demonstrated" (232). Chamas also cites Ghassan Moussawi's exploration of the exclusive LGBTQ+ spaces that are reserved for "subjects with '*economic capital*' and those who are racialised as 'proper' gay subjects" (Moussawi 2020, 31, italics in original). Moreover, scholars such as Ghassan Makarem (2011) and Moussawi (2018, 2020) have also noted the discrimination in the application of laws in Lebanon that are "used to target the working-classes, refugees, trans folk" (Chamas 2023, 233).

We draw from two major approaches in our discussion of understanding sexuality, internet freedom, and social justice: the human rights approach and the human capabilities approach. The global human rights approach emphasizes the importance of recognizing a set of moral protections that must be adopted by state actors. These widely shared protections are recognized through law, including global international law (Forsythe 2017). The international human rights framework reinforces the interaction between a state and its government, on the one hand, and both citizens and noncitizens in the state, on the other. The relationship is refracted through policy to offer a more or less universal set of rights that should be afforded to all humans.

In contradistinction, *human capabilities* is an umbrella term that moves away from the state-based rights paradigm toward a complex understanding of individual liberties. For Amartya Sen, capabilities are "what a person is able to do or be" (2005, 153). Having opportunities to pursue or, alternatively, not pursue particular courses of action are central to Sen's philosophy of freedom, which includes a tentative list of capabilities, such as the freedom to be well nourished, to be educated, and to participate in public life. In addition, Sen offers the notion of "dispositive freedom" to describe one's free and conscious choice *not* to do something. In short, capabilities are sets of opportunities that describe what a person can do or not do, while accounting for significant differences in the human condition among individuals.

From a standpoint of international human rights law, people need to be afforded protection so as to not be considered inferior (Buchanan 2010). This is precisely one of the major weaknesses of the human rights approach, which consistently fails to offer truly equal rights (Buchanan 2010). Equal rights are especially problematic in developing states, which are told by Western states or Western organizations what rights they ought to be protecting. For example, critics remain skeptical of Western notions of lesbian and gay social movements and the idea that similar movements with similar goals (e.g., same-sex marriage) ought to be a part of development (Altman 2012; Puar 2007). There is no such thing as a moral universal core in the real world (Brown 1997; Li and McKernan 2017). In chapter 5 of this volume, Ana Cristina Marques, Salma Talaat, and J. Michael Ryan problematize the "West versus East" dichotomy, "underscoring the importance of going beyond regional dichotomies that associate the 'West' with freedom and the 'East' with oppression; having a better understanding of the influence (or lack thereof) of local, national, and inter/transnational (post) colonial agendas on trans people's rights and their actual experiences; and producing possible pluralities, spaces of resistances, and subterranean discourses (Plummer 2010) of trans people and issues in this region" (p. 163).

Criticisms of the human capabilities approach favor understanding the role of the state rather than individual-level capabilities or entitlements. We argue that access to the internet, a key mechanism for expressions of sexuality, must be conceptualized in the human rights and human capabilities debate as well as through a class lens. The debate is contentious and ongoing. Is access to the internet a human right, or should the internet be considered a mechanism for increasing human capabilities? Sen (2005) offers that human rights and human capabilities go hand in hand and ought to be taken together. According to William Birdsall (2014), however, the human rights and human capabilities approaches are irreconcilable, as observed in real-world policy processes in the United Nations (UN) Development Programme. Which conceptualization makes sense affects how social justice for internet users in the MENA region can be advanced.

Purposes of Internet Use

There are many reasons for MENA region users to log onto the internet and innumerable opportunities for expressing identities related to sexuality. Uses are multiple and include the searches for dates and long-term relationships, refugee status, porn, and other users for sex and hook ups. Queer activism is another activity of internet users. Even a Twitter account tweeting about LGBTQ+ issues is revolutionary in the MENA region. "We have Twitter accounts, Instagram accounts, Facebook accounts, and we are reaching maybe one hundred thousand people every month" (Muedini 2018, 122, quoting a conversation with Renay). The online magazine *Gzone* is used in Turkey to "normalize" the existence of the LGBTQ+ community in the country (Muedini 2018).

Pornography is widespread in the MENA region. Some data find that gay searches dominate porn searches in certain states. For example, gay porn searches such as "daddy love," "gay Iranian," and "gay shower" are at the top of porn search charts in Iran (Grover 2013). In another study, nearly 70 percent of files taken from a sample of teenagers' mobile devices in Saudi Arabia were pornographic, although not specifically gay or straight porn (*BBC News* 2007). There are limited data about pornography in the MENA region because so much of the discourse is shrouded in internet censorship.

Another purpose of internet use among men who have sex with men is to meet up for sex. There are a number of interfaces to seek others and meet up for sex. Gayromeo.com is a worldwide popular gay-dating website where male users create profiles that represent their personal selves (Gagné 2012).

Users can represent themselves however they choose, with full profiles that reflect reality or with only partial information and images or with little information and no images. Key to the organization of the social networking website is the use of geographical location to "place" other users in their country, city, and even neighborhood. Other categories are represented in the online profile, such as physical characteristics, national identity, and specific sexual preferences. However, the security and safety issues stand as a barrier for those who wish to have full profiles that reflect reality. "While digital platforms have enabled LGBT people to express themselves and amplify their voices, they have also become tools for state-sponsored repression" (Human Rights Watch 2023). According to Mathew Gagné, "[Users] communicate their own desires while being gazed at as objects of desire" (2012, 125). Some users seek in-person sex. The process of creating a profile, choosing a personal narrative, and intermingling are subjective and queer. Certain users may resist including a profile picture, for example, for fear of discovery or punishment. Osama Shaeer and Kamal Shaeer found that 5.6 percent of survey participants in a study entitled "The Global Online Sexuality Survey (GOSS): Male Homosexuality among Arabic-Speaking Internet Users in the MENA Region" (2014) regularly engaged in same-sex sexual activity. In their sample of Arabic-speaking web surfers older than eighteen, respondents who reported having a same-sex encounter also reported that their sexual behavior was exclusively undercover. The survey drew respondents from Egypt, Libya, Tunisia, Algeria, Morocco, Sudan, Saudi Arabia, Yemen, Palestine, Lebanon, Jordan, Syria, Iraq, Kuwait, Qatar, United Arab Emirates, and Bahrain. Matthew Hall argues that "contested and marginalized offline identities may be more easily claimed online because there is an absence of face-to-face interaction and there is also the provision of support for, and from, geographically dispersed members of the same community" (2018, 381).

In "The Global Online Sexuality Survey," nearly all respondents who repress their same-sex sexual urges (roughly 65 percent) reported that religion played a role in these repressing behaviors (91 percent) (Shaeer and Shaeer 2014). According to Sharia law, private acts are not subject to penalty, as are announced acts. The survey also distinguished between ego-syntonic attitudes (in harmony with the ego) and ego-dystonic attitudes (internalized homophobia) as well as between practicing and nonpracticing or repressed behavior patterns. Most survey respondents were ego-dystonic (nearly 98 percent) and nonpracticing (67 percent) (Shaeer and Shaeer 2014). In chapter 4 of this book, "Islam and Homosexuality: Identity, Threat, and Sexual Well-Being among Muslim Gay Men," Rusi Jaspal introduces the intersection between Islam and internalized homophobia, where some gay Muslim men feel the urge to "take the right path soon" and "wish to 'become heterosexual'" (p. 146).

Steven Matarelli states, "Using the Internet as a vehicle in the region for social and sexual networking is evident and has been shown to be a useful platform for conducting research particularly in highly sensitive domains" (2013, 1296). The internet makes possible this type of data in part because of the confidentiality of an online survey. Aside from the previously discussed uses for the internet—looking at porn and collecting data—there is still another important aspect to internet use in the MENA region: internet activism.

Methodology of Internet Studies

The internet is an incredibly valuable tool for gathering data in the MENA region. Although anonymity can never be guaranteed, and geography can be difficult to pin down precisely, ethnography and survey data have been robust sites of knowledge in current scholarship and inquiry about the region.

Ethnography is an approach that can easily transition from real-world inquiry into online settings. Virtual ethnography and cyberethnography are burgeoning as more scholars seek rigorous knowledge production, particularly in contexts where in-person data gathering may be difficult or dangerous (Hine 2000). The term *netnography* was coined by Robert V. Kozinets in 2015 to signify ethnographies done through and on the internet, which have been increasing. Further, virtual ethnography is not limited by disciplinary boundaries (Hsu 2014; Powers 2008). The applications for virtual ethnography are limited only by the imaginations of scholars willing to break new ground.

The internet and its many avenues—whether informational or professional websites, weblogs, social networking websites, or even hook-up sites and dating apps—all aid in the construction and reconstruction of the user's identities (Ashford 2009). In other words, a technologically savvy user can combine multiple online expressions of self to create their reality. Technologies continue to offer ample opportunities to rewrite social norms associated with gender and sexuality (Kibby and Costello 2001). Shaimaa Magued's ethnographic work with Egyptian queer activists has underscored the importance of the internet in the expression of sexuality: "Being invisible in real life, social media allowed us to promote a socially and culturally challenging identity and communicate our message without the risk of harassment, attack, or arrest" (2023, 480, quoting an activist).

It is important to note that these rewritings and expressions of self can in some cases only be online. "The recourse to online platforms in reaction to the state crackdown on members, the freedom of sexual identity expression as the advocacy's main goal, and the lack of public awareness about LGBT rights were the main patterns shown by the data" (Magued 2023, 475). Online expressions of LGBTQ+ identities may be the only opportunity individuals have to express their sexuality. In these instances, virtual ethnography likewise may be the only access point to understanding the lived realities of Arab queers threatened by state violence, family estrangement, and homophobic violence and/or ostracized from religious institutions. The Tahrir Institute for Middle East Policy has issued a report condemning the Egyptian state's violence in dealing with LGBTQ+ folks: "LGBTQ individuals are targeted in crackdowns by security forces and subject to maltreatment in prison because of their sexuality; in some circumstances, this treatment amounts to torture. Although not explicitly criminalized in Egypt, same-sex relations and perceived support for LGBTQ issues can be prosecuted under the country's debauchery and prostitution laws" (2019). A *BBC News* article in 2023 described the ways in which the Egyptian police hunt down LGBTQ+ people through dating apps (Shihab-Eldin 2023), which demonstrates that although the internet can be a safer place for sexual minorities to express themselves, states still find ways to track down, torture, and imprison them.

Virtual ethnography, unlike digital ethnography, makes sense of social interactions as they happen online. Tom Boellstorff's (2010) cutting-edge work on users of the multiuser online platform *Second Life* explores how they participate in living online worlds. Another example is an ethnographic account of *World of Warcraft*, which draws out important relationships about how users interact with their technology and participate in extensive, vibrant, and highly imaginative worlds (Nardi 2010). Magued recounts the different ways sexualities are expressed in imaginative worlds on the internet: for example, "Shorouk al-Attar, an Egyptian human rights campaigner in the UK, . . . performs 'The Dancing Queer' act in which she puts on a beard and drag in an expression of dissent against homophobia and transphobia in the Arab world" (2023, 482). These forums may be an ethnographic pinnacle of access to rich networks of interactions and information, but they are also steeped in Western ideas about leisure and gaming as well as about "the West" and "the East." For users, though, the games may be construed as real life and as such are robust sites for social interaction.

Another set of digital artifacts are blog entries. They are called "artifacts" because individuals leave them behind, and so blogs are a lasting representation that can be found later. Blogging offers entries rich with context and much longer content than allowed by some social networking outlets, such as Twitter. *Za'fraan*, which first became public in 2017, is an online expression forum/blog of LGBTQ+ experiences of migration and gives the space for art and poetry publications. One post that caught our attention was titled "Him, in Amman . . . Her, in Beirut," where Maya, a transgender woman from Jordan, takes us into her "journey of transitioning between identities and spaces, with all the pain, loss, and self-actualization that come with it" (Omeran and Kayan 2020, 95). This blog is very popular and has resonated with many people in the MENA region and around the world.

Sima Shakhsari (2012) engaged in cyberethnography of diasporic Iranian bloggers participating in a living "Weblogistan." Even though queers in Iran came to be considered chic in the aftermath of President Mahmoud Ahmadinejad's denial of Iranian queers in 2007, Shakhsari still found limited contours of acceptance for sexual-orientation minorities. Yet another example of methodology is Kristian Daneback and colleagues' (2012) work on sexual education and sexual behaviors using online-survey tools and collecting data from online-survey respondents, often focusing on reproductive and medical experiences to serve as data points in a quantitative approach. They blend online tools and regional studies to understand sexuality in new and productive ways. Dominique Adams-Santos's more recent scholarship asks a very important question: "What happens to sexuality when it materializes on the Internet?" (2020). The author argues that the online context is important in the construction of sexual-selfhood projects. Sociological studies of online dating apps have helped sociologists better understand sexuality through the internet as a mirror to the expressions of sexuality offline (Adams-Santos 2020). Adams-Santos remarks that the use of smartphones has made the expression of sexuality more mobile and has allowed users to produce texts and images from different and diverse offline environments. This transition from the offline to the online has facilitated both the studying of sexualities and the expressing of them.

Yet another method for inquiry is the survey method, which researchers use to gather information on sexuality in the MENA region. Shaeer and Shaeer (2014) are among the first researchers to take on the task of learning more about how Middle Eastern men who have sex with men perceive themselves, their sexuality, and their behaviors and attitudes. Their survey process targeted users based on geographical information given on Facebook. After answering a gateway question (e.g., Are you a man who has had sex with other men?), survey respondents entered a survey geared toward answering questions that might not otherwise be answerable. The anonymity afforded by using an internet survey tool led Shaeer and Shaeer to cutting-edge discoveries. Some of the limitations of this type of inquiry, however, include the digital divide (e.g., who has access to online surveys in the first place), the willingness to self-disclose intimate behaviors even when offered anonymity, and willing participants to complete the survey. Although these issues of selective bias are problematic, surveys of this type are one way to obtain critical data about sexuality in the MENA region that would not necessarily be possible without the anonymity of the internet.

Internet Access in the MENA Region

In the MENA region, internet access was a growing trend in the 1990s. Internet cafés were and to a minimal extent still are used to get online in the region. Wealthier and upper-class users now access the internet from their homes. In this sense, internet access in the MENA region demonstrates a stark example of the digital divide and gender gap in access to technology. The difference between the number of rural users and the number of urban users is dramatic, and poverty prevents many even in urban areas from accessing the internet. A report by the World Bank in 2021 found that in the MENA region women were 33 percent less likely to use the internet than men. The report also found that the gender gap in internet use was particularly large in countries such as Yemen, where only 7 percent of women used the internet compared to 26 percent of men. In 2021, the UN Development Programme issued a report stating that women were 28 percent less likely than men to own a mobile phone, which is often the primary means of accessing the internet (10–11).

In the MENA region, women access the internet at lower rates than women in other global regions owing to several sociopolitical and economic factors. Women's access to education and technological skills and other resources are a central explanation for why women access the internet less frequently than men (Antonio and Tuffley 2014). According to *The Mobile Gender Gap Report 2022*, there is a 16 percent gender gap in internet mobile use in the MENA region, where 56 million women do not have access to the internet or own a mobile phone where the internet can be accessed. Moreover, the two main barriers to using mobile internet are digital illiteracy and the nonaffordability of either buying a smartphone or subscribing to an internet bundle (Shanahan 2022).

Internet penetration, or the rate at which the internet is accessible in a given country, depends on many factors, including availability, infrastructure, cost, and cultural norms. The overall economic health of a particular state affects how widely available the internet is for users. For example, according to an International Telecommunication Union report issued by the UN in 2021, Bahrain and the United Arab Emirates, states with strong economies, have a 97.5 percent and a 92 percent penetration rate, respectively, whereas Syria and Yemen, states bombarded with wars, have penetration rates lower than 30 percent (Syria with 21.4 percent and Yemen with 13 percent) (International Telecommunication Union 2021, 8–9). According to Barney Warf and Peter Vincent (2007), states in the region that have diversified their economies beyond petroleum, have strong telecommunications infrastructure, and have accessible internet cafés tend to have the highest rates of internet penetration. According to data compiled from Facebook and other sources, there are an estimated 156 million users in the MENA region out of a total estimated population of 268.4 million people (Internet World Stats 2022).

Language use is another gap present among MENA region internet users. Sarah Hopkyns, Wafa Zoghbor, and Peter John Hassall focus in their work "The Use of English and Linguistic Hybridity among Emirati Millennials" (2021) on English being the main medium of communication between Emiratis. They unleash an important statistic: "When looking at the third domain of entertainment and online contexts, English also dominates. For entertainment, 68% of respondents often or always used English as opposed to Arabic (37%). The same can be said for writing emails (72%) and surfing the internet (65%) in English, as opposed to Arabic (27% and 35% respectively)" (182). Felix Richter also argues that Arabic is among the languages that are most underrepresented on the internet. "Roughly 1.5 billion people speak English, of which 1.2 billion are internet users. That's equivalent to 25.9 percent of the world's internet users, meaning that almost 3 in 4 users are unable to understand more than 60 percent of all websites, at least without a translation tool" (2022). Certain bloggers, depending on the state and the topic, rely more heavily or exclusively on Arabic. For example, Saudi Arabian bloggers write about religious themes exclusively in Arabic (Etling et al. 2010). Serkan Gorkemli (2012) offers a robust discussion of Turkish–English language differences for processes of "coming out" and "digital closets," descriptions that often do not translate precisely. The language gap is an important consideration for studying regional or country-specific blogs.

Access to English-only websites among Arabic speakers of the MENA region is another concern when thinking about the digital divide. Language use can act as a barrier to internet users there. According to the *Arab Social Media Report* (ASMR in the Media 2017), survey respondents stated that accessibility and connectivity, cost, and lack of content in "my language" were the greatest barriers to internet access. When individuals do not have access to the education or language training to access the internet, they are excluded. The trend is clear: some governments in the region boast English-language websites, which has implications for media access to the region (Curtin and Gaither 2004). In her book *Queer in Translation: Sexual Politics under Neoliberal Islam* (2021), Evren Savci critiques the "English centeredness" in queer-related publications, "assuming their translatability both linguistically and metaphorically" (11). Most information written on the internet regarding safety among users as well as publications on sexual-minority communities are in English, which acts as a barrier to the access of the internet to many queers of the MENA region. There needs to be a decentralization of Western knowledge, different ways of accessing the internet and expressions of sexualities, and a focus on the different experiences of the global South in using the internet to express one's sexuality. This is echoed in Joseph Massad's foundational book *Re-Orienting Desire: The Gay International and the Arab World* (2002), where he affirms that language, race, and sexuality on the internet intertwine to make the MENA region queer subject more prone to state backlash:

> The most prominent of the Web sites, gayegypt.com, is in English and features tips for European and American gay tourists coming to Egypt. Clearly most Egyptian men who practice same-sex contact neither know English nor have the wherewithal to afford Internet access, much less know how to use it. This is important in that the police do not seek to, and cannot if they were so inclined, arrest men practicing same-sex contact but rather are pursuing those among them who identify as "gay" on a personal level and who seek to use this identity as a group identification through social and public activities. The campaign of the Gay International misses this important distinction. The point being that it is not same-sex sexual practices that are being repressed by the Egyptian police but rather the sociopolitical identification of these practices with the Western identity of gayness and the publicness that these gay-identified men seek. (382)

The digital divide also influences place and ease of access in use of the internet, going beyond the issues mentioned earlier. According to the Equaldex website, forty countries around the world censored any LGBTQ+ discussions and promotions in 2023 (Equaldex n.d.). Several MENA region countries have recently banned *Spiderman: Across the Spider-Verse*

(2023) because of a brief appearance of a transgender poster. "The film was listed in cinema programs as recently as last week [early June 2023] in countries such as Kuwait, the UAE, Oman, Saudi Arabia, Qatar, Bahrain, Lebanon, and Egypt, but was abruptly and quietly pulled" (El Hajj and Associated Press 2023).

Inconsistent electric power remains a barrier to internet access. Even access to electricity is an acute problem in rural areas, which tend to have less infrastructure and are poorer, making such access more difficult and more expensive. In sum, the digital divide remains problematic, and the gender gap in access to the internet remains acute (Antonio and Tuffley 2014). However, as access is increasing worldwide, connections and costs are shrinking. In this way, access to the internet also offers locally determined modes of activism and an opportunity for voice, action, and subversive optimism in any locality and any number of online contexts.

Internet Activism and State Backlash

Internet users engage in any number of expressions of sexuality online. When those interactions transition to real space, the state—its religious institutions, governmental authorities, law—push back. Understanding activism throughout the MENA region must include examples of LGBTQ+ individuals taking risks because queer bodies are often sites of state backlash. The following examples illustrate the bravery and courage to stand in the face of oppressive state structures.

What does one do when one is made socially invisible, when the slightest expressions of sexuality are despised and scouted? Queer expressions of sexuality are condemned socially and penalized on the state level in the MENA region. Some members of the LGBTQ+ community in the region have had more space than others to speak out regarding sexuality, such as the Lebanese band Mashrou' Leila through their songs. And yet this presumed "safe space" to speak out or sing about queerness vanishes quickly in the confines of many MENA region countries. In 2017 during the band's concert in Egypt, the LGBTQ+ flag was raised by a couple of fans, who were later imprisoned. This incident resulted in the banning of the band from Egypt for good (this was not the first MENA region banning for Mashrou' Leila, who were previously banned from entering

Jordan in 2016). Ten days after the concert, the band issued a statement on Facebook condemning the imprisonment: "This crackdown is by no means separable from the suffocating atmosphere of fear and abuse experienced by all Egyptians on a daily basis, regardless of their sexual orientation" (Mashrou' Leila 2017). The band has also described such experiences as a "witch hunt" and reminded the Egyptian state and security apparatus that they're signatories of the UN Convention against Torture. Here the internet was the only tool for Mashrou' Leila and others to write about human rights violations in Egypt. The internet was the voice of the imprisoned when every other Egyptian and Middle Eastern media outlet was asking for their imprisonment and penalization for the simple raising of a flag. It was revolutionary, and still is, to write (post/blog/sing/draw) online about queer rights and demand that those who spoke out be freed from unfair imprisonment in the MENA region. The LGBTQ+ community's demand for equality and freedom on the internet is a protest and a revolution in states where revolutions are treated as acts of high national treason: "Activists used the rights frame as a strategic tool for survival in order to adapt to restrictive contexts, formulate their cause into receptive idioms, and reach out to a wider audience. Based on informants' narratives, it can be seen that activists have strategically selected and accommodated social media as a means of action against state repression. Virtual networking allowed them to defy the state's tight security grip over public opinion by providing an alternative medium for diffusion, organizational structures and sites for interaction, and decentralized campaigns and social forums for activism" (Magued 2023, 480).

In another high-profile case, eight Egyptian men were put on trial after posting a YouTube video of what appeared to be a same-sex marriage ceremony. The video highlighted two men exchanging vows and rings. The backlash was swift against the men. After they were arrested, each was subjected to "detection" of homosexuality, which is code for conducting illegal anal examinations (Mudallal 2014). Upon facing imprisonment, the men involved in the ceremony denied that it was related to same-sex marriage. In one interview, participant "Ali" stated, "I'm not the groom, I'm just a normal guy, having a birthday party with one of our friends—nothing more, nothing less. . . . I knew that he wanted a ring, so I brought it as a birthday present" (qtd. in Kingsley 2014). All eight men were sentenced to three years in prison. Since the Queen Boat incident in 2001, where gay Egyptian men were captured at a party after the police followed their internet activities (Massad 2002, 380–81), and the capture and imprisonment of Sarah Hegazi and Malak El Kashef for raising the rainbow flag at the Mashrou' Leila concert in 2017, it is obvious that although there is no law condemning homosexuality or trans-ness in Egypt, the state and the society make sure these expressions of sexuality remain scrutinized and penalized.

The internet in such cases proves to be a double-edged sword: it is both a place to resist the state and a place for the state to crack down against unwanted behaviors and sexual deviance. Using a public forum such as YouTube is in tension with the benefits of anonymity. Although the intention of the people in these stories may not have been activism, posting the video and raising a rainbow flag in a public forum were acts of resistance against the state because they raised the issue of sexuality in a public space. Breaking the silence around same-sex love brings the issue to the forefront and increases gay visibility.

Because of robust internet activism and networking, particularly leading up to and after the Arab Spring, security services in various countries have stepped up their work to infiltrate online activist networks. For example, GayEgypt.com, an online forum to exchange dialogue about religious beliefs and sexuality, closed because of such infiltration (Longman 2014).

Other social media platforms, such as Twitter, are sometimes policed by state authorities. After tweeting about his sexuality and seeking same-sex sexual activity on the forum, an unnamed Saudi man was arrested and charged with 450 lashes and three years in prison (Senzee 2014). Authorities used the man's social media accounts against him and scoured his mobile phone for additional evidence of sexual activity, such as "immoral" photos (Toumi 2014). He was identified after religious authorities used an undercover agent (Senzee 2014). "The Morality Police began its systematic, electronic campaign on some LGBTQ dating applications and websites to arrest LGBTQ individuals through luring them and making arrangements to have sex and then ambushing them" (Egyptian Initiative for

Personal Rights 2017). This ambushing results in arrests that move abuse from the virtual to the physical realm. According to one report in 2023, "Transgender women detainees were routinely held in men's cells, where they faced sexual assault and other ill-treatment. In one case, a transgender woman held in a police station in Egypt said she experienced repeated sexual assault for 13 months" (Human Rights Watch 2023). This example highlights the intersection and tension between social media presence, on the one hand, and the censorship and policing of online forums, on the other. Users run serious risk of homophobic violence if they choose not to remain anonymous.

Grindr is another site for online resistance that is subject to serious backlash from authorities. Grindr is a mobile app that ties male users to their geographical location and identifies potential interested same-sex hook-ups nearby. In Egypt, undercover authorities have been known to create fake profiles in order to arrest unsuspecting users. In response to the Egyptian government's policing of Grindr, the app started to generate warnings based on the location of the users' mobile device: "Speak Safely: Egypt is arresting LGBT people, and police may be posing as LGBT on social media to entrap you. Please be careful about arranging meetings with people you don't know, and be careful about posting anything that might reveal your identity" (qtd. in Mudallal 2014). As an additional measure for protection, Grindr suspended its location data in certain countries, including Egypt (Valle and Lavietes 2023). This example shows the intricate transnational balance between Western app developers and the need for a warning in non-Western contexts. Entrapment is a real fear, but it doesn't stop users, even when the penalties for same-sex encounters are severe.

The travel-writer Bert Archer offers a significant account of the Grindr scene while he was on a trip in Qatar, where men navigate same-sex encounters despite severe potential penalties ranging from one hundred lashes and prison time to death. Archer discussed sexuality with his hook-ups when they were willing to talk. "I asked [one man] if it was tough, having sex with guys here with the laws so strict and scary. He laughed. . . . No, he said, it wasn't tough. There's a quotation inscribed in the entrance hall of Doha's grand Museum of Islamic Art from the 13th-century historian Rawandi: 'He should be aware of his enemies, like a chess player who, while observing his own move, also watches over his opponent's.' These guys seem to have gotten the hang of it" (Archer 2015).

In all these examples, men having sex with men is breaking the rules, but it is also a hushed game with certain rules of engagement. In Archer's anecdote, bodies come together to counter cultural expectations about sex, gender, and sexuality. Whether those actions are a form of resistance or not is tangled with intent. One aspect of these actions seems to be shared across the region: individuals will find a way to have same-sex relations regardless of consequences threatened by the state.

In chapter 1 of this volume, "Sexual Rights Movement(s): Problematics of Visibility," Zeina Zaatari draws the three-phase historical journey of the sexual rights movements in the MENA region. Zaatari remarks, "The chapter understands a social movement as a project that aims to redefine culture rather than only political structures" (p. 23). This distinction is integral to understanding movements beyond politics because we often find that most sexual rights' demands revolve around the everyday life of sexual minorities, who want to lead lives with the freedom to choose what to do with their bodies and which partner(s) they want to be with. Many of the stories told earlier illustrate how men and women operate in online and real spaces, often negotiating those spaces in pursuit of sexual stimulation. Brian Whitaker (2006) offers an up-close and personal story of women in Egypt who live together, passing as "normal" despite their nonheterosexual orientation. Punishments for homosexuality are still stringent, violent, and homophobic in many states. For example, women in Egypt are subject to one hundred lashes for engaging in lesbian sex. For Sahar, whose story Whitaker tells, coming out led to troubled relationships with her family, who did not mind her having gay male friends but were unaccepting of her spending time with other women. They even sent her to a psychiatrist, who recommended extreme rehabilitation measures, such as shock therapy. Sahar went back into the closet and dated men to quell her family's worry about her sexuality.

In another example from Whitaker (2006), Laila cohabitated with her lesbian partner. At first, most of their neighbors assumed they were prostitutes. After the neighbors checked with the doorman, the two women were cleared of suspicion. Few assumed that they could be lesbians, and

Laila and her partner were able to remain closeted, safe, and housed in the same flat. From these stories, lesbians' resistance is couched in silence. In countries where staying in the closet has advantages (El-Menyawi 2006), flying under the radar, even while cohabitating with lesbian partners or other women, is a powerful site of resistance to state policy.

The Euro-American metaphor of "the closet" remains pervasive in transnational activism (Gorkemli 2012). The examples recounted here are not illustrative of coming out, but they are nevertheless powerful instances of resistance. The notion of a closet and the need to come out of it to become a part of gay community reinforces a Western narrative, but applying a Western convention is a narrow view for understanding sexuality in global-local contexts (El-Menyawi 2006). The internet allows for key spaces to participate in activism yet remain anonymous, an important concern for sexual-orientation minorities who must consider their safety, their families (especially if they are in opposite-sex marriages), and personal comfort level as priorities. Coming out might suggest a dangerous visibility for MENA region queers. To further understand the aloofness of the dichotomy between the West and the East, where the West is set as an exemplary model to be followed and the East as the opposite, Gilly Hartal and Orna Sasson-Levy introduce the case of Tel Aviv versus Jerusalem in chapter 3 of this book. The authors condemn studies where "Tel Aviv is portrayed as the westernized, secular, and liberal economic center of Israel, on its way to becoming a global city, whereas Jerusalem is perceived as a local city oriented toward its religious and national past (Alfasi and Fenster 2005) and populated by distinct and even hostile social-religious groups" (p. 106). Hartal and Sasson-Levy argue instead that both cities merge the East and the West differently. Scholars need to step away altogether from comparisons between East and West and focus on what is fitting for Eastern queer communities and their real and lived experiences.

Engaging in behaviors online is one purpose of internet use for MENA region queers, but more formal channels and organizations are also dedicated to promoting education and creating safe spaces for the LGBTQ+ community online. For example, Yasmene Jabar, a trans woman who resided in Jordan for part of her life, created several websites. Café Trans

Arabi and International Transexual Sisterhood were the first websites of their type to be available to MENA region trans women (Zagria 2013). In addition, Jabar was essential in the Trans Eastern Conference in Istanbul in 2005. Café Trans Arabi is still an active website, which offers "Photos, Links, Information, [and] Friendship." International Transsexual Sisterhood offers a similar reprieve: links to information and resources as well as a discussion area called "The Clubhouse," where users can get together to chat and leave messages in discussion forums.[1] But both websites are also glitchy and outdated and in English only.

Another activist, Esra'a al Shafei, and the organization Majal launched Ahwaa.org at the very beginning of the Arab Spring in 2011. The online platform includes more than two thousand discussion forums on a range of topics related to sexuality and sexual expression.[2] The forums are bilingual, and users are represented by an avatar rather than a personal image in the discussions. Ahwaa.org is a safe space where MENA region queers define their lives and experiences, and as such it functions as an anonymous, grassroots, community-based website (al Shafei 2016).

There are other forms of activism, such as the dissemination of information on personal and sexual safety. For example, IraQueer offers a robust and comprehensive "Sexual Health Guide" in addition to a "Security Guide for LGBT+ Individuals," which includes information about how to remain safe as a queer person in Iraq. The "Security Guide" includes key information about how to stay safe when using the internet for hooking up. For example, the section "Grindr, Tinder, Scruff, Hornet, and others" reads: "When using this app or websites, it's crucial to verify the identity of the person(s) you talk to before you meet them. Do not activate your location, and share as little information as possible" (IraQueer 2016). The guide also includes key information about digital safety, such as logging off, creating complex passwords, and keeping identifying information private. In similar style, the website security in-a-box features discussion of

1. Café Trans Arabi, at https://cafe-transarabi.tripod.com; International Transsexual Sisterhood, at https://butterfly-sisterhood.tripod.com/.

2. Ahwaa: An Open Space to Debate LGBTQ-Related Issues in the Middle East, at https://ahwaa.org.

tactics to remain safe from authorities in online contexts (security in-a-box n.d.). Key sections are geared toward tips and tactics for remaining anonymous on social networking sites in addition to creating secure passwords and destroying sensitive online information.

Disseminating information about HIV prevention and working to get that information in the hands of individuals more likely to engage in high-risk sex behaviors are an important channel for online activism in the region. Recognizing high-risk behaviors and condom use is an important step in developing safe-sex education and increasing education about the spread of HIV and other sexually transmitted infections (Noar et al. 2006). Using the internet to develop and implement educational campaigns can create positive outcomes for men who have sex with men. In a more academic vein, S. M. Noar and colleagues (2006) establish a set of predictors for condom use, such as attitudes, norms, self-efficacy, and behaviors. Although these measures are good predictors for condom use, the authors assume that condoms are widely available. Cultural and religious norms are external intervening variables in the MENA region. In addition, according to Ghina Mumtaz and coresearchers, "There is . . . an urgent need to expand HIV surveillance and access to HIV testing, prevision, and treatment services in a rapidly narrow window of opportunity to prevent the worst of HIV transmission among MSM [men who have sex with men] in the Middle East and North Africa" (2011, 15). Matarelli writes that to further support HIV education and awareness,

> harnessing the ubiquitous nature of the Internet provides a platform for positive social change through the creation of a positive social-sexual networking community to reach those at risk. When traditional MSM [men who have sex with men] social gathering sites are lacking, the Internet offers new opportunities to serve as a conduit for the delivery of contemporary HIV education and prevention programs aimed at increasing variety and novelty of low-risk sexual activities. Despite numerous hurdles, adopting Internet-based, non-restricted HIV education and prevention public health programs in the Middle East could instrumentally enhance efforts toward reducing the likelihood of new HIV transmissions in MSM and their sexual partners ultimately contributing to an improved quality of life. (2013, 1296)

Yet although HIV education is important and worthwhile to pursue, such an intervention assumes that men having sex with other men are having insertive sex. Most Arabs, when asked about the kind of sex they have, reported having noninsertive sex, which is associated with less risk than other types of sex (Shaeer and Shaeer 2014).

There are robust examples of LGBTQ+ organizing online. When MENA region queers have access to the internet, these resources are available. Users still must take precautions, such as deleting internet history and using strong passwords to protect their personal information. There are still risks, but these examples highlight how queer resistance takes many forms in many geographical contexts and with multiple perspectives in mind.

Anonymity and Censorship

An undeniable benefit to online expressions of sexuality is anonymity; however, state-sanctioned interventions in the form of censorship persist. Tor, the "Onion Router," keeps users anonymous by moving access around different Tor servers, encrypting along the way by means of "onion routing." "Onion routing uses successive layers of encryption to route messages through an overall network, such that each node knows the previous and the next node in the route but nothing else" (Feigenbaum and Ford 2015, 60). Tor is conceptualized as an onion with layers because it adds layers of protection between the user and the online content.

Despite these layers, there are four distinct ways to intervene and strip Tor users of their anonymity: global traffic analysis, active attacks, intersection attacks, software exploits, and self-identification (Feigenbaum and Ford 2015). States have become proficient in these methods for cracking the code of anonymity and criminalizing internet users. Joan Feigenbaum and Bryan Ford's (2015) map of the "Republic of Repressistan" uses small red images reminiscent of devils to show blockages between points of free-flowing information. The suffix *-istan* is problematic, of course, because it promotes the notion that the MENA region is the only region that censors internet users. Yes, censorship does exist in the MENA region, but it also exists in many forms and to varying degrees across the globe.

According to the website Equaldex, which was first launched in 2014 and is considered a collaborative-knowledge base for the LGBTQ+ movement, "Homosexuality is illegal in 64 countries and punishable by death in 9." According to the website, most countries that criminalize homosexuality fall in Africa and the Middle East (Equaldex n.d., data for 2023). The criminalization of homosexuality, however, goes beyond the MENA region; for example, homosexuality is punishable by death or life imprisonment in the following countries: the death penalty is applied in Afghanistan, Brunei, Iran, Saudi Arabia, United Arab Emirates, Yemen, Mauritania, Somalia, and Uganda, life imprisonment is sentenced in Gambia, Bangladesh, Sudan, Tanzania, and Zambia (Equaldex n.d., data for 2023).

Annabelle Sreberny and Gholam Khiabany discuss the finer points of censorship in the Arabic blogosphere in their book *Blogistan: The Internet and Politics in Iran* (2010). Bloggers in Iran practice high-context and highly coded use of language to avoid censors. Even terms such as *women* and *sex* have been highly censored and criminalized in Iran. Promoting censorship suggests supporting state criminalization of women's sexuality or of sexual-orientation minorities. In some cases, that means arrest, imprisonment, and worse for sexual-orientation minorities in the MENA region. For sexual-orientation minority and queer internet users, anonymity is a prerequisite for self-expression. Threats to anonymity may have dire consequences, such as homophobic violence with varying severity depending on state policy and laws.

Continued internet democratization in the region, particularly after the Arab Spring, requires an historical and contemporary understanding of digital-infrastructure politics (Hussain and Shaikh 2015; see also Sutherlin 2012 and Wagner and Gainous 2007). Only then can scholars and activists trace the specific ways state-sanctioned censorship (e.g. "shutting down the internet," "using a 'kill switch'") has come into play in fomenting widespread social resistance to state actors. Some states, such as Saudi Arabia, have an internally planned and heavily regulated internet infrastructure; Egypt, in contrast, has utilized private corporations to establish its mobile-device networks (Hussain and Shaikh 2015). Beyond infrastructure, the notion that internet freedom and the dismantling of state-sanctioned censorship are part of democratization projects is increasingly common in Western democratization efforts. Specifically, the idea of promoting freedom among internet users has gained traction among Western organizations that are promoting freedom from censorship in the Middle East (MacKinnon 2012). However, moving away from a liberal, Western understanding of democratization, and amid a harsh crackdown on freedoms in MENA region countries, some activists in the region have remained committed to standing up for the community and for the continued dissemination of the message: "In light of the inability to develop a physical repertoire of disruptive actions among supporters, activists opted for a virtual platform that evaded the state censorship. In their testimonies, respondents underlined their awareness of the sensitivity of their activities, which led them to refuse foreign funds, keep their activism underground, and use pseudonyms in the call for freedom and individual rights on social media" (Magued 2023, 481).

Human Rights and Human Capabilities

Encouraging and emphasizing these two human rights in tandem—the right to internet freedom and the right to express one's sexuality—have a multiplier effect for individual experiences. Cosmopolitan notions of these human rights should also be considered in a broader nexus, including rights to education for girls, access to contraceptives, and HIV/AIDS awareness. Taken together, these types of social, political, and cultural shifts have the potential to dramatically improve individual lives. How will the expansion of civil liberties and human rights, specifically those related to internet freedom and sexuality, sexual orientation, and gender expression, parallel online revolutions and continued democratization in the region?

When Sarah Hegazi was detained for raising a rainbow flag at the Mashrou' Leila concert, the fight for her by different nongovernmental organizations and queer communities was framed as a human rights issue. Scholars employ human rights frameworks to suggest that political homophobia employed by the state requires rights-based resistances (Boellstorff 2004; Bosia and Weiss 2013). The internet is one tool with the potential for facilitating movement against homophobic state structures.

There are robust explanations for identifying the complex problems of homophobia and homocolonialism and for suggesting theoretical paths forward (Rahman 2014), but few scholars are willing to make concrete predictions about what the path forward will look like. One difficulty in determining potential solutions is thinking through the key differences between human rights and human capabilities (Sen 2005). Another problem is maintaining acute awareness of westernized conceptions of freedom of speech, censorship, sexuality, and sexual orientation within a Middle Eastern context (MacKinnon 2012; Puar 2007).

Human Rights Framework

Rights emerge from dignity, self-actualization, and function, not the other way around. Sexuality remains relegated to the margins of international-relations inquiry and human rights discourse (Langlois 2016). Sexuality, freedom of sexual expression and imagination, and freedom of gender expression are aspects of the human condition that are repressed in the MENA region.

Depending on place and perspective, intervention and activism take different shapes. To offer an example of adopting a human rights framework, Joke Swiebel describes the limitations of LGBTQ+ activism in the United Nations and European Union using a social movement framework. According to Swiebel, "Right-wing Catholics and fundamentalist Islamic states have formed a formidable alliance that systematically tries to block recognition of LGBT rights as a UN issue" (2009, 25). It was not until 2016 that the United Nations finally settled on a definition of sexual orientation and included that language in a mandate to protect "against violence and discrimination based on sexual orientation and gender identity."[3]

In other words, if LGBTQ+ activists move around a rights-based approach, the state will inevitably resist that approach. Conservative or homophobic states will not likely be compelled by these international institutions to resist homophobic violence, particularly when the perceived

3. UN Human Rights Council, "Resolution 32/2. Protection against Violence and Discrimination Based on Sexual Orientation and Gender Identity," 2016.

dictates come from Western democracies. The failure of the rights-based approach is its dependence on state action and reaction. Another criticism of this approach is that it remains tied to westernized language and westernized conceptions of sexual identity (Puar 2007).

Yet questions of state power persist in the granting of human rights to citizens. Some argue that human rights and gay rights are inextricably linked. "For the average gay Arab, the personal and political intersect daily, and queer rights cannot be separated from human rights issues that affect everyone in the MENA region" (al Shafei 2016). According to Shaimaa Magued, "The authoritarian revival in the Middle East and the banning of social movements coincided with the bourgeoning of unconventional forms of contention inspired by the uprising. Inscribed into the premises of global human rights advocacy, the Egyptian revolution's cyber-mobilization persisted as a mobilization technique in spite of the end of hopes for democratization. Minority groups witnessing the revolution's spirit sustained their activism through the adoption of a rights frame that has successfully functioned through online platforms and virtual solidarity networks" (2023, 483).

Internet freedom and individual sexuality are better understood in conjunction with one another because the two are often deeply connected on the individual level, affecting how a user accesses and uses the internet and how they choose to express their sexuality online. If pursuing self-actualization through sexuality and sexual expression falls under the umbrella of promoting human dignity, then access to the technology that allows uncensored expressions of the self is something worth fighting to achieve. Achieving freedom of expression in all forms is a part of achieving human dignity for all (Nussbaum 2006).

Repression in the real world leads to the necessary consideration of online expression as a mode of dignity. Censorship and state backlash have continued to silence queer voices in the region. At least two conceptualizations result from thinking about the internet in a human rights framework: (1) the internet and access to the internet as a human right and (2) the internet as a mechanism to achieve human rights. In early 2023, the UN Office of the High Commissioner for Human Rights issued a declaration to the UN Human Rights Council that it is "time to reinforce universal access to the internet as a human right, not just a privilege," arguing that lack of internet access from a young age deprives children of knowing about the world, receiving education, and achieving successes (*United Nations News* 2023).

According to the human-rights-based approach adopted by Stephen Wicker and Stephanie Santoso (2013), governments can both give the right for citizens to access internet technology and take it away (e.g., through censorship and internet shutdowns). For these authors, it makes little sense to approach the issue of internet access from a capabilities' perspective because the issue at hand is government censorship rather than an individual's capacity to realize self-expression or sexuality.

Human Capabilities Framework

Contrary to the human rights framework, the human capabilities framework conceptualizes the role of humanity not as a reaction to the state but as individual modes of being a fully realized human. According to Amartya Sen's (2005) and Martha Nussbaum's (2006) capabilities approaches, there remains an ethical imperative to acknowledge the person a priori, without the need for the person's rights to be granted by a government or state apparatus. Capabilities, such as bodily health, thought, emotion, and affiliation, among others, are fundamental to human dignity (Nussbaum 2006; Sen 2005). Based on this framework, can the internet be thought of as a mechanism to achieving human capabilities in the context of sexuality, sexual orientation, and self-expression?

For Michael Bosia (2014) and others, the notion of bodily autonomy is a more progressive and meaningful path toward answering that question. Linking sexual identity to human rights reinforces problematic Western conceptions of gay rights (El-Menyawi 2006; Puar 2007). Focusing on capabilities such as bodily autonomy, however, allows for a more open mode of emphasizing freedom of expression. In addition, conceptualizations of human rights and resistance react to the state. In the context of the MENA region, according to Hassan El-Menyawi (2006), a rights-based approach is not necessarily the most effective path to achieve bodily autonomy.

Yet when the human capabilities framework is applied to internet access, it ignores the mechanics of how the internet is built, distributed, accessed, and censored by the state (Hussain and Shaikh 2015). So long as the state regulates information flow, censorship practices, and the penalizing of noncompliant citizens, the human capabilities framework falls short of intervening in these processes. In other words, conceptualizing freedom and dignity related to sexual orientation aligns nicely with the human capabilities framework, whereas conceptualizing internet access aligns with the human rights framework. The tension between human rights and human capabilities vacillates between state resistance and the inclusion of considerations for sexuality, sexual orientation, and gender expression within broader conversations about human dignity.

The capability framework does not adequately capture the need for internet freedom as a mechanism to facilitate the free expression of sexuality. If sexuality, freedom of sexual expression, and freedom of gender expression have a place at the table of capabilities, how does one conceptualize a human rights framework in the MENA region? In the context and scope of this chapter, thinking about how the internet facilitates these aspects of the human condition shapes the need for internet access as a central tenant of a development and human rights framework. The two perspectives, human rights and human capabilities, remain contentious because their roots run in distinctly different directions and with competing aims. In short, the human capabilities approach has roots in philosophy and public policy, whereas the human rights approach remains rooted in organizational practices and experiences (Birdsall 2014).

Promoting internet access for all is an undertaking that must include considerations of access and limitations to the internet. The layers of the digital divide (sex/gender, poverty, state infrastructure, language) are an ongoing concern. Promoting access to the internet as a unitary path forward for sexual liberation in the MENA region may be beneficial to some but would also be mired in problems for others that arise from the digital divide. Further, suggesting "high-speed internet access for all" when other aspects of human rights development, such as girls' education and deep poverty, have not been met is a Western and classist suggestion. In chapter 7 of this volume, "Identity, Mental Health, and Coping among Sexual Minorities in the Middle East and North Africa: The Case of Lebanon," Rusi Jaspal, Ismaël Maatouk, and Moubadda Assi argue that "stigma at multiple levels (i.e., institutional, communal, and social) can result in threats to social and psychological well-being and precipitate modifications to one's sense of identity" (p. 236). How do we look at the human first and the human's capabilities in the MENA region when the human is facing a loss of identity and internalized homophobia? Access to the internet can be the way in which alternative identities or, in this case, real identities are expressed and portrayed, in contrast to the way queer communities keep constructing masked identities in real spaces so that they are not criminalized.

Despite the difficulties just explained, access to the internet should be imagined as a human right and not a capability for two reasons. The first is that LGBTQ+ rights are human rights, as established by the UN Development Programme as a part of its Sustainable Development Goals (Martínez-Solimán 2015). Although problematic in the context of Western development, a human rights framework allows for a clear path forward to interacting with states to increase internet access and negotiate decreasing censorship. The second reason is that interventions to promote internet access and resist censorship are key to contemporary activist movements. Nongovernmental organizations (e.g., OpenNet Initiative) have a role to play in facilitating these changes, too. Activism and subversive optimism are also pathways forward to translating online experiences into real lived experiences of individuals in the MENA region and must continue to directly confront state structures to promote change in the region.

Therefore, access to internet freedom must be considered in the human rights framework to combat state interference with freedom of expression, which includes expression of sexuality. Increasing access in the region must happen before the internet can be used as a mechanism for promoting human dignity through the free expression of sexuality and sexual orientation online. While the two can happen in tandem, increasing infrastructure and reducing censorship must continue to take priority in the human rights development framework.

Conclusion

MENA region internet users are heavily censored, propelling the need for continued activism from the closet and measures of anonymity. Expressions of sexuality online range widely, from seeking porn and hook-ups to engaging in various forms of activism. In many instances, knowledge related to sexuality and expressions of sexuality is made possible through survey data and e-ethnography.

Overall, internet access must be considered a human right in the human rights versus human capabilities debate. In most states in the MENA region, state forces engage in internet surveillance, which can often translate into violence against users (e.g., through entrapment). Therefore, many users opt to remain anonymous to stay protected. As a result, MENA region internet users are often confined to online closets. Working within a human rights framework and conceptualizing access to the internet as a human right entangled with the freedom to express sexuality through the internet are key contributions to the debate. Future research in this area must either adopt or challenge this framework.

References

Adams-Santos, Dominique. 2020. "Sexuality and Digital Space." *Sociology Compass* 14, no. 8: art. e12818. At https://doi.org/10.1111/soc4.12818.

Alfasi, Nurit, and Tovi Fenster. 2005. "A Tale of Two Cities: Jerusalem and Tel Aviv in an Age of Globalization." *Cities* 22, no. 5: 351–63. At https://doi.org/10.1016/j.cities.2005.05.006.

Altman, Dennis. 2012. "Globalization of the International Gay/Lesbian Movement." In *Handbook of Lesbian and Gay Studies*, edited by Diane Richardson and Steven Seidman, 415–25. Thousand Oaks, CA: Sage.

Antonio, Amy, and David Tuffley. 2014. "The Gender Digital Divide in Developing Countries." *Future Internet* 6: 673–87.

Archer, Bert. 2015. "My Experience Using Hook-up Apps in Qatar Where Gay Sex Is Punishable by Death." *Vice Online*, Dec. 6. At https://www.vice.com/en_us/article/my-experience-using-gay-hook-up-apps-in-qatar-where-homesexuality-can-get-you-executed.

Ashford, Chris. 2009. "Queer Theory, Cyber-Ethnographies and Researching Online Sex Environments." *Information & Communications Technology Law* 18, no. 3: 297–314.

ASMR in the Media. 2017. *Arab Social Media Report*. Dubai: Dubai School of Government's Governance and Innovation Program. At https://www.arabsocialmediareport.com/home/index--primenuid-1-mnu-pri.html.

BBC News. 2007. "Middle East: Porn Dominates Saudi Mobile Use." Apr. 25. https://news.bbc.co.uk/2/hi/middle_east/6592123.stm.

Birdsall, William. 2014. "Development, Human Rights, and Human Capabilities: The Political Divide." *Journal of Human Rights* 13: 1–21.

Boellstorff, Tom. 2004. "Gay Language and Indonesia: Registering Belonging." *Journal of Linguistic Anthropology* 14, no. 2: 248–68.

———. 2010. *Coming of Age in* Second Life: *An Anthropologist Explores the Virtually Human*. Princeton, NJ: Princeton Univ. Press.

Bosia, Michael J. 2014. "Strange Fruit: Homophobia, the State, and the Politics of LGBT Rights and Capabilities." *Journal of Human Rights* 13: 256–73.

Bosia, Michael J., and Meredith Weiss. 2013. "Political Homophobia in Comparative Perspective." In *Global Homophobia: States, Movements, and the Politics of Oppression*, edited by Meredith Weiss and Michael J. Bosia, 1–29. Champaign: Univ. of Illinois Press.

Brown, Chris. 1997. "Universal Human Rights: A Critique." *International Journal of Human Rights* 1, no. 2: 41–65.

Buchanan, Allen. 2010. "The Egalitarianism of Human Rights." *Ethics* 120, no. 4: 679–710.

Chamas, Sophie. 2023. "*Lil Watan*: Queer Patriotism in Chauvinistic Lebanon." *Sexualities* 26, nos. 1–2: 230–51. At https://doi.org/10.1177/13634607211047523.

Curtin, Patricia A., and T. Kenn Gaither. 2004. "International Agenda-Building in Cyberspace: A Study of Middle East Government English-Language Websites." *Public Relations Review* 30, no. 1: 25–36.

Daneback, Kristian, Sven-Axel Månsson, Michael Ross, and Christine M. Markham. 2012. "The Internet as a Source of Information about Sexuality." *Sex Education* 12, no. 5: 583–98.

Egyptian Initiative for Personal Rights (EIPR). 2017. "Crackdown on Homosexual Conduct in Egypt Escalates: EIPR Calls for Immediate Release of All Those Arrested on the Basis of Their Sexual Orientation." Press release, Sept. 27. https://eipr.org/en/pressrelease/2017/09/27/3035.

Equaldex. n.d. "Censorship of LGBT Issues by Country." At https://www.equaldex.com/issue/censorship.

Etling, Bruce, Rob Faris, John Palfrey, and John Kelly. 2010. "Mapping the Arabic Blogosphere: Politics and Dissent Online." *New Media & Society* 12, no. 8: 1225–43.

Feigenbaum, Joan, and Bryan Ford. 2015. "Seeking Anonymity in an Internet Panopticon." *Communications of the ACM* 58, no. 10: 58–69.

Forsythe, David. 2017. *Human Rights in International Relations.* Cambridge: Cambridge Univ. Press.

Gagné, Mathew. 2012. "Queer Beirut Online." *Journal of Middle East Women's Studies* 8, no. 3: 113–37.

Gorkemli, Serkan. 2012. "'Coming Out of the Internet': Lesbian and Gay Activism and the Internet as a 'Digital Closet' in Turkey." *Journal of Middle East Women's Studies* 8, no. 3: 63–88.

Grover, Dominic. 2013. "Web Porn Searches Mock Anti-gay Laws in Muslim World and Africa." *International Business Times*, Mar. 28. At https://www.ibtimes.co.uk/sex-porn-search-451425.

El Hajj, Nick, and Associated Press. 2023. "*Spider-Man: Across the Spider-Verse* Censored in Muslim Countries." *Fortune*, June 16. At https://fortune.com/2023/06/16/spider-man-verse-censorship-middle-east-muslim-countries-trans-character-flag/.

Hall, Matthew. 2018. "Disability, Discourse and Desire: Analyzing Online Talk by People with Disabilities." *Sexualities* 21, no. 3: 379–92. At https://doi.org/10.1177/1363460716688675.

Hartal, Gilly, and Orna Sasson-Levy. 2024. "Middle Eastern LGBT Westernization? The Case of Jerusalem and Tel Aviv." In *Sexuality in the Middle East and North Africa: Contemporary Issues and Challenges*, edited by J. Michael Ryan and Helen Rizzo, 104–34. Syracuse, NY: Syracuse Univ. Press.

Hine, Christine. 2000. *Virtual Ethnography.* Washington, DC: Sage.

Hopkyns, Sarah, Wafa Zoghbor, and Peter John Hassall. 2021. "The Use of English and Linguistic Hybridity among Emirati Millennials." *World Englishes* 40, no. 2: 176–90. At https://doi.org/10.1111/weng.12506.

Hsu, Wendy. 2014. "Digital Ethnography toward Augmented Empiricism: A New Methodological Framework." *Journal of Digital Humanities* 3, no. 1. At https://journalofdigitalhumanities.org/3-1/digital-ethnography-toward-augmented-empiricism-by-wendy-hsu/.

Human Rights Watch. 2023. "Middle East, North Africa: Digital Targeting of LGBT People: Arbitrary Arrests, Torture Follow Online Abuses, Illegal Phone Searches." *Human Rights Watch*, Feb. 21. At https://www.hrw.org/news/2023/02/21/middle-east-north-africa-digital-targeting-lgbt-people.

Hussain, Muzammil M., and Sonia Shaikh. 2015. “Three Arenas for Interrogating Digital Politics in Middle East Affairs.” In “The Digital Age in the Middle East,” edited by Akram Khater and Jeffrey Culang. Special issue, *International Journal of Middle East Studies* 47, no. 2: 366–68.

International Telecommunication Union (ITU). 2021. *Measuring Digital Development: Facts and Figures 2021.* Geneva: ITU. At https://www.itu.int/en/ITU-D/Statistics/Documents/facts/FactsFigures2021.pdf.

Internet World Stats. 2022. “MENA Region Internet Statistics, Population, Facebook and Telecommunications Reports.” At https://www.internetworldstats.com/stats5.htm.

IraQueer. 2016. “IraQueer Security Guide.” At https://www.iraqueer.org/uploads/1/2/4/0/124034920/security_guide_-_english.pdf.

Jaspal, Rusi. 2024. “Islam and Homosexuality: Identity, Threat, and Sexual Well-Being among Muslim Gay Men.” In *Sexuality in the Middle East and North Africa: Contemporary Issues and Challenges*, edited by J. Michael Ryan and Helen Rizzo, 137–60. Syracuse, NY: Syracuse University Press.

Jaspal, Rusi, Ismaël Maatouk, and Moubadda Assi. 2024. “Identity, Mental Health, and Coping among Sexual Minorities in the Middle East and North Africa: The Case of Lebanon.” In *Sexuality in the Middle East and North Africa: Contemporary Issues and Challenges*, edited by J. Michael Ryan and Helen Rizzo, 236–58. Syracuse, NY: Syracuse Univ. Press.

Kibby, Marjorie, and Brigid Costello. 2001. “Between the Image and the Act: Interactive Sex Entertainment on the Internet.” *Sexualities* 4, no. 3: 353–69.

Kingsley, Patrick. 2014. “Egypt Jails Eight Men after ‘Gay Marriage’ Ceremony on Nile.” *The Guardian*, Nov. 3. At https://www.theguardian.com/world/2014/nov/03/egypt-jails-eight-men-gay-marriage-ceremony-nile.

Kozinets, Robert V. 2015. *Netnography: The Essential Guide to Qualitative Social Media Research*. Thousand Oaks, CA: Sage.

Langlois, Anthony J. 2016. “International Relations Theory and Global Sexuality Politics.” *Politics* 36, no. 4: 385–99.

Li, Yingru, and John McKernan. 2017. “‘Achieved Not Given’: Human Rights, Critique and the Need for Strong Foundations.” *International Journal of Human Rights* 21, no. 3: 252–69.

Longman, James. 2014. “Gay Community Hit Hard by Middle East Turmoil.” *BBC News*, Oct. 29. At https://www.bbc.com/news/world-middle-east-29628281.

MacKinnon, Rebecca. 2012. *Consent of the Networked: The Worldwide Struggle for Internet Freedom*. New York: Basic.

Magued, Shaimaa. 2023. "The Shift to Cause Framing in Egyptian LGBT Advocacy after the January 25 Revolution." *Current Sociology* 71, no. 3: 470–88. At https://doi.org/10.1177/00113921211024693.

Makarem, Ghassan. 2011. "The Story of HELEM." *Journal of Middle East Women's Studies* 7, no. 3: 98–112.

Marques, Ana Cristina, Salma Talaat, and J. Michael Ryan. 2024. "The (Im)Possibilities of Being Trans in the MENA Region." In *Sexuality in the Middle East and North Africa: Contemporary Issues and Challenges*, edited by J. Michael Ryan and Helen Rizzo, 161–94. Syracuse, NY: Syracuse University Press.

Martínez-Solimán, Magdy. 2015. "Ending LGBTI Discrimination Is Key to Achieving SDGs." United Nations Development Programme in Yemen: Our Perspectives, Sept. 9.

Mashrou' Leila. 2017. "Statement on Fan Imprisonment." Facebook, Sept. 27. At https://www.facebook.com/mashrou3leila/posts/10155495830387854.

Massad, Joseph. 2002. *Re-Orienting Desire: The Gay International and the Arab World*. New York: Columbia Univ. Press.

Matarelli, Steven. 2013. "Sexual Sensation Seeking and Internet Sex-Seeking of Middle Eastern Men Who Have Sex with Men." *Archives of Sexual Behavior* 42: 1285–97.

El-Menyawi, Hassan. 2006. "Activism from the Closet: Gay Rights Strategizing in Egypt." *Melbourne Journal of International Law* 7, no. 1: 28–51.

Moussawi, Ghassan. 2018. "Queer Exceptionalism and Exclusion: Cosmopolitanism and Inequalities in 'Gayfriendly' Beirut." *Sociological Review* 66, no. 1: 174–90.

———. 2020. *Disruptive Situations: Fractal Orientalism and Queer Strategies in Beirut*. Philadelphia: Temple Univ. Press.

Mudallal, Zainab. 2014. "An Alarming Crackdown on LGBT Rights Is Hitting Grindr and Other Online Corners of the Arab World." *Quartz Online*, Sept. 28. At https://qz.com/271925/an-alarming-crackdown-on-lgbt-rights-is-hitting-grindr-and-other-online-corners-of-the-arab-world/.

Muedini, Faton. 2018. *LGBTI Rights in Turkey: Sexuality and the State in the Middle East*. Cambridge: Cambridge Univ. Press.

Mumtaz, Ghina, Nahla Hilmi, Willi McFarland, Rachel L. Kaplan, Francisca Ayodeji Akala, Iris Semini, Gabriele Riedner, et al. 2011. "Are HIV Epidemics among Men Who Have Sex with Men Emerging in the Middle East and

North Africa? A Systematic Review and Data Synthesis." *PLOS Medicine* 8, no. 8: 1–15. At https://doi.org/10.1371/journal.pmed.1000444.

Nardi, Bonnie. 2010. *My Life as a Night Elf Priest: An Anthropological Account of World of Warcraft*. Ann Arbor: Univ. of Michigan Press.

Noar, S. M., R. S. Zimmerman, P. Palmgreen, M. Lustria, and M. L. Horosewski. 2006. "Integrating Personality and Psychological Theoretical Approaches to Understanding Safer Sexual Behavior: Implications for Message Design." *Health Communication* 19, no. 2: 165–74.

Nussbaum, Martha C. 2006. *Frontiers of Justice: Disability, Nationality, Species Membership*. Cambridge, MA: Harvard Univ. Press.

Omeran, Layle, and Kayan. 2020. "*Za'faraan*: A Space for Creative Expression of LGBTQ Folks in the MENA/SWANA Region." *Journal of Middle East Women's Studies* 16, no. 1: 94–99. At https://doi.org/10.1215/15525864-8016604.

Plummer, Ken. 2010. "Generational Sexualities, Subterranean Traditions, and the Hauntings of the Sexual World: Some Preliminary Remarks." *Symbolic Interaction* 33, no. 2: 163–90. At https://doi.org/10.1525/si.2010.33.2.163.

Powers, Amanda C. 2008. "Social Networking as Ethical Discourse: Blogging a Practical and Normative Library Ethic." *Journal of Library Administration* 47, nos. 3–4: 191–209.

Puar, Jasbir. 2007. *Terrorist Assemblages: Homonationalism in Queer Times*. Durham, NC: Duke Univ. Press.

Rahman, Momin. 2014. *Homosexualities, Muslim Cultures, and Identities*. Basingstoke, UK: Palgrave MacMillan.

Richter, Felix. 2022. "Infographic: English Is the Internet's Universal Language." *Statista Daily Data*, Feb. 21. At https://www.statista.com/chart/26884/languages-on-the-internet/.

Ryan, J. Michael, and Helen Rizzo. 2024. "Sexuality in the Middle East and North Africa: Contemporary Issues and Challenges." Introduction to *Sexuality in the Middle East and North Africa: Contemporary Issues and Challenges*, edited by J. Michael Ryan and Helen Rizzo, 1–19. Syracuse, NY: Syracuse Univ. Press.

Savci, Evren. 2021. *Queer in Translation: Sexual Politics under Neoliberal Islam*. Durham, NC: Duke Univ. Press.

security in-a-box. n.d. "Tools and Tactics for the LGBTI Community in the Middle-East and North Africa." Accessed in 2017, updated in 2020. At https://securityinabox.org/en/lgbti-mena/.

Sen, Amartya. 2005. "Human Rights and Capabilities." *Journal of Human Development* 6, no. 2: 151–66.

Senzee, Thom. 2014. "Saudi Man's 'Gay' Tweets Earn 450 Lashes, Jail Time." *Advocate Online*, July 24. At https://www.advocate.com/world/2014/07/24/saudi-mans-gay-tweets-earn-450-lashes-jail-time.

Shaeer, Osama, and Kamal Shaeer. 2014. "The Global Online Sexuality Survey (GOSS): Male Homosexuality among Arabic-Speaking Internet Users in the Middle East." *Journal of Sexual Medicine* 11: 2414–20.

Al Shafei, Esra'a. 2016. "What's the Real Story of the Gay Middle East?" *Medium*, Jan. 26. At https://fellowsblog.ted.com/the-real-story-of-the-gay-middle-east-fc0ed6d02e76.

Shakhsari, Sima. 2012. "From Homoerotics of Exile to Homopolitics of Diaspora: Cyberspace, the War on Terror, and the Hypervisible Iranian Queer." *Journal of Middle East Women's Studies* 8, no. 3: 14–40.

Shanahan, Matt. 2022. "The Mobile Gender Gap Report 2022." GSMA, June 22. At https://www.gsma.com/mobilefordevelopment/blog/the-mobile-gender-gap-report-2022/.

Shihab-Eldin, Ahmed. 2023. "How Egyptian Police Hunt LGBT People on Dating Apps." *BBC News*, Jan. 30. At https://www.bbc.com/news/world-middle-east-64390817.

Sreberny, Annabelle, and Gholam Khiabany. 2010. *Blogistan: The Internet and Politics in Iran*. New York: I. B. Tauris.

Sutherlin, John. 2012. "Middle East Turmoil and Human Rights: How Will the 'New' Regimes Expand Civil Liberties?" *Perspectives in Global Development and Technology* 11: 75–87.

Swiebel, Joke. 2009. "Lesbian, Gay, Bisexual and Transgender Human Rights: The Search for an International Strategy." *Contemporary Politics* 15, no. 1: 19–35.

Tahrir Institute for MENA Region Policy (TIMEP). 2019. "TIMEP Brief: LGBTQ Human Rights in Egypt." July 3. At https://timep.org/reports-briefings/timep-brief-lgbtq-human-rights-in-egypt/.

Toumi, Habib. 2014. "Gay Man Sentenced for Twitter Debauchery in Saudi Arabia." *Gulf News: Saudi Arabia*, July 23. At https://gulfnews.com/news/gulf/saudi-arabia/gay-man-sentenced-for-twitter-debauchery-in-saudi-arabia-1.1363181?.

United Nations Development Programme (UNDP). 2021. *Gender Equality in Digitalization*. Istanbul: UNDP Istanbul Regional Hub. At https://www.undp.org/eurasia/publications/gender-equality-digitalization.

United Nations News. 2023. "It May be Time to Reinforce Universal Access to the Internet as a Human Right, Not Just a Privilege, High Commissioner Tells Human Rights Council." Mar. 10. At https://www.ohchr.org/en/news/2023/03/it-may-be-time-reinforce-universal-access-internet-human-right-not-just-privilege-high.

Valle, Jay, and Matt Lavietes. 2023. "Grindr Sends Egypt Users a Warning after Alleged Entrapments and Arrests." *NBC News*, Mar. 23. https://www.nbcnews.com/nbc-out/out-news/grindr-sends-egypt-users-warning-alleged-entrapments-arrests-rcna76349.

Wagner, Kevin, and Jason Gainous. 2007. "Digital Uprising: The Internet Revolution in the Middle East." *Journal of Information Technology & Politics* 10, no. 3: 261–75.

Warf, Barney, and Peter Vincent. 2007. "Multiple Geographies of the Arab Internet." *Area* 39, no. 1: 83–96.

Whitaker, Brian. 2006. "Behind the Veil: Lesbian Lives in the Middle East." *Al-bab Online*, July. At https://al-bab.com/behind-veil-lesbian-lives-middle-east.

Wicker, Stephen B., and Stephanie M. Santoso. 2013. "Access to the Internet Is a Human Right: Connecting Internet Access with Freedom of Expression and Creativity." *Communications of the ACM* 56, no. 6: 43–46.

World Bank. 2021. "Individuals Using the Internet (% of Population)—MENA Region & North Africa." At https://data.worldbank.org/indicator/IT.NET.USER.ZS?locations=ZQ.

Zaatari, Zeina. 2024. "Sexual Rights Movement(s): Problematics of Visibility." In *Sexuality in the Middle East and North Africa: Contemporary Issues and Challenges*, edited by J. Michael Ryan and Helen Rizzo, 23–66. Syracuse, NY: Syracuse Univ. Press.

Zagria. 2013. "Yasmene Jabar (1956–): Artist, Activist, Comedienne." *A Gender Variance Who's Who* (blog), Nov. 28. At https://zagria.blogspot.com/2013/11/yasmene-jabar-1956-artist-activist.html#.WO-lZFKZP-Y.

3

Middle Eastern LGBT Westernization?

The Case of Jerusalem and Tel Aviv

Gilly Hartal and Orna Sasson-Levy

"This Knesset is the home of all Israeli citizens. It is the true fortress of human rights and individual freedom. . . . This Knesset, led by this chairman, will not harm them or any child or family. P-e-r-i-o-d. . . . And if there is a boy or girl watching the swearing-in ceremony today, know that it doesn't matter who you are or where you are from, you can achieve anything you want." This excerpt is taken from the speech of Amir Ohana, a gay man and Israel's chairman of the Knesset (Israel's Parliament) since 2022, at his swearing-in ceremony. His statements present Israel as a liberal state in which individuals have equal opportunities to reach positions of power and influence. The appointment of a gay man to such an important and prominent political role feeds into a narrative of Israel as a progressive state vis-à-vis LGBT rights that stands in contrast to the "primitive" and traditional Middle East, especially Iran and the Palestinian Authority.[1] Yet the very coalition of which Ohana is a member includes Avi Maoz (Noam party), who works to remove LGBT content from educational institutions; Orit Struck and Simcha Rotman (Religious Zionism party), who advocate for a law that will allow hotel owners or doctors to refuse service to gay people because of religious beliefs; and members of his own

1. We use LGBT rather than LGBTQ+ it was the common terminology in Israel during the time we did our research.

party who support canceling pride parades. This contradiction reflects a broad tension between progress and challenges for the LGBT community in contemporary Israeli society (Blus-Kadosh et al. 2023).

Israeli progressiveness toward LGBT individuals is a relatively new and limited framework. Until the late 1980s, Israel was a conservative place for LGBT individuals, who were excluded from the public sphere. Their status changed in 1988 with the amendment of the penal code that prohibited homosexual intercourse. Since then, LGBT individuals have gained legal recognition and achieved acceptance mainly in Tel Aviv, reaffirming Kath Weston's (1995) claim that large urban spaces serve as places of tolerance and acceptance of LGBT culture.

The relationship between global cities and LGBT cultures as well as cities' status as spaces of belonging for LGBT individuals, organizations, and culture have been well documented. Sexuality is a primary and fundamental force in everyday life in cities (Hubbard 2011; Hubbard, Collins, and Gorman-Murray 2016; Oswin 2016) and serves as a fertile ground for generating modes of belonging to national collectives. Scholars have noted that since the start of the 2000s there has been a major turnaround in which municipalities, governments, and businesses have begun to support LGBT inclusion and promote homonormative initiatives (Bell 2001; Bell and Binnie 2004; Markwell 2002; Mowlabocus 2021; Rushbrook 2002). Such homonational practices and discourses are most prominent in the West, specifically in places where LGBT equality is established and normalized. This understanding of "LGBT normalization" in the West is questioned by some scholars, however (see, for example, Browne and Nash 2014; Nash and Browne 2015). Indeed, in Israel as elsewhere, a recent populist backlash has emerged that resists sexual and gender rights (Nash and Browne 2020; Rothschild 2023; chapter 5 in this volume).

Moreover, in Israel, LGBT inclusion serves to portray the state as tolerant and liberal, while simultaneously marking other states as intolerant, undemocratic, and illiberal. This process, known as "pinkwashing," legitimizes violent policies toward Middle Eastern Arab countries and conceals Israel's human rights violations toward Palestinians (Hartal and Sasson-Levy 2021). As Ana Cristina Marques, Salma Talaat, and J. Michael Ryan write in chapter 5 in this volume, Westerners see LGBT individuals from

Islamic Middle East and North African (MENA) countries as victims of oppressive and homophobic Islamic beliefs, but they don't recognize how European colonialism and Western postcolonialism had already undermined acceptance of gender and sexual diversity in these countries. The protection of LGBT rights is then used to justify Western imperialism and militarism. Thus, sexual minorities are used as political weapons to animate both imperialism and nationalistic ideologies (see also the introduction to this volume).

Moreover, the "urban," or large metropolitan centers, does not constitute a homogenous category (see, for example, Oswin 2016). Looking at the two largest cities in Israel—Tel Aviv and Jerusalem—reveals profound differences. These differences have not only been a focus of vast sociological and geographical research (Alfasi and Fenster 2005; Fenster 2004; Vinitzky-Seroussi 1998) but are especially blatant in LGBT research (Hartal and Sasson-Levy 2017; Misgav and Hartal 2019). In this study, Tel Aviv is portrayed as the westernized, secular, and liberal economic center of Israel, on its way to becoming a global city, whereas Jerusalem is perceived as a local city oriented toward its religious and national past (Alfasi and Fenster 2005) and populated by distinct and even hostile social-religious groups.

Discussing the nuanced politics and the way sexual belonging is forged within each of these urban spaces, we argue that these cities are indeed very different from each other, but the differences are not based solely on an East (Jerusalem)–West (Tel Aviv) division. Rather, from an LGBT perspective we show that both cities relate to their Middle Eastern location, albeit by merging East and West differently.

Thus, in this chapter we ask how homonationalism operates in the two cities. By "homonationalism," we refer to the coupling of LGBT folks with nationality and normativity and to that coupling's derived processes of inclusion of some LGBT individuals within mainstream society, which involves adopting the hegemonic ideology and (in Israel) militarist discourses. We study the two Middle Eastern cities in the larger context of Israel, which associates itself (especially when discussing sexualities) with the West rather than with the surrounding Middle East. Thus, our main goal is to examine the way sexual politics, nationalism, and neoliberal economics play distinct roles and are manifested differently in the contexts of

Tel Aviv and Jerusalem. More specifically, we ask how homonationalism and sexual citizenship interact in different urban spaces.

The study is based on data collected (by Gilly Hartal) for two ethnographic studies: the first focuses on LGBT spaces in Israel, and the second focuses on gay tourism to Tel Aviv. The Tel Aviv part of the research was collected during participant observations at the Gay Center between October 2011 and October 2012 and sixteen open-ended interviews in Hebrew with the Gay Center's staff and key activists. Twenty-two additional interviews were conducted in Hebrew and English in 2016 for the study on gay tourism to Tel Aviv, along with four months of participant observations between May and August 2016. The Jerusalem part included five months of participant observations between January and May 2010. These observations were accompanied by ten open-ended interviews in Hebrew with leading activists in the Jerusalem Open House, the only LGBT community space in West Jerusalem. All interviews lasted from two to four hours and were recorded and transcribed, and transcriptions were sent to the participants for approval. Translations to English were made by the authors. Although it is unusual, all participants gave written consent for the use of their real names because they all are well-known local public figures who wanted credit for their statements. Also, the activist LGBT community in Israel is small, and most of the activists are known to each other. Since almost all activists in the research field were interviewed, their statements are recognizable. However, by now, most of the participants have left their positions or are former activists.

In what follows, we examine the concepts of sexual citizenship and homonationalism, specifically discussing their scope within the Middle East and the criticism they have induced. Following this theoretical framework, we present the cities, producing an analysis of the local politics and its Middle Eastern projections, then discuss what the Israeli case has to offer to other debates on the subject of sexual citizenship and homonationalism in the Middle East.

Moving between Sexual Citizenship and Homonationalism

As an "incorporations regime" (Soysal 1994), citizenship is an ensemble of institutional practices and cultural norms that define groups' and individuals' belonging to a political collective. The theory that links citizenship to sexuality argues that citizenship has always been associated with heterosexuality (Bell and Binnie 2000; Richardson 1998). Although citizenship represents unity and equality, in many countries gays and lesbians are not eligible for equal civic rights. In other (mostly neoliberal) states, LGBT individuals' citizenship has been perceived as unsettled because they are not inherently seen as part of the nation but are not unequivocaly excluded from it. Indeed, although LGBT individuals are not formally denied the right to vote or participate in politics, their power to exercise political influence has been circumscribed in most parts of the world (Cossman 2010).

The political discrimination against LGBT people is the main source for the emergent concept of sexual citizenship, which marks sexuality as part of citizenship and employs citizenship as a locus for sexual identities and practices (Bell and Binnie 2006). The concept of sexual citizenship calls for citizenship to include the rights of LGBT individuals. Expansion of sexual citizenship occurs both through juridical enfranchisement and via "symbolic incorporation into a national community" (Seidman 2001, 323; see also Richardson 2000) in the public sphere. To achieve that expansion, sexual citizenship must entail changing heteronormative cultural and social norms (such as family formations and the welfare state's organizing principles).

However, sexual citizenship not only signifies a struggle for inclusion but also, as critical scholars argue, is an attempt at the normalization, discipline, and promotion of gay commodification and marketization (Evans 1993; Phelan 2001). Brenda Cossman (2010) argues that what makes the struggle for sexual citizenship particularly successful in the West is that it does not fundamentally challenge hegemony. Similarly, Steven Seidman asserts that "gays have claimed not only to be normal, but to exhibit valued civil qualities such as discipline, rationality, respect for the law and family values, and national pride" (2001, 323). Normalization thus neutralizes sexual difference and renders it an exception that does not prove the rule, portraying LGBT individuals as ideal citizens who exhibit national pride and normativity, thus replicating heteronormativity (Stychin 2001) and reproducing hierarchies of exclusion and inclusion (Bell and Binnie 2004).

This criticism, as important as it is, reflects a Western perspective located in places "where 'we have won'" (Browne and Nash 2014). In many other places, citizenship is still something yet to be achieved and cannot be undervalued. As Jeffrey Weeks (1998) argues, making demands on a culture that denies you is a radical act. Because citizenship is a disciplinary discourse, any desire to reiterate heterosexual citizenship is constituted by both struggles for belonging and subversion. The common understanding of the citizen as an abstract and universal subject hides Orientalist constructions that enhance othering processes of whoever doesn't fit Western narratives of citizenship (Isin 2002). These Orientalist discourses portray Middle Eastern sexualities through the "modernity versus tradition" binary, enforcing a stubborn structure that locates the West as progressive and the East as traditional (Kuntsman and al-Qasimi 2012). Within this equation, not only geographic location but also ideological identification, economic power, and democratization processes play a role.

The formation of sexual citizenship in the Middle East and specifically in Israel manifests differently than it does in the West. This difference has been commonly discussed within the analytical framework called "homonationalism" (Puar 2015; Ritchie 2010). Jasbir Puar coined the term *homonationalism* to reflect a combination of nationality and normativity: nationality being a mode of belonging to the nation-state and normativity in its specific meaning as "the new homonormativity" (Duggan 2003)—neoliberal sexual politics and its practice by LGBT individuals. Homonationalism should be understood not as an identity or a positionality but as a disciplining ideology and regulatory regime within the structure of citizenship; it is an assemblage of political, social, and economic forces: "Homonationalism . . . is rather a facet of modernity and a historical shift marked by the entrance of (some) homosexual bodies as worthy of protection by nation-states. . . . Part of the increased recourse to domestication and privatization of neoliberal economies and within queer communities, homonationalism is fundamentally a deep critique of lesbian and gay liberal rights discourses and how those rights discourses produce narratives of progress and modernity that continue to accord some populations access to citizenship—cultural and legal—at the expense of the delimitation and expulsion of other populations" (Puar 2013, 337; see also Puar

2007). Dynamic binary processes of inclusion and exclusion occur within homonationalism. While specific groups are marked with the "correct" belonging and thus legitimized, others are branded perverse and thus distanced from the public sphere (Hartal and Sasson-Levy 2021). That is, inclusion in mainstream society also creates exclusion by ignoring the inequality of sections of the LGBT community.

Moreover, LGBT subgroups who receive equal rights by adopting hegemonic ideology strengthen LGBT individuals' legitimate belonging to the nation. The Israeli military is a case in point. From its inception in 1948, the military did not have restrictions regarding the enlistment of LGBT soldiers, despite Israel's antisodomy law, though until 1993 there were restrictions to their promotion (Levy 2007). Thus, in contrast to many other countries, Israel did not deem homosexuality "incompatible" with army service (Belkin and Levitt 2001), and the Israeli military was ahead of civilian society in legitimizing both homosexuality (Kama 2000) and transgender identities (Yerke 2020). The military's inclusiveness resulted from a combination of perceived existential threat from the surrounding countries and a national narrative of individual sacrifice for collective goals (Shafir and Peled 2002). Both Israeli politicians and the military have worked to maintain an image of the military—and by extension of Israeli society as a whole—as affirming, inclusive, and nondiscriminatory toward LGBT individuals (Mandelbaum 2018).

Expanding the nation's boundaries and including LGBT folks—that is, a deviant group—within it allow the state to portray itself as tolerant and liberal while simultaneously marking Others as intolerant, undemocratic, and illiberal. In Israel, public officials and others champion gay rights to claim that Israel is a liberal state in contrast to the "primitive" and Oriental Middle East, especially Iran and the Palestinian Authority. At its most extreme, this pinkwashing deploys the hard-won gains of Israel's gay community in order to legitimize violent policies toward countries portrayed as intolerant of LGBT and other minorities (see chapters 1 and 5 in this volume). In other words, states are now judged as premodern or modern by their treatment of homosexuals. A state's treatment of LGBT individuals is then an index of its tolerance that obscures any other human rights violations or abuse (Franke 2012; Gross 2015; chapter 5 in this volume). It also erases the existence of Palestinian gay rights organizations, such as Aswat and alQaws (Atshan 2020), that have linked LGBT activism with the Palestinian struggle for freedom and justice (Darwich and Maikey 2014) and thus have rejected alliances with Israeli LGBT organizations and the narrative of Israel as a haven for Palestinian gays (Atshan 2020).

At the same time, the imprecise or overuse of homonationalism as a master narrative has come under fire in recent years (Ritchie 2015; Zanghellini 2012). Some of the arguments specifically highlight the paradox of using homonationalism as a totalizing analytical framework outside Western/white contexts (Winer and Bolzendahl 2021). Yet Jason Ritchie (2015) contends that it is the oversimplifications of homonationalism that also make it tenable, popular, and, to some extent, universal. C. Heike Schotten (2016) shares the critique of homonationalism, claiming the diverse formations of it cause a blurring of its unique location-based particularities, making it unproductive in articulating a grounded, distinctive analysis. Criticizing from a different perspective, Joseph Massad (2002) claims that while understandings of sexuality are presumed to be universal, in actuality they are culturally based. Sexual discourses are specific, divergent, place and time based, and therefore projections of lesbian and gay identities onto non-Western individuals can be dangerous: "Gays and lesbians are universal categories that exist everywhere in the world, and based on this prediscursive axiom, the Gay International sets itself the mission of defending them by demanding that their rights as 'homosexuals' be granted where they are denied and be respected where they are violated. In doing so, however, the Gay International produces an effect that is less than liberatory" (Massad 2002, 363). Framing a large portion of queer activism as the act of imposing Western categories not suited to localized/non-Western cultures, Massad sets the stage for a critique of homonationalism.

Echoing Massad's critique of the universalizing of the gay subject, Neville Hoad claims that homosexuality is "an identity that travels," underlining that outside Western contexts the colonial legacy constructed sexual identity narratives (2000, 151; see also Najmabadi 2014). But while Hoad sees the construction of gay identities as violently imposed by the capitalist West on postcolonial spaces, Oswin Natalie (2008) argues that constructions of Western sexualities and non-Western ones are always formed in relation to one another. For example, Xavier Livermon in his analysis shows how whereas the white queer body is emblematic of human rights and progressive discourses, thus promoting South Africa as a queer-friendly tourist destination, the Black queer body remains a "threat to African culture and tradition" (2012, 302). Livermon (2012) also shows how in South Africa local vernacular terms that at times challenge Western understandings of sexuality to describe sexual positioning, acts, and performances are reworked into sexual identity categories. Lisa Rofel (2007) echoes this critique in her discussion of sexualities in China, where she aims to disrupt neoliberalism-based homogeneous global sexual identities and reveal a globalized logic that has colonized sexual imagination.

The "LGBT" subject proliferation, widely documented in the West, has not been chronicled in the Middle East to nearly the same extent. According to Edward Said (1978), homoeroticism in the Middle East underwrites the attractiveness and practices of Orientalism. Considering that the foundational understanding of LGBT subjectivity is Western based, an Orientalist portrayal of LGBT individuals in the Middle East reproduces West–East binaries. Unlike Islamophobic discourses that accompanied US imperialism, which are criticized through the concept of homonationalism (Mikdashi 2016), Middle Eastern understandings of sexualities are influenced by Western narratives of progress but at the same time are glocalized—that is, shaped simultaneously both by a global framework and by local traditions of sexuality. As Zeina Zaatari writes in chapter 1 of this volume, Palestinian LGBT organizations resist the Western narrative of gay liberation and its associated mandate for visibility. This perspective is a sign of the refusal to be defined by the West as the only point of reference.

Tel Aviv Homonational West–East Blend

Tel Aviv has been frequently framed as a homonational space by both scholars and activists (Eisner 2012; Gross 2015; Gunther and Collejfe 2004; Hartal and Sasson-Levy 2017; Misgav 2016). In 2008, the municipality established the Gay Center. Funded by the municipality, the center operates a commercial café and runs community events, group activities, self-help gatherings, a health clinic, an information center, a theater, and the local pride parade. The building, which is currently undergoing a major reconstruction, is located inside a park in downtown Tel Aviv, where real estate is very expensive. The city is not only welcoming to Israeli LGBT individuals but was declared the world's best gay travel destination in 2012, leading to an increase in LGBT (mainly gay men) tourists, who visit the city during summertime and the pride parade (Hartal and Sasson-Levy 2021).[2] This homonationalist framing is produced through both top-down and bottom-up power models (Hartal and Sasson-Levy 2017). We open this section with a discussion of Tel Aviv's homonational actions and then focus on the city's marketing practices to gay (mostly men) tourists, revealing the construction of an East–West blend. Such branding connects Tel Aviv to its Middle Eastern roots but at the same time keeps it from being "too Middle Eastern." Within this context of homonational space produced as an East–West exception, we ask: What kind of mechanisms lie at the basis of this linkage, and what does the linkage entail? We contrast this space with inherent differences in Jerusalem's LGBT space and its linkage to the Middle East.

Avi, a veteran activist, explained LGBT politics' centrality to Tel Aviv municipal politics:

> The important thing is that there is a large strong municipality that takes [it] upon itself [to produce annual pride events]. . . . That's the story. The Tel Aviv pride parade is stunning. What a magnificent mobilization of the municipality. . . . I don't care what they get in return. They send five hundred municipal workers to manage my business . . . to clean up after the parade or whatever. . . . This is exactly what we want, this reflects our success. . . . Look, even today in Tel Aviv, politically, you cannot ignore it [the commitment to LGBT issues]. I don't think that you can get elected to any kind of official job without relating to the [LGBT] community, it's like . . . every fourth person on the street [in Tel Aviv] is [LGBT]. (second and last ellipses indicate pauses)

Avi's words reveal the activists' direct identification with the municipal establishment. He is enthusiastic about municipal involvement in LGBT

2. For Tel Aviv as the world's best gay travel destination in 2012, see Heller 2012.

activities. Furthermore, Avi reflects on a process in which some municipal politicians are in fact LGBT politician-activists who began their political careers within LGBT organizations and currently serve on their boards. These politicians have made clear that promoting LGBT belonging in Tel Aviv is imperative, which in turn has culminated in wide support of the municipality. This promotion has morphed into a commitment toward LGBT individuals in Tel Aviv and even a wider sense of responsibility for LGBT individuals in Israel. And, indeed, LGBT individuals have great power within local politics.

LGBT politics in Tel Aviv is based on a conception of Tel Aviv as *the* gay capital of Israel, thus marking LGBT politics and spaces as respectable, cultural, and family friendly (contrary to common stereotypes about LGBT individuals and spaces as filthy, hypersexual, and dangerous). Simultaneously, however, LGBT belonging in Tel Aviv is grounded in a power structure and boundaries that lead to the marginalization of others (Hartal 2015; Markwell 2002; Puar 2002). This sociospatial politics, which is based on inner hierarchies in the community (strong–weak, men–women, gay–LGBT), produces and reproduces homonationalism, which enables homonormative gay men to achieve and sustain power positions, ensuring their control over the LGBT politics and resources in Tel Aviv.

Rather than constituting a local formation of gayness, Israeli LGBT individuals and organizations see themselves as the descendants of North American LGBT individuals and struggles. Ofri Ilany (2015) contends that since the 1970s the representation of Israeli Jewish homosexuality has become white and North American, describing a Western liberal lifestyle. This Western narrative is not limited to LGBT rights struggles and politics but also reflects personal identifications and performances (such as choices of favorite music and style as well as sexual practices and preferences). The LGBT struggle for rights and the struggle's practices (such as the determination on visible presence in the public sphere) are inspired by but also legitimized by Western discourses of human rights. Specifically, the Stonewall riots that took place in 1969 in New York City are a constitutive narrative for activists immersed in the Israeli LGBT struggles.

At the same time, Israeli public officials and others have been widely criticized for pinkwashing Israel, using gay rights to claim that Israel is a liberal state by stressing its progressive human rights legislation. In this process, Tel Aviv becomes a space of wide acceptance, a bubble of LGBT inclusivity, away from the dangers of backwardness and its homophobia. Through the production of gay tourist campaigns, the Tel Aviv municipality and the Aguda (Association for LGBTQ Equality in Israel) also take part in pinkwashing. Lior Meyer, the director of brand marketing and communications at Tel Aviv Global & Tourism, a company owned by the Tel Aviv municipality, described how "[the gay tourism campaigns] contributed to the self-perception of Tel Aviv as a city that loves to show itself off as cosmopolitan, . . . a bit like Israel, [which] loves to show itself within the space of the Middle East, as how Bibi [Benjamin Netanyahu, Israel's prime minister] puts it: we are a villa in the jungle. So, like that. Not from an arrogant place, but . . . we love to see ourselves as enlightened and liberal and very open, and gays are an easy way to achieve this" (ellipses indicate pauses). The well-known phrase "villa in the jungle," coined by Prime Minister Ehud Barak in 1996,[3] is utilized both to portray the desire of the State of Israel to become a Western/European white space as well as to reveal what this desire camouflages and represses (Bar Yosef 2013)—namely, Israeli Mizrahi-ness, Arab-ness, and links to Africa and the Middle East. On a wider scale, it symbolizes the drive to construct Israel as a "bubble" that purposely disregards its location within the Middle East (Zaban 2015). Furthermore, the metaphor of "the jungle" echoes nineteenth- and twentieth-century European colonial claims about the barbarism of the region (Said 1978). Thus, this phrase "encapsulates the Israeli construction of identity and sense of place as being white, 'European-like,' democratic and enlightened; a 'villa' that dominates a white and modern territory surrounded by walls and borders that are supposedly impenetrable" (Yacobi 2015, 2).

In contrast, the companies that promote gay tourism portray Tel Aviv as not "just another" Western city. Rather, they paint Tel Aviv in Oriental colors, marketing it as an exotic and authentic Middle Eastern heaven:

3. Ehud Barak, "Address by Foreign Minister Ehud Barak to the Annual Plenary Session of the National Jewish Community Relations Advisory Council," Feb. 11, 1996.

located in the Middle East but not Black like Africa and not backward like Arab states (Hartal and Sasson-Levy 2021).

Shai Doitsh, the initiator and "engine" of gay tourism in Tel Aviv and former Aguda chairperson, explained the secret of the gay tourism campaign's success: "[Tel Aviv] was the new guy. . . . Not just the new guy . . . 'I'm not another European city, I have an Oriental flavor, I'm Middle Eastern.' I'd say to them: 'We are Europeans with a Middle Eastern temper. We're different, we're gnarled, we have stubble and chest hair.' . . . And today Israeli DJs are touring parties around the world, . . . and the logo says 'Tel Aviv, Israel' because Tel Aviv became a hot brand around the world" (ellipses indicate pauses). Doitsh understood the potential of mixing Europe with a touch of Orientalism to create a winning and easy-to-promote product.

Lior Meyer added: "When you market, the tension between what you expect and what you actually get is your greater strength. Now, in Tel Aviv, let's look at one extreme: [at one end] the element of . . . the Israeli-Palestinian conflict and war and the Middle East and [at] the absolute other extreme the subject of Tel Aviv and pride. The surprise on their [tourists'] faces . . . the fact is that this completely dissolves what they think they know of this place and enables you to create a whole different narrative, and this is a great marketing strength" (ellipses indicate pauses). The story Meyer told distinguishes between Tel Aviv and Israel: westernization processes are part of Tel Aviv, while the Oriental processes are located within the State of Israel but not directly tied to Tel Aviv's urban space. At the same time, Tel Aviv is framed as an integral part of the Middle East to promote its attractiveness to Western (male) gay tourists. This notion of Tel Aviv as an amalgam of East and West, modern and backward, is not a unique perspective; it has manifested in the past—for example, in the United Nations Educational, Scientific, and Cultural Organization's declaration of the city as a World Heritage Site.[4] In promoting gay tourism, the municipality and other commercial agencies stress Tel Aviv's Middle

4. The World Heritage Site list is at https://whc.unesco.org/en/list/1096/, viewed Apr. 21, 2017.

Eastern location and character, which are still evident there but in new and compelling ways.

Thus, we argue that even though Tel Aviv can be framed as a homonational and global space, it is not constructed as a Western space per se. Rather, neoliberal economic forces involved in the promotion of gay tourism to the city have brought about a unique blend of East–West discourses. This mix makes the city a sexy, attractive space for tourists, a city that shifts its focus from its Western ideological identification back to its Middle Eastern geographic location. This shift reveals the importance of neoliberal forces within LGBT discourses in the Middle East, which heretofore were understood and analyzed mostly through perspectives such as religion, Orientalism, digital technology, and activism (Boone 2010; Kuntsman and al-Qasimi 2012; Moussawi 2013; Naber and Zaatari 2014; Walsh-Haines 2012).

Jerusalem as a Mosaic

Jerusalem, Israel's capital, is often portrayed as a religious city oriented toward its past and its history (Vinitzky-Seroussi 1998). It is considered a holy city to the three major monotheistic religions and a segregated and contested space (Adelman and Elman 2014; Alfasi and Fenster 2005; Vinitzky-Seroussi 1998). The city is divided along the intersecting religious, political, ethnic, and gendered splits in Israeli society (Fenster 2005), separated into social, cultural, and spatial fragments that (re)produce symbolic and physical boundaries such as walls and enclosed neighborhoods (Gedaliah and Sharkansky 2010). These boundaries expose the religious, ethnic, and national significance of divisions within Israeli society, separating religious Israeli Jews from secular ones, Palestinians from Israeli Jews, and isolating ultra-Orthodox spaces. Moreover, because the Green Line and the Separation Wall pass through the city (Weizman 2007, 161), the city encompasses loaded political and physical boundaries that reinforce the social segregation.

In the LGBT context, Jerusalem is thought of as a highly political space where being an LGBT individual is problematic in both public and private spaces (Adelman 2014; Hartal 2016; Wagner 2013). Public Jerusalem spaces and the municipal establishment itself create a sense of discomfort and unbelonging for LGBT people (David, Hartal, and Pascar 2018; Hartal and Misgav 2021). The Jerusalem Open House (JOH), located in the city center, is an LGBT organization, a community center, and a safe, empowering, and visible space. The JOH organizes the annual Jerusalem pride parade; it holds community meetings and runs an open clinic for HIV/AIDS testing. The organization often copes with issues that are unique to Jerusalem, focusing on LGBT visibility in an intolerant space and responding to the Palestinian and ultra-Orthodox communities living in the city.

The JOH's spatial politics reveal consolidating practices and discourses that we have termed "the politics of holding" (Hartal 2016). Because Jerusalem is home to Jewish religious lesbians, Palestinian gays, local LGBT youth, and others with various sexual identities, this politics aims to give space to all factions of the Jerusalem LGBT community, holding them together and at the same time restraining them from dissolving, contesting, or competing.[5] However, rather than bringing these communities together, creating a united fabric, JOH politics is similar to a mosaic in that it makes room for each of the factions, maintaining peaceful interactions between them but at the same time maintaining the factions' different, sometimes contradictory political stances. In this sense, one of the central goals the JOH takes upon itself is to escape the all-encompassing homonational imperative and to construct itself through sexual citizenship in ways that do not reflect modes of homonormativity or compliance with a government agenda.

As we mentioned earlier, the city of Jerusalem is characterized by a prominent religious (Jewish, Christian, and Muslim) objection to LGBT public presence. Since the JOH's inception, this objection has materialized

5. By "Palestinian gays," we refer to the activists in alQaws for Sexual & Gender Diversity in Palestinian Society. The activists could be Christian or Muslim, religious or secular, but all define themselves as Palestinians. We do not detail the heterogeneity of this group because they see themselves as one Palestinian organization and are not divided according to other axes of identity. Conversely, we depict ultra-Orthodox Jewish and Hevruta, the religious Jewish LGBT group, as having a more nuanced sense of Jewish religiosity because this was the base of the organization.

violently several times. In 2005, Yishai Schlissel, an ultra-Orthodox man, stabbed three pride parade marchers. Ten years later, in 2015, Schlissel, only three weeks out of prison, once again stabbed marchers during the parade, killing sixteen-year-old Shira Banki and injuring six other marchers.

Within this general atmosphere of homophobia and violence, it is difficult for LGBT individuals to openly enter the JOH community center and participate in its activities (Hartal and Misgav 2021). For example, Jewish religious LGBT individuals had difficulties accessing the JOH because of the demands between 2005 and 2008 not to hold the pride parade in Jerusalem, which came for the most part from the ultra-Orthodox community in Jerusalem. In this context, every religious-looking man was immediately suspected of hostile homophobia, thus making it hard for religious homosexuals to enter the center.

In response to such difficulties, the JOH has developed a "politics of holding" (Hartal 2016), which emphasizes the consolidation of public and private LGBT politics and aims to contain contradictory points of view and to incorporate LGBT individuals' diverse embodiments as well as rival political standpoints. This politics offers a dialectic mode of holding through a constant effort to balance normative politics and discourses of inclusion. It is an attempt to frame the LGBT community space in Jerusalem as a shelter, which is simultaneously at odds with ongoing blockages, social boundaries, and sociospatial normative divisions and with attempts to increase LGBT visibility. Hagai Elad asks in a journal article: "How can we persuade a religious lesbian that the JOH is her home as well? How would a Palestinian gay guy feel the JOH is open for him too? We are making an effort to create a community framework in which everyone can participate, that includes putting a pride mezuzah [a symbol of a Jewish home] on the front door, a dairy kitchen [keeping a kosher kitchen], signs in Arabic" (2008, 261, our translation). The local heterogeneity of Jerusalem, which incorporates Israeli Jewish, Palestinian, right- and left-wing political stances as well as secular, religious, and Orthodox LGBT individuals, makes it difficult to produce a unified LGBT politics.

At the organization's plenary in 2011, JOH activists discussed its role in creating an inclusive space. A veteran activist said, "The first thing is that this is a home for all LGBT people. . . . We really need to address the needs of ultra-Orthodox LGBT people, even LGBT people who are extremely right wing, . . . who do not want to give rights to anyone. . . . This place, in my view, is first and foremost for LGBT people. . . . Among us, we have all types [of LGBT individuals], all opinions—this is everyone's home" (ellipses indicate pauses). Yonatan, the JOH director, described in an interview what was required for the preservation of the JOH's accessibility as a result of this state of affairs: "In the process of reducing the great flames of 2008 in relation to the great violence . . . we did something very deliberate through quiet and constant communication with representatives of the ultra-Orthodox community; we undertook a process with ourselves as well, a process of down shifting. We do less communication; . . . we are placing boundaries. . . . Part of it is realizing . . . that there will be less media coverage of all topics of the parade" (ellipses indicate pauses).

Yonatan's desire not to provoke media attention meant giving up a degree of visibility. However, visibility is not something he unequivocally endorsed against the accessibility of the JOH; rather, it seems that what was important is the nature of media visibility. Yonatan preferred nonadversarial visibility, which aims for inclusion and the creation of an all-encompassing space for LGBT individuals. The contradiction between accessibility and visibility is caused by Jerusalem's social structure and its ideological fractures. The consolidation of accessibility and visibility poses a political challenge to the JOH, a challenge that constructs the politics of holding. Yonatan elaborated:

> In Tel Aviv everyone is former something . . . there is no such thing as real and original Tel Avivians. In Tel Aviv, there are ex-religious, ex-whatever. . . . It turns out it's much more fun to talk about the parties and who had sex with whom. . . . And here [in Jerusalem] the heterogeneity, the fact that everyone is entrenched in their own identity, may be a bit too much . . . the specific Kippa [yarmulke] color. . . . This is what makes this city so interesting because in the end we have to live together. . . . These cities can be what they are only because of this profound contrast. (ellipses indicate pauses)

Whereas Tel Aviv is portrayed as a space with no roots, no past, symbolizing the identity categories that were abandoned in favor of a fun

LGBT party life, Jerusalem is portrayed as a mosaic, a local assemblage of identities and intersectional specifications connecting past and present. These strategies reflect how the Israeli state wants to portray itself as both distinct from the Middle East and sharing with it a rich and diverse history and tradition. Having to establish and protect pluralism, the JOH works to enhance tolerance in the city but without aiming to create unification or assimilation. This effort is embedded in the politics of holding, which makes room for diverse identifications and experiences and offers all Jerusalem LGBT individuals a space of belonging.

Yaron and Yonatan gave two different examples of the effort not to leave anyone out and to take others' points of view into consideration. Yaron, the community coordinator, recalled in an interview a situation in which JOH activists were called to participate in a neighborhood protest against the encroachment of the ultra-Orthodox community: "Someone called us from Kiryat Yovel to invite us to protest there and told us, 'We want to invite you [the JOH's activists] for a Shabbat, to fill the place up with rainbow flags.' They don't do this because they want LGBT visibility [in their neighborhood]; they do it because they want to annoy the ultra-Orthodox people who come to live there. We need to explain to them that we don't want to [help them] because we don't want to annoy the ultra-Orthodox communities who live in the neighborhood; we want to befriend everyone." The ultra-Orthodox community's well-known opposition to the LGBT community was almost dragged into a "spatial occupation" debate, but the JOH's activists declined the invitation. Yaron stressed that accessibility was a guiding principle in decision making, articulating what he thought it meant for the JOH to be an inclusive space, a home for LGBT individuals in Jerusalem irrespective of nationality, ethnicity, class, gender, religion, or religiosity. In this sense, the JOH is a space for LGBT convergence, transcending political boundaries. At a JOH board meeting, Yonatan demonstrated this position:

> We [the JOH] were invited to participate in a regional [LGBT] activity in Turkey, and this is something that never happens. Usually, if someone is trying to have a regional seminar which includes LGBT representatives from the Arab world, then Israeli organizations are not invited. . . . So

> we were invited. . . . The first thing I said to them was, "Kudos to you for inviting us." The second thing was that if us coming meant that the Arab LGBT organizations would not attend, then please invite Tel Aviv [LGBT organizations], not us. We don't like that corner, we don't. We will not have someone not come because we are there. (ellipses indicate pauses)

Yonatan positioned the JOH as an organization that doesn't want to reproduce power relations that would lead to exclusions of Arab LGBT organizations. While portraying this position, he placed Tel Aviv LGBT politics at an oppositional viewpoint in its identification with Israeli (pinkwashing) nationalist politics. JOH's position places it in the political role of opposition to the government, thus preventing the development of local homonational politics.

The politics of holding is also prevalent in the JOH's internal structure and politics. As a result of the JOH's goal to serve as a home for marginalized LGBT individuals, two local groups emerged, but they subsequently left the JOH for an independent future. Hevruta, a male religious gay organization, and alQaws for Sexual & Gender Diversity in Palestinian Society, a Palestinian organization, began inside the JOH but later chose to go their own way. Hevruta moved to Tel Aviv, the most comfortable space for Israeli Jewish LGBT individuals in Israel, and alQaws physically stayed part of the JOH but as a separate and independent organization. Both groups left the JOH as a result of their own growth and the consolidation of their leadership. The two groups implement opposing politics: the Israeli Jewish religious group members are associated with right-wing, conservative politics, while the Palestinian group is associated mostly with leftist, queer, antioccupation politics and with the Boycott, Divestment, and Sanction movement.[6]

In an interview, Eyal, the first chairman of Hevruta, asserted that leaving the JOH and establishing an autonomous organization originated for three main reasons: migration of religious gay folks to Tel Aviv, which

6. The global Boycott, Divestment, and Sanctions campaign to end the Israeli occupation and colonization of Palestinian or Arab land, to gain equality for Arab Palestinian citizens of Israel, and to demand respect for the right of return of Palestinian refugees.

transferred Hevruta's center of gravity and increased the need for meetings in Tel Aviv; disagreements with the JOH regarding the usage of designated monetary contributions to Hevruta; and a need for autonomy and self-determination, which led to the establishment of Hevruta as a nongovernmental organization, separate from the JOH's infrastructure. Eyal made clear that "as long as we were within the JOH, we had to explain why we were not the JOH. We are Hevruta, an independent group functioning within the JOH," and that associating Hevruta with the JOH reflected badly on Hevruta. This association tied Hevruta to the secular JOH's leftist stances, which are opposed to Hevruta's political views.

As for alQaws, the ethnography on which this chapter is based was unsuccessful in setting up interviews with its activists. At first, this seemed to be because alQaws members visited the JOH at different times. After two months of no luck in connecting with them for interview, it became apparent that this was a refusal on their part, even though it was not bluntly articulated, because of the researcher's (Gilly's) identity as a Jewish Israeli woman doing research at an Israeli university. Thus, even though alQaws's offices and some of its activities are located inside the JOH's space, and although, just like Hevruta, the organization originated as a JOH group, and alQaws' chairwoman was a former coordinator for the Palestinian community at the JOH, there was no direct contact by the researcher with the group during the research period. This alone is very indicative of alQaws's political stand and its relations with the JOH and its activists. The members of alQaws have written elsewhere that organizing based on LGBT identity alone did not meet the needs of Palestinian members of the LGBT community; their activism and alliance had to incorporate their ethnicity and nationality. Their separatist strategy came from a need to create a safe space to explore, support, and advocate for their complex and intersectional identities (Maichi 2009; chapter 1 in this volume). This move was a sign of the politization of the Palestinian LGBT movement, which resulted in its separation from the Israeli LGBT movement (Atshan 2020). Thus, alQaws strives to distance itself from the Jerusalem organization even while residing in its building. This politics, it is important to note, is completely approved by the JOH, which is happy to provide a space for Palestinian LGBT people and organizations.

Despite this political opposition between Hevruta and alQaws, the JOH cultivated both groups spatially and organizationally, being a home at the same time to both religious Israeli Jewish gays and Palestinian queers. This clear tension was managed for many years in which no direct disputes surfaced—an indication of a politics of holding. This politics reflects the JOH's awareness of its location within Jerusalem and more generally within the Middle East, leading the activists to focus the organization on creating a sense of belonging—whether spatial or social. Stemming from a Middle Eastern reflexivity, the JOH clearly realizes that any attempt to create a unified LGBT (national or secular) identity would destroy the possibility of sexual citizenship for LGBT Jerusalemites.

We argue that Jerusalem reveals a different kind of politics in comparison to Tel Aviv, one that aims to create a safe and inclusive space for all LGBT communities (ultra-Orthodox, Palestinian, etc.). In such a contested space as Jerusalem, it is impossible to ignore the city's sociopolitical density. Thus, while the LGBT space creates room for all, it does not enable social interactions between the different groups that compose the LGBT community in Jerusalem. Such space-management practices are implemented throughout the city, where walls, divisions, and separations are the rule. The assumption underlying this politics is that it is the only possible way to metaphorically make room for all local LGBT communities, to establish an inclusive politics in a homonational era, and to strive to escape homonormativity.

Discussion

The spatial perspective offers a fresh overview of LGBT political belonging, highlighting that being an LGBT individual in Tel Aviv or in Jerusalem creates differentiated logics for thinking through space and sexual citizenship. The Middle Eastern angle produces a more nuanced understanding of urban spaces as products of a trendy homonational configuration. At the same time, in a critical view of this popular framework, the application of homonationalism to the Jerusalem space reveals a profoundly different kind of spatial politics in which the Middle Eastern aspects of the Israeli space work in a different way.

Our discussion of LGBT politics is anchored in discourses on sexual citizenship and homonationalism, the way the two are portrayed, and their specific political practices within LGBT spaces. We have shown that Tel Aviv and Jerusalem present very different LGBT politics in relation to their Middle Eastern location, revealing specific understandings of East and West and differentiated formations of national belonging. Our findings resonate with Canton Winer and Catherine Bolzendahl's observation that homonationalist discourses create "liminal spaces that include a blend of East and West (and thus a blend of enlightenment and homophobia)" (2021) and that complicate simple East–West binaries.

Tel Aviv has succeeded in presenting itself as a global city, an attractive mecca for gay tourism, through a process of combining East and West. The westernization processes of Tel Aviv, which derive from global human rights discourses, manifest as vocal gay parades and the self-perception of Tel Aviv LGBT activism as a direct continuation of the Stonewall riots. Middle Eastern culture, however, is also embedded in the marketing of Tel Aviv as an Oriental space, introducing new ways of commodifying Tel Aviv through its positioning within the Middle East. The construction of a Middle Eastern cultural perspective has helped to induce gay tourism and bring in money for the city, bolstering its self-perception as a global space. Paradoxically, this globalization is maintained through an adoption of practices that portray the city as a space combining the East and the West, persistently linking Tel Aviv to the Middle East. Constructing the city this way has increased its market value and revealed that homonationalism is constituted through neoliberal processes that in fact produce the LGBT understanding of being in the Middle East as a profitable process of homonormativity and homonationalism powered and promoted via neoliberal market forces (Hartal 2020).

Jerusalem, in contrast, is entrenched in the Middle East in a different way. Much like other Middle Eastern cities, the city of Jerusalem encapsulates the major rifts in Israeli society in a small geographic space. Because this "holy" city comprises Israeli Jews and Palestinians of many different social, ethnic, and religious groups, the local LGBT politics in the city aims to make it a comfortable "home" for all LGBT individuals. Aiming for inclusive politics, this practice is tailored to help the local activists manage the city's sociospatial structure, which encompasses ultra-Orthodox, secular, and Palestinian LGBT people in a space that is generally intolerant to LGBT public visibility. The "politics of holding" (Hartal 2016) adopted by Jerusalem activists and its derivative practices makes room for all facets of the local LGBT community but does not bring them together. Homonationalism and homonormativity are not the main issues that concern this kind of politics; on the contrary, such mechanisms of political belonging risk the inclusive space. The Middle Eastern location of the JOH in Jerusalem is a starting point for practices that create sexual citizenship. Belonging is achieved via allowing different groups to reside together without forcing artificial togetherness among them. Moreover, the JOH achieves sexual citizenship by maintaining political vagueness to allow political precision for each different group. Hence, the JOH's modes of incorporation are not derived from cultural assimilation or a homonational melting-pot policy but rather from a politics of holding of differences without erasing them. Thus, LGBT organizations adjust their strategies to adapt to the local landscape (Browne, Nash, and Gorman-Murray 2018).

This comparative analysis of sexual politics in Israeli urban spaces can be extended to better understand both other homonational discourses and other Middle Eastern cities. For example, studying Euro-American journalistic articles, gay travelogues, and an international gay tour guide of Beirut, Ghassan Moussawi argues that Beirut is advertised as the "'Paris of the Middle East,' 'Switzerland of the Middle East,' 'San Francisco of the Arab World'" (2013, 863). This marketing characterizes Beirut as primarily Middle Eastern or Arab, with a Western scent dabbed onto it to make it "both exotic and familiar" (Moussawi 2013, 863).

Tel Aviv is presented in the media as a "gay mecca," located in "the West" but laced with Middle Eastern flavor. In fact, the city had so successfully cast itself as Western that marketing gurus needed to tie it to the Orient again in order to create a new gay vibe. The gay tourist campaign—bringing Tel Aviv back to its Middle Eastern context, encapsulating a mixture of West and East, LGBT assimilation and westernization with a grain of Orientalism—became a winning advertising ensemble.

The modes of being in the Middle East taken up here work in different ways in each urban space. At the heart of this difference lies the constitution of national belonging as a basis for political action. In Tel Aviv, homonationalism serves to create profit and assimilation, whereas in Jerusalem sexual citizenship helps avoid disputes and maintain "tempered" visibility—only enough visibility to sustain a space of belonging but never discussing the form this belonging should take.

Moreover, in each space the Middle East is taken up differently. In the Jerusalem Open House, the Middle Eastern context is the starting point of its politics. In discussing political practices, the JOH activists take into consideration not only its Middle Eastern location but also the ramifications of the organization's politics for other Middle Eastern societies. In Tel Aviv, the Middle Eastern culture enables a new neoliberal formation for profit. In this neoliberal formation, Middle Eastern identities are commodified and contribute to homonational processes.

This comparative analysis shows that although processes that create LGBT spaces, practices, and identities are shaped by global (mostly Western) discourses, they are interpreted and manifested differently in various contexts. The interplay of economics, politics, religion, and nationalism in each space shapes the specific form of sexual politics and belonging in a Middle Eastern city.

Thus, the Middle Eastern context produces both similarities (religious, patriarchal, and conflicted societies) and major differences between the two cities. The similarities call for mutual cultural influence and reciprocity in developing LGBT politics. However, it seems that the differences and the social distance, at least between Israel and its surrounding countries, are perceived as so profound that they prevent interactions among LGBT communities and minimize LGBT collective activism that has the potential to transgress national political borders.

References

Adelman, Madelaine. 2014. "Sex and the City: The Politics of Gay Pride in Jerusalem." In *Jerusalem: Conflict and Cooperation in a Contested City*, edited by Madelaine Adelman and Miriam Elman, 233–60. Syracuse, NY: Syracuse Univ. Press.

Adelman, Madelaine, and Miriam Elman, eds. 2014. *Jerusalem: Conflict and Cooperation in a Contested City.* Syracuse, NY: Syracuse Univ. Press.

Alfasi, Nurit, and Tovi Fenster. 2005. "A Tale of Two Cities: Jerusalem and Tel Aviv in an Age of Globalization." *Cities* 22, no. 5: 351–63. At https://doi.org/10.1016/j.cities.2005.05.006.

Atshan, Sa'ed. 2020. *Queer Palestine and the Empire of Critique.* Stanford, CA: Stanford Univ. Press.

Bar Yosef, Eitan. 2013. *A Villa in the Jungle: Africa and the Zionist Imagination* (in Hebrew). Tel Aviv: Hakibbutz Hameuchad.

Belkin, Aaron, and Melissa Levitt. 2001. "Homosexuality and the Israeli Defense Forces: Did Lifting the Gay Ban Undermine Military Performance?" *Armed Forces & Society* 27, no. 3: 541–65.

Bell, David. 2001. "Fragments of a Queer City." In *Pleasure Zones: Bodies, Cities, Spaces*, edited by David Bell, Jon Binnie, Ruth Holiday, Robyn Longhurst, and Robin Peace, 84–102. Syracuse, NY: Syracuse Univ. Press.

Bell, David, and Jon Binnie. 2000. *The Sexual Citizen: Queer Politics and Beyond.* Cambridge: Polity Press.

———. 2004. "Authenticating Queer Space: Citizenship, Urbanism and Governance." *Urban Studies* 41, no. 9: 1807–20. At https://doi.org/10.1080/0042098042000243165.

———. 2006. "Geographies of Sexual Citizenship." *Political Geography* 25, no. 8: 869–73. At https://doi.org/10.1016/j.polgeo.2006.09.002.

Blus-Kadosh, Inna, Avner Rogel, Ruth Blatt, and Gilly Hartal. 2023. "Progress and Challenges of the LGBT+ Community in Israel." In *The Palgrave International Handbook of Israel*, edited by P. R. Kumaraswamy, 1–16. Singapore: Palgrave Macmillan.

Boone, Joseph A. 2010. "Modernist Re-Orientations: Imagining Homoerotic Desire in the 'Nearly' Middle East." *Modernism/Modernity* 17, no. 3: 561–605. At https://doi.org/10.1353/mod.2010.0017.

Browne, Katherine, Catherine J. Nash, and Andrew Gorman-Murray. 2018. "Geographies of Heteroactivism: Resisting Sexual Rights in the Reconstitution of Irish Nationhood." *Transactions of the Institute of British Geographers* 43, no. 4: 526–39.

Browne, Katherine, and Catherine J. Nash. 2014. "Resisting LGBT Rights Where 'We Have Won': Canada and Great Britain." *Journal of Human Rights* 13, no. 3: 322–36. At https://doi.org/10.1080/14754835.2014.923754.

Cossman, Brenda. 2010. "Sexing Citizenship, Privatizing Sex." *Citizenship Studies* 6, no. 4: 483–506. At https://doi.org/10.1080/1362102022000004127.

Darwich, Lynn, and Haneen Maikey. 2014. "The Road from Antipinkwashing Activism to the Decolonization of Palestine." *Women's Studies Quarterly* 42, nos. 3–4: 281–85. At https://doi.org/10.1353/wsq.2014.0057.

David, Yossi, Gilly Hartal, and Lital Pascar. 2018. "The Right to Jerusalem: The Danger of Queer Safe Spaces." *Borderlands Ejournal* 17, no. 1: 1–26. At https://www.proquest.com/scholarly-journals/right-jerusalem-danger-queer-safe-spaces/docview/2159685427/se-2?accountid=14483.

Duggan, Lisa. 2003. *The Twilight of Equality? Neoliberalism, Cultural Politics and the Attack on Democracy.* Boston: Beacon Press.

Eisner, Shiri. 2012. "Love, Rage and the Occupation: Bisexual Politics in Israel/Palestine." *Journal of Bisexuality* 12, no. 1: 80–137. At https://doi.org/10.1080/15299716.2012.645722.

Elad, Hagai. 2008. "In Jerusaelm, from the Path of the Pride Parade You Can See the Separation Wall." In *Where, Here: Language, Identity, Place* (in Hebrew), edited by Israel Katz, Zeev Degani, and Tamar Gross, 252–76. Tel Aviv: Hakibbutz Hameuchad.

Evans, T. David. 1993. *Sexual Citizenship.* New York: Routledge.

Fenster, Tovi. 2004. *The Global City and the Holy City: Narratives on Knowledge, Planning and Diversity.* London: Pearson.

———. 2005. "The Right to the Gendered City: Different Formations of Belonging in Everyday Life." *Journal of Gender Studies* 14, no. 3: 217–31. At https://doi.org/10.1080/09589230500264109.

Franke, Katherine. 2012. "Dating the State: The Moral Hazards of Winning Gay Rights." *Colombia Human Rights Law Review* 49, no. 1: 1–46. At https://ssrn.com/abstract=2186595.

Gedaliah, Auerbach, and Ira Sharkansky. 2010. *Planning and Politics in Jerusalem* (in Hebrew). Jerusalem: Floersheimer Institute for Policy Studies.

Gross, Aeyal. 2015. "The Politics of LGBT Rights in Israel and Beyond: Nationality, Normativity, and Queer Politics." *Columbia Human Rights Law Review* 46, no. 2: 81–152.

Gunther, Scott, and Wellesley Collejfe. 2004. "Building a More Stately Closet: French Gay Movements since the Early 1980s." *Journal of the History of Sexuality* 13, no. 3: 326–47.

Hartal, Gilly. 2015. *The Gendered Politics of Absence: Homonationalism and Gendered Power Relations in Tel Aviv's Gay-Center.* London: Ashgate.

———. 2016. "The Politics of Holding: Home and LGBT Visibility in Contested Jerusalem." *Gender, Place and Culture: A Journal of Feminist*

Geography 23, no. 8: 1193–206. At https://doi.org/10.1080/0966369X.2015.1136813.

———. 2020. "Israel's LGBT Movement and Interest Groups." In *Oxford Research Encyclopedias: Politics*, online, edited by W. R. Thompson. Oxford: Oxford Univ. Press. At https://doi.org/10.1093/acrefore/9780190228637.013.1295.

Hartal, Gilly, and Chen Misgav. 2021. "Queer Urban Trauma and Its Spatial Politics: A Lesson from Social Movements in Tel Aviv and Jerusalem." *Urban Studies* 58, no. 7: 1463–83.

Hartal, Gilly, and Orna Sasson-Levy. 2017. "ReReading Homonationalism: An Israeli Spatial Perspective." *Journal of Homosexuality* 65, no. 10: 1391–414. At https://doi.org/10.1080/00918369.2017.1375364.

———. 2021. "The Progressive Orient: Gay Tourism to Tel Aviv and Israeli Ethnicities." *Environment and Planning C: Politics and Space* 39, no. 1: 11–29.

Heller, Aaron. 2012. "Tel Aviv Emerges as Top Gay Tourist Destination." *AP News*, Jan. 24. At https://apnews.com/article/lifestyle-business-middle-east-religion-israel-23831e37389d41fa81ca3f5f9b072c20.

Hoad, Neville. 2000. "Arrested Developments or the Queerness of Savages: The Existing Evolutionary Narratives of Difference." *Postcolonial Studies* 3, no. 2: 133–58.

Hubbard, Phil. 2011. *Cities and Sexualities*. New York: Routledge.

Hubbard, Phil, Alan Collins, and Andrew Gorman-Murray. 2016. "Introduction: Sex, Consumption and Commerce in the Contemporary City." In "Sex, Consumption and the City," edited by Phil Hubbard, Alan Collins, and Andrew Gorman-Murray. Special issue, *Urban Studies* 54, no. 3: 567–81. At https://doi.org/10.1177/0042098016682685.

Ilany, Ofri. 2015. "'A Common Affliction in the East': Descriptions of Homosexual Intercourse during the Mandate Period" (in Hebrew). *Zmanim* 121: 8–21.

Isin, Engin F. 2002. *Being Political: Geneologies of Citizenship*. Minneapolis: Univ. of Minnesota Press.

Kama, Amit. 2000. "From Terra Incognita to Terra Firma: The Logbook of the Voyage of Gay Men's Community into the Israeli Public Sphere." *Journal of Homosexuality* 38, no. 4: 133–62.

Kuntsman, Adi, and Noor al-Qasimi. 2012. Introduction to "Queering Middle Eastern Cyberscapes," edited by Adi Kuntsman and Noor al-Qasimi. Special issue, *Journal of Middle East Women's Studies* 8, no. 3: 1–13.

Levy, Yagil. 2007. "The Right to Fight: A Conceptual Framework for the Analysis of Recruitment Policy toward Gays and Lesbians." *Armed Forces & Society* 33, no. 2: 186–202.

Livermon, Xavier. 2012. "Queer(y)ing Freedom: Black Queer Visibilities in Post-apartheid South Africa." *GLQ: A Journal of Lesbian and Gay Studies* 18, nos. 2–3: 297–343.

Maichi, Hanin. 2009. "Forming a Social Movement." In *Community Work: Methods for Social Change* (in Hebrew), edited by Elisheva Sadan, 297–306. Tel Aviv: Hakibbutz Hameuchad.

Mandelbaum, Moran M. 2018. "'I'm a Proud Israeli': Homonationalism, Belonging and the Insecurity of the Jewish-Israeli Body National." *Psychoanalysis, Culture & Society* 23, no. 2: 160–79.

Markwell, Kevin. 2002. "Mardi Gras Tourism and the Construction of Sydney as an International Gay and Lesbian City." *GLQ: A Journal of Lesbian and Gay Studies* 8, no. 1: 81–99.

Marques, Ana Cristina, Salma Talaat, and J. Michael Ryan. 2024. "The (Im)Possibilities of Being Trans in the MENA Region." In *Sexuality in the Middle East and North Africa: Contemporary Issues and Challenges*, edited by J. Michael Ryan and Helen Rizzo, 161–94. Syracuse, NY: Syracuse Univ. Press.

Massad, Joseph. 2002. "Re-Orienting Desire: The Gay International and the Arab World." *Public Culture* 14: 361–85.

Mikdashi, Maya. 2016. "Fear and Loathing in Orlando." *Jadaliyya*, June 14. At https://www.jadaliyya.com/pages/index/24635/fear-and-loathing-in-orlando.

Misgav, Chen. 2016. "Radical Activism and Autonomous Contestation 'from Within': The Gay Centre in Tel Aviv." In *Companion for the Geography of Sex and Sexuality*, edited by Gavin Brown and Katherine Browne, 105–16. London: Ashgate.

Misgav, Chen, and Gilly Hartal. 2019. "Queer Movements in Tel Aviv and Jerusalem: A Comparative Discussion." In *Routledge Handbook on Middle East Cities*, edited by Yacobi Haim and Mansour Nasara, 57–74. New York: Routledge.

Moussawi, Ghassan. 2013. "Queering Beirut, the 'Paris of the Middle East': Fractal Orientalism and Essentialized Masculinities in Contemporary Gay Travelogues." *Gender, Place & Culture* 20, no. 7: 858–75. At https://doi.org/10.1080/0966369X.2012.753586.

Mowlabocus, Sharif. 2021. *Interrogating Homonormativity: Gay Men, Identity and Everyday Life*. New York: Palgrave Macmillan.

Naber, Nadine, and Zeina Zaatari. 2014. "Reframing the War on Terror: Feminist and Lesbian, Gay, Bisexual, Transgender, and Queer (LGBTQ) Activism in the Context of the 2006 Israeli Invasion of Lebanon." *Cultural Dynamics* 26, no. 1: 91–111. At https://doiorg/10.1177/0921374013510803.

Najmabadi, Afsaneh. 2014. *Professing Selves: Transsexuality and Same-Sex Desire in Contemporary Iran*. Durham, NC: Duke Univ. Press.

Nash, Catherine J., and Katherine Browne. 2015. "Best for Society? Transnational Opposition to Sexual and Gender Equalities in Canada and Great Britain." *Gender, Place & Culture* 22, no. 4: 561–77. At https://doi.org/10.1080/0966369X.2014.885893.

———. 2020. *Heteroactivism: Resisting Lesbian, Gay, Bisexual and Trans Rights and Equalities*. London: Zed.

Oswin, Natalie. 2008. "Critical Geographies and the Uses of Sexuality: Deconstructing Queer Space." *Progress in Human Geography* 32, no. 1: 89–103. At https://doi.org/10.1177/0309132507085213.

———. 2016. "Planetary Urbanization: A View from Outside." *Environment and Planning D: Society and Space* 36, no. 3: 540–46. At https://doi:10.1177/0263775816675963.

Phelan, Shane. 2001. *Sexual Strangers: Gays, Lesbians, and Dilemmas of Citizenship*. Philadelphia: Temple Univ. Press.

Puar, Jasbir K. 2002. "A Transnational Feminist Critique of Queer Tourism." *Antipode* 34, no. 5: 935–45.

———. 2007. *Terrorist Assemblages: Homonationalism in Queer Times*. Durham, NC: Duke Univ. Press.

———. 2013. "Rethinking Homonationalism." *International Journal of Middle East Studies* 45: 336–39.

———. 2015. *The "Right" to Maim: Disablement and Inhumanist Biopolitics in Palestine*. Durham, NC: Duke Univ. Press.

Richardson, Diane. 1998. "Sexuality and Citizenship." *Sociology* 32, no. 1: 83–100. At https://doi.org/10.1177/0038038598032001006.

———. 2000. "Constructing Sexual Citizenship: Theorizing Sexual Rights." *Critical Social Policy* 20, no. 1: 105–35. At https://doi.org/10.1177/026101830002000105.

Ritchie, Jason. 2010. "How Do You Say 'Come Out of the Closet' in Arabic? Queer Activism and the Politics of Visibility in Israel-Palestine." *GLQ: A Journal of Lesbian and Gay Studies* 16, no. 4: 557–75. At https://doi.org/10.1215/10642684-2010-004.

———. 2015. "Pinkwashing, Homonationalism, and Israel-Palestine: The Conceits of Queer Theory and the Politics of the Ordinary." *Antipode* 47, no. 3: 616–34.

Rofel, Lisa. 2007. *Desiring China: Experiments in Neoliberalism, Sexuality, and Public Culture.* Durham, NC: Duke Univ. Press.

Rothschild, Leehee. 2023. "New Skin for an Old Ceremony—the Gay Revolution and the Formation of Israeli Heteroactivism." In "Heteroactivism, Homonationalism, and National Projects," edited by Stefanie C. Boulila and Katherine Browne. Special issue, *ACME: An International Journal of Critical Geographies* 22, no. 3: 1115–40. At https://acme-journal.orgindex.php/acme/article/view/2201.

Rushbrook, Dereka. 2002. "Cities, Queer Space, and the Cosmopolitan Tourist." *GLQ: A Journal of Lesbian and Gay Studies* 8, no. 1: 183–206.

Ryan, J. Michael, and Helen Rizzo. 2024. "Sexuality in the Middle East and North Africa: Contemporary Issues and Challenges." Introduction to *Sexuality in the Middle East and North Africa: Contemporary Issues and Challenges*, edited by J. Michael Ryan and Helen Rizzo, 1–19. Syracuse, NY: Syracuse Univ. Press.

Said, Edward. 1978. *Orientalism.* New York: Vintage.

Schotten, C. Heike. 2016. "Homonationalism." *International Feminist Journal of Politics* 18, no. 3: 351–70.

Seidman, Steven. 2001. "From Identity to Queer Politics: Shifts in Normative Heterosexuality and the Meaning of Citizenship." *Citizenship Studies* 5, no. 3: 321–28. At https://doi.org/10.1080/13621020120085270.

Shafir, Gershon, and Yoav Peled. 2002. *Being Israeli: The Dynamic of Multiple Citizenship.* Cambridge: Cambridge Univ. Press.

Soysal, Yasemin Nuhoğlu. 1994. *Limits of Citizenship: Migrants and Postnational Membership in Europe.* Chicago: Univ. of Chicago Press.

Stychin, Carl F. 2001. "Sexual Citizenship in the European Union." *Citizenship Studies* 5, no. 3: 285–301. At https://doi.org/10.1080/13621020120085252.

Vinitzky-Seroussi, Vered. 1998. "'Jerusalem Assassinated Rabin and Tel Aviv Commemorated Him': Rabin Memorials and the Discourse of National Identity in Israel." *City & Society* 10, no. 1: 183–203. At https://doi.org/10.1525/city.1998.10.1.183.

Wagner, Roy Roi. 2013. "On (Not) Choosing between Mobility and Visibility: Crossing Sexual and National Borders in Israel/Palestine." *Borderlands Ejournal* 12, no. 2. At https://www.academia.edu/7184297/On_not_choosing

_between_mobility_and_visibility_Crossing_sexual_and_national_borders_in_Israel_Palestine.

Walsh-Haines, Grant. 2012. "The Egyptian Blogosphere: Policing Gender and Sexuality and the Consequences for Queer Emancipation." *Journal of Middle East Women's Studies* 8, no. 3: 41–62. At https://doi.org/10.2979/jmiddeastwomstud.8.3.41.

Weeks, Jeffrey. 1998. "The Sexual Citizen." *Theory, Culture & Society* 15, no. 3: 35–52. At https://doi.org/10.1177/0263276498015003003.

Weizman, Eyal. 2007. *HOLLOW LAND: Israel's Architecture of Occupation*. London: Verso.

Weston, Kath. 1995. "Get Thee to a Big City: Sexual Imaginary and the Great Gay Migration." *GLQ: A Journal of Lesbian and Gay Studies* 2, no. 3: 253–77.

Winer, Canton, and Catherine Bolzendahl. 2021. "Conceptualizing Homonationalism: (Re-)Formulation, Application, and Debates of Expansion." *Sociology Compass* 15, no. 5: art. e12853. At https://doi.org/10.1111/soc4.12853.

Yacobi, Haim. 2015. *Israel and Africa: A Genealogy of Moral Geography*. London: Routledge.

Yerke, Adam. 2020. "Stronger Together: The Global Shift to Transgender-Inclusive Armed Forces." In *Trans Lives in a Globalizing World: Rights, Identities, and Politics*, edited by J. Michael Ryan, 147–66. London: Routledge.

Zaatari, Zeina. 2024. "Sexual Rights Movement(s): Problematics of Visibility." In *Sexuality in the Middle East and North Africa: Contemporary Issues and Challenges*, edited by J. Michael Ryan and Helen Rizzo, 23–66. Syracuse, NY: Syracuse Univ. Press.

Zaban, Hila. 2015. "Living in a Bubble: Enclaves of Transnational Jewish Immigrants from Western Countries in Jerusalem." *Journal of International Migration and Integration* 16, no. 4: 1003–21. At https://doi.org/10.1007/s12134-014-0398-5.

Zanghellini, Aleardo. 2012. "Are Gay Rights Islamophobic? A Critique of Some Uses of the Concept of Homonationalism in Activism and Academia." *Social & Legal Studies* 21, no. 3: 357–74. At https://doi.org/10.1177/0964663911435282.

Part Two. Gender and Sexual Minorities

4

Islam and Homosexuality

Identity, Threat, and Sexual Well-Being among Muslim Gay Men

Rusi Jaspal

For decades, social scientists have conducted research into identity processes among gay men of religious faith (Coyle and Rafalin 2000; Harris et al. 2020; Jaspal and Cinnirella 2010; Maatouk and Jaspal 2022).[1] In this work, it has become clear that contemplating the relationship between sexuality and religion can be a source of psychological distress. In many religious traditions, there is an emphasis on heterosexual marriage—the sacred, spiritual, and physical union of a man and a woman. Homosexuality is often represented as a contravention of this religious expectation. This chapter focuses on the relations between religion and sexuality—two facets of identity that are often interconnected—among Muslim gay men in particular. It examines some of the social and psychological challenges to sexual well-being observed in previous research into Muslim gay men. The chapter considers sexual well-being in the broadest sense, focusing not only on physical sexual health outcomes but also on those outcomes relating to one's emotional, psychological, and social well-being. The application of tenets of identity process theory and social representations

1. The term *gay* is often construed as a Western construct. Some individuals reject this category for self-description (Carlson 1997), but in this chapter it is deemed appropriate for use because participants in many of the cited research studies self-identified as gay.

theory from social psychology can enhance our understanding of the interrelations between religion and sexuality among Muslim gay men and enable us to understand the implications for their overall sexual well-being. Crucially, the synthesis of existing theory and research constitutes an important step toward developing measures to enhance well-being in this population.

Theological Considerations

Like most religious traditions, Islamic ideology appends hegemonic status to heterosexuality, and it is widely interpreted as opposing homosexuality. This stance is ingrained in the major ideological channels of communication, such as Islamic holy scripture (the Qur'an), Islamic law (Sharia), and the verbal teachings of the Prophet Mohammed (hadith), all of which appear to outlaw homosexuality (Bouhdiba 1998). Theological opposition to homosexuality is based on what is regarded by most Islamic scholars as the Qur'an's explicit prohibition of same-sex sexuality. The story of Lot in the Qur'an has been widely cited as evidence of God's condemnation of homosexuality. The Qur'an makes seven explicit references to Lot and the people of Sodom and Gomorrah, whose destruction by God is often attributed to their engagement in homosexual practices, as exemplified in the following passage:

> What! Of all creatures do ye come unto the males,
> And leave the wives your Lord created for you?
> Nay but ye are forward folk . . .
> And we rained on them a rain. And dreadful is the rain of those who have been warned.
>
> (sura 26:165, translated in Pickthall 1930)

Although there has been some variation in the interpretation of the story of Lot (Kugle 2010), one passage in the Qur'an more clearly demonstrates the illegality of homosexuality: "And as for the two of you who are guilty thereof [of homosexuality], punish them both. And if they repent and improve, then let them be. Lo! Allah is ever relenting, Merciful" (sura 4.16 translated in Pickthall 1930). In Islam, the Qur'an legislates all aspects of social life, but interpretations of the text have varied in accordance with time and place, and some interpretations have been favored over others in particular denominations of Islam. Yet in their reading of the story of Lot, many mainstream Muslim scholars understand it as saying that homosexuality is an aberration and violation of nature as well as a revolt against God.

Although there has been some discussion of the authenticity and accuracy of the hadith (teachings attributed to the Prophet Mohammed), they are frequently invoked by Islamic scholars to substantiate the dominant Islamic position on homosexuality: "The Prophet said: If you find anyone doing as Lot's people did, kill the one who does it, and the one to whom it is done."[2] Like other hadith, this one represents homosexual acts as both immoral and illegal and homosexuals as deserving of capital punishment. They construct both the active and passive individuals as equally culpable, although in societal thinking the passive role appears to be more stigmatized (Karimi and Bayatrizi 2019; Schmidtke 1999). Although the Qur'an does not make overt reference to lesbian sexuality, some hadith suggest that lesbian sexual activity is sinful in that it is comparable to *zina* (adultery) and thus punishable by death.

Most Islamic countries prohibit homosexuality, and in some of them it is punishable by death. Very few Islamic or Muslim-majority countries have decriminalized homosexuality, and even in these few countries' societies there is little legal support for LGBT individuals, and extrajudicial punishments are common. The Islamic Republic of Iran, which is governed by its own interpretation of Sharia law, has a particularly harsh legal stance on homosexuality. Iranian law dictates that anal intercourse will be punished with death by hanging (Karimi and Bayatrizi 2019). According to Sharia law, individuals can be convicted of homosexuality only if they confess four times or if four "righteous" Muslim men can testify that they have witnessed a homosexual act taking place. In Islamic societies, both judicial and extrajudicial measures taken against homosexuality

2. Sunan Abi Dawud 4462, book 39, hadith 4447, "Prescribed Punishments (Kitab al-hudud)," Sunnah.com: Sayings and Teachings of Prophet Muhammad (صلى الله عليه و سلم), at https://sunnah.com/abudawud/40/112.

communicate a clear message to society that homosexuality is immoral, illegal, and, thus, punishable.

However, there is also a "reverse discourse" concerning the Islamic position on homosexuality, with some scholars arguing that there is indeed scope for its theological accommodation. For instance, Jim Wafer indicates that the mildness of the Qur'anic passages alluding to homosexuality vis-à-vis other religious infractions perhaps indicates that "the Prophet took a lenient attitude toward sex between males" (1997, 89). Some have contested the dominant interpretation of the story of Lot, arguing that Sodom's destruction reflected God's condemnation of the people's promiscuity, violence, inhospitality, and so on rather than of homosexuality per se (Jamal 2001; Kugle 2010). Accordingly, Khalid Duran (1993) has indicated that gay Muslims need to seek out a theological accommodation of their sexuality based on a new Sharia that emphasizes the principles of freedom and justice that are central to Islam. However, it is noteworthy that such theological accommodation remains unacceptable to many mainstream Muslim scholars. Andrew Kam-Tuck Yip's statement that "there are at present limited efforts in Islamic theology which offer non-heterosexual Muslims resources to construct a reverse discourse" (2005, 50) remains relevant today.

Social Representations and Identity Processes

There is a growing tradition of research into the interface of religion and sexuality among gay men of Islamic faith, and this work highlights the complex social and psychological struggles that can characterize their experiences and identities (Jaspal and Cinnirella 2010, 2012; Yip 2004, 2005). To explore how gay Muslims construct and negotiate their sexual and religious identities, two theories from social psychology—social representations theory and identity process theory—are especially useful. Together, the two theories enable the analyst to understand the social norms, values, and images that contribute to understandings of homosexuality in particular social contexts and the social psychological processes that underpin how gay Muslims themselves construct their identities consisting of their religion and sexuality.

Social representations theory (Moscovici 1988) can provide a useful framework for understanding social perceptions of homosexuality among Muslims. At a basic level, a social representation can be defined as a collective "elaboration" of a given social object (i.e., homosexuality) that enables individuals to think and talk about it. This elaboration consists of emerging beliefs, values, ideas, images, and metaphors used to conceptualize this object. Two principal social psychological processes converge in the creation of a social representation:

- *Anchoring* refers to the process whereby a novel, unfamiliar phenomenon is integrated into existing ways of thinking. For instance, in research with gay Muslims, it has been found that homosexuality is sometimes linked to "liberal Western culture," which can lead some to reject homosexuality as a norm associated with a cultural outgroup (Jaspal and Cinnirella 2010, 2012).
- *Objectification* refers to the process whereby an abstract phenomenon is rendered concrete and tangible. The use of metaphors is a key objectification process. For example, some individuals refer to homosexuality as a disease, which implies that it is possible to cure it (Stychin 1995) and thus can lead to the endorsement of so-called gay conversion therapies.

Glynis Breakwell (2014) has outlined the processes that underpin people's relationship with a social representation. Individuals differ in the extent to which they are aware of, understand, accept, and assimilate to their thinking about a social representation. For instance, although an individual may be aware of homosexuality, they may not understand it and may erroneously link it to other stigmatized behaviors, such as pedophilia (Kort 2012). This error could have important implications for how they subsequently behave toward gay people and in turn how gay Muslims themselves construct and manage their identities. For instance, gay Muslims may construe their sexuality as shameful and thus attempt to conceal it from others.

Identity process theory (Breakwell 1986; Jaspal and Breakwell 2014) focuses on the social-psychological mechanisms underpinning identity construction, threat, and protection. It encompasses multiple levels of analysis, including the intrapsychic, intergroup, and societal levels. The theory enables the analyst to understand how particular social positions and events may affect identity and how identity is protected in the face of possible challenges. For instance, gay Muslims may struggle to maintain a sense of connection with their religion given the knowledge that other Muslims perceive homosexuality to be incompatible with Islamic norms and values.

Identity process theory proposes that identity is constructed through two universal processes: (1) assimilation-accommodation and (2) evaluation. Assimilation-accommodation refers to the absorption of new information in the identity structure (e.g., "I am gay") and to the adjustment that takes place for that information to become part of the structure (e.g., "I am gay, so maybe I cannot be a Muslim"). The evaluation process confers meaning and value upon the contents of identity (e.g., "Being Muslim is a good thing, but being gay is not").

These processes function to create particular desirable end states for identity, or "identity principles," which include:

- Continuity—the perception that one's past, present, and future are connected
- Self-esteem—personal and social worth
- Distinctiveness—uniqueness and differentiation from others
- Self-efficacy—competence and control
- Psychological coherence—the perception that relevant aspects of identity are compatible

The significance of these principles in the context of sexuality and religion among British Pakistani Muslim men has been discussed elsewhere (Jaspal and Cinnirella 2010). The theory suggests that when the identity processes cannot provide appropriate levels of the identity principles, identity is threatened, and the individual will engage in strategies to alleviate the threat (Breakwell 1986). Some strategies function at the intrapsychic level, such as *denial* that one is actually gay or *reconceptualization* of what it means to be gay. Others function at the interpersonal or intergroup levels, such as *isolation* of oneself from others or *relinquishment* of particular social group memberships.

A consistent finding in identity process theory research into identity among gay Muslims is that they may face identity threat due to (1) the perceived incompatibilities between their religion and their sexuality (threatening *psychological coherence* [Jaspal and Cinnirella 2010, 2012]); (2) the inability to construct a coherent narrative connecting past, present, and future in relation to being gay (threatening *continuity* [Jaspal and Cinnirella 2012]); and (3) the negative value and affect habitually appended to their sexuality, which nonetheless is recognized as a key component of the self-concept (threatening *self-esteem* [Bhugra 1997]). Identity threat is generally harmful to psychological well-being.

When one's religion is construed as "core," as it often is for Muslims, self-identification as gay can place gay Muslims in a threatening position because of the perception that homosexuality is rejected by other Muslims. This perception can cause identity threat, and, consequently, individuals will attempt to cope with this aversive psychological state (Jaspal and Cinnirella 2010). Social representations evidently play a key role: if individuals are *aware* of social representations that stigmatize their sexual orientation, they may plausibly be threatened by these representations. This sense of threat is particularly acute if individuals themselves *accept* these social representations (i.e., if they believe them to be true), as is the case for some gay Muslims who append importance to their religion.

In the remainder of this chapter, three major themes that have emerged from qualitative interview research into identity construction among gay Muslims are discussed: how gay Muslims make sense of homosexuality, the threats to psychological coherence that can arise when they think about their religion and sexual orientation, and the ways in which they seek to maintain a sense of belonging in their religious group, where the legitimacy of their group membership may be questioned. The potential implications of identity threat for sexual well-being among gay Muslims are also considered.

Making Sense of Homosexuality

Some gay and bisexual men report very early awareness of their sexual orientation (i.e., "I have always known"), while others are able to identify a particular point at which they became aware (e.g., "I realized I was gay when I was twenty"). Becoming aware of one's sexual orientation is a complex process influenced by multiple social and psychological factors (Jaspal 2022b). Although the individual may be aware of their same-sex attractions, they may dismiss them as a "phase," reconceptualize them as nonsexual, or suppress them so that the individual can deny their sexual orientation. This can mean that the individual simply does not regard their sexual orientation as an element of identity but rather as something else—a behavioral trait, for instance. By denying the reality of their sexual orientation, they are able to maintain their previous (desired) self-image and essentially protect their sense of continuity.

Gay Muslims may struggle to make sense of their sexual orientation and the feelings, emotions, and desires associated with it. Individuals attempt to define and append meaning to their sexual orientation, which in turn will shape the way they decide to categorize themselves. Possible self-categories include, inter alia, gay, homosexual, bisexual, and heterosexual. Several scholars have accurately noted that the category "gay" is a Western construct, which individuals from some cultures may therefore reject as an inaccurate descriptor of their identity (e.g., Carlson 1997). In Western societies, being gay is sometimes understood as a group-level category, which implies a sense of commonality and solidarity between members of this category (Lin and Israel 2012). According to this perspective, the individual perceives a sense of affiliation to the group and shares some key norms, values, and practices with other members of that group. In contrast, some gay Muslims construe homosexuality in terms of an individual characteristic rather than in terms of membership in a social group. In other words, they may describe their sexual orientation as an entirely personal characteristic and eschew any sense of social identification with other gay men. Some may even stigmatize and denigrate other gay men—in interviews, some have made reference to the "promiscuous lifestyles" of gay men. In short, they may feel that it is unnecessary and even problematic to express one's sexuality publicly and that one's sexuality should be concealed. In some cases, this feeling reflects individuals' internalized homophobia in that they uncritically accept the stigma socially appended to homosexuality (Maatouk and Jaspal 2022). This view decreases the likelihood of developing friendships with other gay men and may deprive some gay Muslims of social support networks that might ordinarily enable those experiencing identity threat to cope effectively.

Given that many gay Muslims perceive their religion as an important element of identity, they may come to view their sexual orientation through a religious lens and draw upon theological explanations for it. In attempting to make sense of their sexual orientation, gay Muslims may make theologically informed attributions, which in turn can have implications for the ways in which they evaluate their sexual orientation.

Some individuals may attribute their sexual orientation to God, and, given the perception that God is perfect, this attribution can enable them to deduce that God's creation (namely, the homosexual or homosexuality) cannot possibly be imperfect or wrong. This reasoning amounts to a form of anchoring—a link is established between homosexuality and divinity. Moreover, homosexuality is metaphorically represented as God's *creation*, which is an example of objectification. In view of the centrality of their religion, this understanding can enable gay Muslims to evaluate homosexuality positively. For instance, some may distance the notion of sex from their homosexual relationships and instead emphasize the importance of companionship, security, and intimacy in these relationships. In interviews, some gay Muslims have lamented the focus on sexual behavior in social representations of their sexual orientation and note that it was promiscuity, not homosexuality, that invited disapproval from God. Incidentally, this argument echoes alternative interpretations of the story of Lot offered as part of the "reverse discourse" against the mainstream Islamic stance on homosexuality (Kugle 2010). This positive evaluation of homosexuality may increase the likelihood of assimilating and accommodating one's sexual orientation. Given that this social representation can contribute favorably to self-esteem (and possibly to other principles of identity), gay Muslims who accept it may more readily assimilate and accommodate their sexuality in their self-concept.

Conversely, some gay Muslims may attribute their sexual orientation to malevolent forces, such as Satan, and deduce from this the notion that homosexuality is imperfect and perhaps even sinful. In previous work (Jaspal and Cinnirella 2010), interviewees have expressed the notion that homosexuality is a Satanic corruption, which they, as followers of God, must attempt to resist. In such cases, homosexuality is anchored to images of evil and sin. When perceived as a "Satanic corruption," the reality of one's homosexuality is likely to threaten self-esteem. This attributional style can therefore preclude the assimilation and accommodation of one's sexuality in the self-concept. People wish to distance from their self-concept those identity elements that challenge the integrity of identity. As a means of coping with the possible threat to identity, some gay Muslims hope to "take the right path soon"; that is, they may resist what they construe to be Satanic temptations and wish to "become heterosexual." The principal aim is to align their sexual orientation with the perceived norms, values, and expectations associated with their religion, which can increase the acceptability of so-called conversion therapies. Yet by anchoring homosexuality to sin, individuals may face a threat to psychological coherence. Indeed, some may come to question the feasibility of reconciling self-identification as Muslim and engagement in homosexual behavior.

In making sense of their sexual orientation, some individuals consider the extent to which they wish to disclose it to other people. In Western societies, there is a coercive norm of "coming out" as gay. When celebrities come out as gay, this is often represented as a positive personal and societal step forward. Much social sciences research highlights the social and psychological benefits of "coming out" (Allen 2022; Lasala 2000; Pistella et al. 2016; Rosario et al. 2001). In short, being open about one's sexual identity is widely regarded in the West as a desirable end state. However, this is not necessarily the case for gay men in Muslim societies, where "coming out" can bring about a series of social, legal, and, indeed, psychological challenges. Gay Muslims may be fearful of "bringing shame on the family" by disclosing their sexual identity and of the negative social consequences that this disclosure could entail (Maatouk and Jaspal 2022). Given that homosexuality is widely perceived to be incompatible with Islamic norms and values, some individuals have expressed the fear that their coming out could be construed as an act of apostasy—that is, the de facto renunciation of their religion.

These factors may collectively render the prospect of coming out challenging or even impossible (Jaspal and Siraj 2011). The more feasible alternative may be for some gay Muslims to develop ways of constructing and manifesting their sexuality that do not threaten their physical and psychological well-being (see Jaspal 2014b). Yet the psychological perception of identity incompatibility may persist.

Threats to Psychological Coherence

The psychological coherence principle of identity motivates the individual to seek a sense of compatibility in relation to identity elements that, for whatever reason, become interconnected. As indicated earlier in this chapter, gay Muslims may regard their sexual orientation through the lens of their religion and may therefore make religious attributions in seeking to make sense of it. It is clear that some struggle to derive a sense of coherence between these identity elements (Jaspal and Cinnirella 2010). In attempting to establish coherence between their religion and their sexual orientation, some gay Muslims may come to question the authenticity of their Muslimness.

Although some individuals are unaware of specific passages in holy scripture concerning the Islamic stance on homosexuality, they may continue to believe that same-sex behavior is incompatible with their religion. Individuals may not necessarily possess firsthand knowledge of holy scripture, but they draw upon negative social representations of homosexuality that are grounded in Islamic theology. Some gay Muslims describe the Prophet Mohammed's alleged disgust toward homosexuality in the hadith as well as God's intolerance of homosexuality, which resonates with the story of Lot in the Qur'an. Gay Muslims generally value their religion, which may lead them to accept uncritically the messages that they perceive to be associated with this element of identity. Internalized homophobia is associated with threats to identity (Jaspal, Lopes, and Breakwell 2022).

Interviewees in previous studies (e.g., Jaspal 2012) have described the threat to coherence metaphorically by making statements such as "my worlds were clashing" and "I was fighting with myself." These statements suggest a degree of internal conflict. However, as gay Muslims struggle to reconcile their sexual orientation and their faith, they may attenuate the significance of or deny altogether the identity aspect, which they consider to be of lesser importance. In many cases, their sexual orientation is relegated to an inferior position within the identity structure. Accordingly, individuals may view themselves as heterosexual while acknowledging occasional engagement in homosexual behavior. The perception of homosexuality as a behavior rather than as a characteristic of identity essentially obviates the need to acknowledge the threat to psychological coherence. After all, it is easier to compartmentalize (that is, to separate out in one's mind) behaviors and identities. Moreover, behaviors can seem more mutable than identities. Indeed, participants in previous research have anchored homosexual behavior to harmful behaviors such as smoking and the consumption of alcohol and, thus, view it as a behavior that they can change.

In explicating their engagement in homosexual "behaviors," some gay Muslims may identify a source external to the self to which their sexual orientation can be attributed (see Kelley 1967 for a description of external attribution). Indeed, as noted earlier, some gay Muslims may attribute their sexual orientation to either God or Satan. In addition, previous studies have described a tendency for some Muslim gay men who live in the United Kingdom to attribute their sexual orientation to "Western culture" (Jaspal and Cinnirella 2010). This attributional style enabled them to distance their sexual orientation from the self and to argue that, owing to Western cultural influences (specifically the "normalization" of homosexuality in the West), they had "fallen" into homosexual practices. There was a perception among some interviewees that if they had grown up in Islamic societies, they would not have "become" gay. Similarly, some of the Iranian Muslim gay men who participated in interview studies attributed their homosexual behavior to their migration to Britain, where it was reportedly easier to meet other men for sex (Jaspal 2014b). This attributional style enables individuals to objectify their sexual orientation as a "sinful behavior" and to distance the behavior from the self, which can provide a short-term strategy for coping with threat. Previous research (e.g., Jaspal and Cinnirella 2010) has found that some Muslim gay men construct their homosexuality as a behavior rather than as a component of identity, possibly as a means of minimizing threats to psychological coherence.

However, those gay Muslims who, for whatever reason, cannot deny their sexual orientation and who acknowledge the difficulties in "resisting" it, may come to question the authenticity of their Muslimness. In view of the belief held by some that Islam and homosexuality are fundamentally incompatible, they may question whether they actually are "good" or "true" Muslims. Given the social, cultural, and, indeed, psychological importance of their religion, this questioning can compromise the continuity principle of identity. It is important to note that Islam constitutes an important element of identity for many gay Muslims, one that they wish to maintain. Doubts surrounding the authenticity of their Muslimness can essentially represent a rupture among past, present, and future. Loss of one's religion may amount to a perceived loss of community. Some express the hope that they will eventually be forgiven for what they perceive to be sinful and immoral behavior, while others express their desire to "become straight."

Gay Muslims employ various strategies for aligning their sexual orientation and religion to enhance psychological coherence. These strategies include self-distancing from the gay community, contemplating an arranged heterosexual marriage, and seeking religious guidance to "become" heterosexual. Yet the recognition that it is impossible to change their sexual orientation in real terms may lead some to perceive decreased self-efficacy; they feel helpless and resign themselves to the psychologically undesirable reality of their homosexual orientation. This reality becomes an "undesired self" (Carroll, Shepperd, and Arkin 2009). In short, the strategies deployed to enhance psychological coherence can be ineffective in the long term and result in threats to other identity principles.

Maintaining a Sense of Belonging

In view of the coercive social representation of homosexuality as a sin, some gay Muslims may fear exclusion from their religious ingroup. For many Muslims, their religion constitutes an important source of social connectedness. It can constitute a "meaning system" as its norms and tenets guide most aspects of social life, and it consequently becomes a "lens" for viewing the surrounding social world. In many Islamic societies in the Middle East, Islam underpins both societal norms and the legislative system. Religion is often entwined with other elements of identity (e.g., ethnicity, nationality). Because religion is so important, gay Muslims may fear ostracism from this group membership. The prospect of ostracism may undermine feelings of belonging.

In an era of elevated Islamophobia in the West, many Muslims in Western societies report feeling isolated and excluded (Carr 2016). Furthermore, recent research suggests that ethnic- and religious-minority groups more generally face racism and other forms of exclusion on the gay scene, which can inhibit access to social support in this context (Jaspal 2017). In the face of exclusion, ethnic- and religious-minority individuals may become more immersed in their ethnoreligious ingroup as this group membership comes to constitute a strong and reliable source of belonging, which can make some gay Muslims even more reliant on their religious ingroup. In previous research, one interviewee described his fear of being "kicked out of the community" and of "being alone in the world," while another noted that he was "not networked or well connected" outside of his religious and family networks (Jaspal 2012, 775). This illustrates not only the desire for belonging but also one's fear of losing it.

Gay Muslims employ strategies for attempting to maintain a sense of connection with their religious group in the face of threats to belonging. Psychologists have described the strategy of "compartmentalization," which refers to the psychological process of keeping elements of identity separate in the mind to reduce dissonance (Breakwell 1986). However, compartmentalization may not be sustainable as a long-term strategy in this group. Some individuals do report initially compartmentalizing their sexual orientation and religion to reduce the "interconnectedness" of these identity elements that they perceive to be incompatible. However, in some contexts, compartmentalization ceases to be an option.

In a research interview for a previous study, a gay Muslim described his experience of sitting in a mosque during Friday prayers and suddenly becoming aware of his sexual orientation and the implications that this had for his religious affiliation (Jaspal 2012, 775). Compartmentalization ceased to constitute a viable strategy. The interviewee described the onset of his feelings of insecurity and inauthenticity in relation to his religion. Furthermore, some social and interpersonal issues can further undermine the efficacy of compartmentalization. Given the religious expectation for a heterosexual (often arranged) marriage in Muslim societies, some Muslim gay men may be pressured into considering marital offers (Jaspal 2014a). This situation can severely undermine the compartmentalization strategy as social cues of this nature essentially force the individual to take a stance on the source of their dissonance.

Some engage in the strategy of hyperaffiliation to the religious ingroup. Hyperaffiliation can be defined as "accentuated social and psychological identification with a social group in response to threatened group membership" (Jaspal and Cinnirella 2014, 266). For example, religious events may provide prime opportunities for "proving" the authenticity of one's Muslimness. A possible strategy is the diligent observance of fasting due to the belief that it compensates for one's homosexuality. Another possible strategy is sexual abstinence during Ramadan. Hyperaffiliation can transiently make individuals feel more connected to their religious community.

Furthermore, there are socially oriented methods of safeguarding religious authenticity and belonging. In seeking to demonstrate the authenticity of one's Muslimness in public settings, individuals may forcefully express views that they perceive to be central to their religion. One example is the manifestation of (sometimes self-directed) homophobia. When self-directed, it amounts to internalized homophobia. The expression of homophobia may also constitute a means of "convincing" other people within one's social ingroup that one's personal views align with those of the ingroup and that one's group affiliation is authentic, which can enhance a sense of belonging.

The chapter has so far focused on the implications of the sexuality–religion interface for identity processes and, in particular, illustrates possible threats to psychological coherence and belonging. In the remainder of this chapter, the implications of threatened identity for sexual well-being are considered.

Sexual Well-Being

Sexual identity issues can have important direct and indirect effects on sexual well-being. Sexual well-being has social, psychological, emotional, and physical dimensions. It concerns not only the physical absence of sexually transmitted infections (STIs) but also the cognitive, emotional, and social construal of one's sexuality (see chapter 6 by Inas Abdelwahed in this volume). The potential physical implications of a negative cognitive, emotional, and social construal of one's sexuality are significant. According to the Health Adversity Risk Model (Jaspal and Bayley 2020; Jaspal, Lopes, Wignall, et al. 2021), threats to identity may indirectly lead to engagement in sexual risk-taking behaviors, while the desire to protect identity may be associated with disengagement from sexual health services. Ethnic- and religious-minority gay men in the United Kingdom are more likely to be concerned about the possible negative consequences of disclosing their sexual identity to significant others, such as rejection, which can lead them to prioritize concealment of their identity over and above their (physical) sexual health (Jaspal 2018; Jaspal and Siraj 2011; Jaspal and Williamson 2017). This can mean that individuals prefer to meet sexual partners on mobile social networking applications, such as Grindr, where they can remain anonymous. Similarly, research has shown that some ethnoreligious-minority gay men express a preference for using gay saunas for the same purpose—there is less risk of nonvoluntary disclosure of their sexual orientation to others (Jaspal and Papaloukas 2021). Some Muslim gay men may avoid gay bars and nightclubs because of the perceived incompatibility between Islam and the norm of alcohol consumption in these venues. Although interviewees generally perceived their homosexual behavior as problematic from the perspective of their religious identity, they sought to limit their engagement in "sinful" behavior by at least adhering to the Islamic norm of not consuming alcohol. Yet there are also reports of substance use among some individuals; they associate their drug use with the desire to "disconnect" from the reality of their sexual orientation. Drug use (often in sexualized settings) may operate as a form of psychological escapism as it can enable individuals to disconnect from the threatening reality of rejection and disownment (see Jaspal 2022a for greater insight into drug use in sexualized settings, often referred to as "chemsex").

Prejudice faced by some Muslim gay men can have negative outcomes for their sexual well-being. It is clear that the experience of racism is associated with decreased self-esteem and that decreased self-esteem may in turn give rise to engagement in sexual risk-taking behaviors (Ayala et al. 2012). In one study of racism on the gay scene, interviewees described experiences of rejection from non-Muslim gay men as well as overt stigma due to Islamophobia, which undermined feelings of belonging and thus inhibited the formation of interpersonal relationships in these contexts (Jaspal 2017). Some individuals also described the low self-confidence and vulnerability that this rejection could induce. More specifically, some Muslim gay men feel unable to negotiate condom use with their sexual partners, fearing that this could lead to further rejection, and they may thereby take sexual risks that could expose them to HIV and other STIs.

Along these same lines, the experience of homophobia both from within their ethnoreligious group and from society in general is also associated with decreased self-esteem, which may also be translated into sexual risk-taking (Thomas et al. 2014). Fear of involuntary disclosure of their sexual identity, which could in turn induce threats to belonging, self-esteem, and continuity, may lead some gay Muslims to focus simply on enacting their sexual identity covertly so that their significant others do not find out about it. In the process, they may become more focused on protecting their identity than their sexual health. For some, the aim is simply to have sex covertly, and, thus, condoms and other precautionary measures are frequently overlooked in the process. More generally, long-term exposure to multiple forms of discrimination—homophobic, Islamophobic, and racial—may take its toll on self-esteem, leading some gay Muslims to develop internalized homophobia.

Internalized homophobia—that is, the individual's acceptance of stigma in relation to their sexual orientation (Herek, Gillis, and Cogan 2009) and the low self-esteem that tends to accompany this internalization—may constitute a barrier to sexual health screening, which in turn can have an adverse impact on overall sexual health. Internalized homophobia inhibits the assimilation and accommodation of one's sexual orientation in identity, and, consequently, some may continue to view themselves as exclusively heterosexual. They may therefore have limited exposure to sexual health messaging directed specifically at gay and bisexual men and thus fail to recognize their own risk of poor sexual health.

It has been observed that individuals tend to "other" risk; that is, they attribute it to people "unlike themselves" (Joffe 2007). Some Muslim gay men may therefore see sexual health screening as relevant only to "others," not to themselves. Furthermore, given the association of sexual health screening with homosexuality, engagement with sexual health services may represent a threat to the continuity of their self-identity, which may precipitate a rupture in the self-narrative they have constructed over time. It may compel the individual to acknowledge an aspect of their identity and behavior that they in fact wish to deny. Moreover, some interviewees have expressed fear of being seen (especially by other ethnoreligious in-group members) in a sexual health clinic (see also McKeown et al. 2012). Being seen could represent a threat not only to individual continuity given the acknowledgment of sexual identity but also to the continuity of their "public" image as heterosexual.

Conclusions

In this chapter, it has been shown that there is a strong and coercive *negative social representation of homosexuality* in Muslim societies. This negative representation is grounded in Islamic theology and draws upon Qur'anic scripture and the hadith. Many Muslims—both heterosexual and nonheterosexual—are aware of and uncritically accept this negative representation. They may cite this representation to substantiate the argument that homosexuality is not permitted in Islamic societies. Crucially, some gay Muslims may accept negative social representations of homosexuality because of their own internalized homophobia.

Muslim gay men may experience threats to identity as they struggle to reconcile their internalized homophobia with the reality that they cannot change their sexual orientation. More specifically, they may experience threats to (1) self-esteem due to the stigma of homosexuality; (2) continuity as they begin to contrast their past (heterosexual) identity with their emerging or current (gay) identity; and (3) psychological coherence as they struggle to reconcile their sexual orientation and their religion, which are represented and perceived to be contradictory. In addition, they may struggle to derive feelings of belonging given that there remains the risk of ostracism from relevant ingroups because of their sexual orientation. Threats to these and other principles of identity can undermine social and psychological well-being. In response to threat, Muslim gay men use a variety of coping strategies with varying levels of long-term effectiveness. Moreover, some of these strategies can lead to secondary threats to identity.

In addition to considering the sexual identity issues associated with Muslim gay men, this chapter outlines some of the possible challenges to sexual well-being in this group. There is evidence that some Islamic countries face a growing HIV burden, which has been largely ignored by health authorities (Mumtaz, Chemaitelly, and Abu-Raddad 2021). Sexual identity issues appear to be related to this elevated risk of HIV and other STIs. Sexual well-being is complex—a threat to identity may eventually result in adverse health outcomes and vice versa.

The observations made in this chapter reiterate the importance of challenging homophobia at a global level. Homophobia can have profoundly negative implications for identity, leading to ineffective coping strategies and engagement in sexually risky behaviors. Although the topic of homosexuality is controversial in Muslim societies, efforts must be made to promote understanding of sexual-minority identities and to reduce prejudice against them. There is also a need to provide social and psychological support to Muslim gay men so that they can be encouraged to engage in more efficacious coping strategies with long-term benefits. Health-care practitioners should be trained to work with gay Muslim clients in identity-affirmative ways (Jaspal 2018). Programs and interventions should focus on promoting greater sexual health awareness and understanding among Muslim gay men so that they can be empowered to engage in positive sexual health behaviors and reduce their risk of exposure to HIV and other STIs. Indeed, research in the United Kingdom shows low levels of HIV knowledge in ethnic and religious minorities, including Muslim gay men (Jaspal, Lopes, Jamal, et al. 2019).

It is important to note that physical well-being is inextricably entwined with social and psychological well-being. Identity and the social backdrop against which it is constructed play a fundamental role in how people make sense of their experiences. Thus, it is essential to challenge social representations that potentially threaten the identities of Muslim gay men. This challenge may in turn facilitate a more accepting and affirmative context in which Muslim gay men can construct their identities and take steps to enhance their sexual well-being.

References

Abdelwahed, Inas. 2024. "An Overview of Sexual and Reproductive Health: Social Determinants and Challenges." In *Sexuality in the Middle East and North Africa: Contemporary Issues and Challenges*, edited by J. Michael Ryan and Helen Rizzo, 197–235. Syracuse, NY: Syracuse Univ. Press.

Allen, Junior Lloyd. 2022. "'And Then I Came Out . . . ': A Thematic Analysis of Gay Men's Recalled Memories of Coming Out and Its Impact on Their Mental Health and Well-Being." *Journal of Gay & Lesbian Social Services* 35, no. 4: 488–510. At https://doi.org/10.1080/10538720.2022.2140242.

Ayala, George, Trista Bingham, Junyeop Kim, Darrell P. Wheeler, and Gregorio A. Millett. 2012. "Modeling the Impact of Social Discrimination and Financial Hardship on the Sexual Risk of HIV among Latino and Black Men Who Have Sex with Men." *American Journal of Public Health* 102, no. 2: 242–49.

Bhugra, Dinesh. 1997. "Coming Out by South Asian Gay Men in the United Kingdom." *Archives of Sexual Behavior* 26, no. 5: 547–57.

Bouhdiba, Abdelwahab. 1998. *Sexuality in Islam*. London: Saqi.

Breakwell, Glynis Marie. 1986. *Coping with Threatened Identities*. London: Methuen.

———. 2014. "Identity and Social Representations." In *Identity Process Theory: Identity, Social Action and Social Change*, edited by Rusi Jaspal and Glynis Marie Breakwell, 118–34. Cambridge: Cambridge Univ. Press.

Carlson, Dennis. 1997. "Gayness, Multicultural Education and Community." In *Beyond Black and White: New Faces and Voices in U.S. Schools*, edited by Maxine Seller and Lois Weis, 233–56. Albany: State Univ. of New York Press.

Carr, James. 2016. *Experiences of Islamophobia: Living with Racism in the Neoliberal Era*. London: Routledge.

Carroll, Patrick J., James A. Shepperd, and Robert M. Arkin. 2009. "Downward Self-Revision: Erasing Possible Selves." *Social Cognition* 27, no. 4: 550–78.

Coyle, Adrian, and Deborah Rafalin. 2000. "Jewish Gay Men's Accounts of Negotiating Cultural, Religious and Sexual Identity: A Qualitative Study." *Journal of Psychology and Human Sexuality* 12: 21–48.

Duran, Khalid. 1993. "Homosexuality in Islam." In *Homosexuality and World Religions*, edited by Arlene Swidler, 181–98. Harrisburg, PA: Trinity Press.

Harris, Helen, Gaynor Yancey, Veronica L. Timbers, and Carolyn Cole. 2020. "LGBTQI+ and Christian? Who Decides?" *Journal of Religion & Spirituality in Social Work: Social Thought* 39, no. 4: 452–73.

Herek, Gregory M., J. Roy Gillis, and Jeanine C. Cogan. 2009. "Internalized Stigma among Sexual Minority Adults: Insights from a Social Psychological Perspective." *Journal of Counseling Psychology* 56: 32–43.

Jamal, Amreen. 2001. "The Story of Lot and the Qur'an's Perception of the Morality of Same-Sex Sexuality." *Journal of Homosexuality* 41, no. 1: 1–88.

Jaspal, Rusi. 2012. "'I Never Faced Up to Being Gay': Sexual, Religious and Ethnic Identities among British South Asian Gay Men." *Culture, Health and Sexuality: An International Journal for Research, Intervention and Care* 14, no. 7: 767–80.

———. 2014a. "Arranged Marriage, Identity and Psychological Wellbeing among British Asian Gay Men." *Journal of GLBT Family Studies* 10, no. 5: 425–48.

———. 2014b. "Sexuality, Migration and Identity among Gay Iranian Migrants to the UK." In *Queering Religion, Religious Queers*, edited by Yvonne Taylor and Ria Snowdon, 44–60. London: Routledge.

———. 2017. "Coping with Perceived Ethnic Prejudice on the Gay Scene." *Journal of LGBT Youth* 13, no. 2: 172–90.

———. 2018. *Enhancing Sexual Health, Self-Identity and Wellbeing among Men Who Have Sex with Men: A Guide for Practitioners*. London: Jessica Kingsley.

———. 2022a. "Chemsex, Identity and Sexual Health among Gay and Bisexual Men." *International Journal of Environmental Research and Public Health* 19, no. 19: art. 12124. At https://doi.org/10.3390/ijerph191912124.

———. 2022b. "Social Psychological Aspects of Gay Identity Development." *Current Opinion in Psychology* 48: art. 101469. At https://doi.org/10.1016/j.copsyc.2022.101469.

Jaspal, Rusi, and Jake Bayley. 2020. *HIV and Gay Men: Clinical, Social and Psychological Aspects*. London: Palgrave.

Jaspal, Rusi, and Glynis M. Breakwell. 2014. *Identity Process Theory: Identity, Social Action and Social Change*. Cambridge: Cambridge Univ. Press.

Jaspal, Rusi, and Marco Cinnirella. 2010. "Coping with Potentially Incompatible Identities: Accounts of Religious, Ethnic and Sexual Identities from British Pakistani Men who Identify as Muslim and Gay." *British Journal of Social Psychology* 49, no. 4: 849–70.

———. 2012. "Identity Processes, Threat and Interpersonal Relations: Accounts from British Muslim Gay Men." *Journal of Homosexuality* 59, no. 2: 215–40.

———. 2014. "Hyper-affiliation to the Religious Ingroup among British Pakistani Muslim Gay Men." *Journal of Community and Applied Social Psychology* 24, no. 4: 265–77.

Jaspal, Rusi, Barbara Lopes, and Glynis M. Breakwell. 2022. "Minority Stressors, Protective Factors and Mental Health Outcomes in Lesbian, Gay and Bisexual People in the UK." *Current Psychology* 42: 24918–34. At https://doi.org/10.1007/s12144-022-03631-9.

Jaspal, Rusi, Barbara Lopes, Zahra Jamal, Carmen Yap, Ivana Paccoud, and Parminder Sekhon. 2019. "HIV Knowledge, Sexual Health and Behaviour among Black and Minority Ethnic Men Who Have Sex with Men in the UK: A Cross-Sectional Study." *Sexual Health* 16, no. 1: 25–31. At https://doi.org/10.1071/SH18032.

Jaspal, Rusi, Barbara Lopes, Liam Wignall, and Claire Bloxsom. 2021. "Predicting Sexual Risk Behaviour in British and European Union University Students in the United Kingdom." *American Journal of Sexuality Education* 16, no. 1: 140–59. At https://doi.org/10.1080/15546128.2020.1869129.

Jaspal, Rusi, and Periklis Papaloukas. 2021. "Identity, Connectedness and Sexual Health in the Gay Sauna." *Sexuality Research & Social Policy* 18, no. 1: 54–63.

Jaspal, Rusi, and Asifa Siraj. 2011. "Perceptions of 'Coming Out' among British Muslim Gay Men." *Psychology and Sexuality* 2, no. 3: 183–97.

Jaspal, Rusi, and Iain Williamson. 2017. "Identity Management Strategies among HIV-Positive Colombian Gay Men in London." *Culture, Health and Sexuality: An International Journal for Research, Intervention and Care* 19, no. 2: 1374–88. At https://dx.doi.org/10.1080/13691058.2017.1314012.

Joffe, Helene. 2007. "Identity, Self-Control, and Risk." In *Social Representations and Identity: Content, Process, and Power*, edited by Gail Moloney and Ian Walker, 197–213. London: Palgrave Macmillan.

Karimi, Aryan, and Zohreh Bayatrizi. 2019. "Dangerous Positions: Male Homosexuality in the New Penal Code of Iran." *Punishment & Society* 21, no. 4: 417–34.

Kelley, Harold H. 1967. "Attribution Theory in Social Psychology." In *Nebraska Symposium on Motivation*, vol. 15, edited by David Levine, 192–238. Lincoln: Univ. of Nebraska Press.

Kort, Joe. 2012. "Homosexuality and Pedophilia: The False Link." *Huffington Post*, May 10. At https://www.huffingtonpost.com/joe-kort-phd/homosexuality-and-pedophi_b_1932622.html.

Kugle, Scott Siraj al-Haqq. 2010. *Homosexuality in Islam: Critical Reflection on Gay, Lesbian, and Transgender Muslims.* Oxford: Oneworld.

Lasala, Michael C. 2000. "Gay Male Couples: The Importance of Coming Out and Being Out to Parents." *Journal of Homosexuality* 39, no. 2: 47–71.

Lin, Yen-jui, and Tania Israel. 2012. "Development and Validation of a Psychological Sense of LGBT Community Scale." *Journal of Community Psychology* 40, no. 5: 573–87.

Maatouk, Ismael, and Rusi Jaspal. 2022. "Internalized Sexual Orientation Stigma and Mental Health in a Religiously Diverse Sample of Gay and Bisexual Men in Lebanon." *Journal of Homosexuality* 70, no. 8: 1441–60. At https://doi.org/10.1080/00918369.2022.2030617.

McKeown, Eamonn, Rita Doerner, Simon Nelson, Nicola Low, Angela Robinson, Jane Anderson, and Jonathan Elford. 2012. "The Experiences of Ethnic Minority MSM Using NHS Sexual Health Clinics in Britain." *Sexually Transmitted Infections* 88, no. 8: 595–600.

Moscovici, Serge. 1988. "Notes towards a Description of Social Representations." *European Journal of Social Psychology* 18: 211–50.

Mumtaz, Ghina, Hiam Chemaitelly, and Laith J. Abu-Raddad. 2021. "The HIV Epidemic in the Middle East and North Africa: Key Lessons." In *Handbook of Healthcare in the Arab World*, edited by Ismail Laher, 3053–79. Geneva: Springer.

Pickthall, Marmaduke. 1930. *The Meaning of the Glorious Koran: An Explanatory Translation.* New York: Knopf.

Pistella, Jessica, Marco Salvati, Salvatore Ioverno, Fiorenzo Laghi, and Robert Baiocco. 2016. "Coming-Out to Family Members and Internalized Sexual Stigma in Bisexual, Lesbian and Gay People." *Journal of Child and Family Studies* 25, no. 12: 3694–701.

Rosario, Margaret, Joyce Hunter, Shira Maguen, Marya Gwadz, and Raymond Smith. 2001. "The Coming-Out Process and Its Adaptational and Health-Related Associations among Gay, Lesbian, and Bisexual Youths: Stipulation and Exploration of a Model." *American Journal of Community Psychology* 29, no. 1: 133–60.

Schmidtke, Sabine. 1999. "Homoeroticism and Homosexuality in Islam: A Review Article." *Bulletin of the School of Oriental and African Studies* 62, no. 2: 260–66.

Stychin, Carl. 1995. *Law's Desire: Sexuality and the Limits of Justice.* London: Routledge.

Thomas, François, Marie Cozette Mience, Joanic Masson, and Amal Bernoussi. 2014. "Unprotected Sex and Internalized Homophobia." *Journal of Men's Studies* 22, no. 2: 155–62.

Wafer, Jim. 1997. "Mohammad and Male Homosexuality." In *Islamic Homosexualities: Culture, History and Literature*, edited by Stephen O. Murray and Will Roscoe, 87–96. New York: New York Univ. Press.

Yip, Andrew Kam-Tuck. 2004. "Embracing Allah and Sexuality? South Asian Non-heterosexual Muslims in Britain." In *South Asians in the Diaspora: Histories and Religious Traditions*, edited by Knut A. Jacobsen and P. Pratap Kumar, 294–310. Leiden, Netherlands: Brill.

———. 2005. "Queering Religious Texts: An Exploration of British, Non-heterosexual Christians' and Muslims' Strategy of Constructing Sexuality-Affirming Hermeneutics." *Sociology* 39: 47–65.

5

The (Im)Possibilities of Being Trans in the MENA Region

Ana Cristina Marques, Salma Talaat, and J. Michael Ryan

Trans individuals as well as women, gay, lesbian, bisexual, and intersex individuals living in the Middle East and North Africa (MENA) tend to be seen "under western eyes" (Mohanty 1988, 49) as victims of backward, retrograde cultures, oppressive and homophobic Islamic beliefs, and weak states (Hélie 2012).[1] Contrary to the main trend in the "global North" and other parts of the world, such as Nepal and Argentina—where laws are being changed to recognize gender identity as a human right and to protect trans people from discrimination, harassment, and other forms of violence and where ongoing processes of depathologization of trans people and identities are occurring (Ryan 2018)—several MENA region countries, such as Tunisia, Algeria, Iraq, and Saudi Arabia, forbid gender-confirmation surgery and/or legal gender recognition or do not have specific legislation to address trans people's issues and needs, as in the

1. In this chapter, we are using the term *trans* as a socially and culturally constructed "umbrella" category that refers to people who self-identify as a gender that is different from the socially expected gender correlated with the sex they were assigned at birth (Ryan 2018; Stryker [2008] 2017). However, trans people are not necessarily thought of as transgressing gender normativities. Although some trans people wish to disrupt gender binaries, other trans people wish to be recognized as men or women (Ryan 2019; Stryker [2008] 2017).

case of Yemen (Equaldex n.d.).[2] When MENA countries, such as Turkey and Iran, do account for legal gender recognition, highly medicalized and pathologizing procedures tend to be demanded. In several MENA region countries where gender-confirmation surgery is "allowed" and often "forcibly" prescribed for intersex people—as in Lebanon, Egypt, and the United Arab Emirates (UAE)—legal gender recognition is made difficult for many trans people due to a lack of clear legislation. Furthermore, in countries that do not de facto criminalize trans people—such as Tunisia, Egypt, and Iraq—there is nevertheless lack of protective legislation against hate crimes and discrimination that could afford some level of protection to trans people. This lack is compounded by other legislation, often associated with Sharia law (even when the states are secular), that forbids attacks on the public order and/or any sexual activity that falls outside the heteronormative married couple, including sex work and same-sex practices, and this legislation is often used to persecute and arrest trans people. In a context where sexual orientation is often conflated with gender identity, trans people are particularly subject to homophobia and transphobia (Fortier 2019). Trans people are thus often subject to discrimination, harassment, and violence, while often having difficulty in accessing the support of state institutions, such as the police or medical care, and/or the support of their families. These social institutions can instead be the perpetrators of violence and discrimination.

However, it is important to consider that far from having homogeneous gender orders, the MENA region encompasses different realities, and Islam can be subject to diverse interpretations—ranging from the more "conservative" to the more "progressive" (Zaharin and Pallotta-Chiarolli 2020). Further, even within one country the lives of trans people may vary significantly according to the other social positions they occupy (e.g., social class and level of education). Moreover, in the case of several MENA countries and regions that have had (post)colonial experiences

2. Equaldex is an online project that traces the situation of LGB/T rights around the world based on several indicators, such as "homosexual activity," "censorship of LGBT issues," "right to change legal gender," and "legal recognition of nonbinary gender." It is available at https://www.equaldex.com, accessed June 15, 2023.

and/or are subject to foreign funding and/or participation in (post)conflict nation building, national and regional gender politics that frame trans people's experiences need to be understood in their interactions with international and local gender norms (Nay 2019). In addition, despite the several obstacles that trans people and trans-inclusive organizations face within the region, it is important to recognize their agency in trying, with more or less room for action, to create safe spaces of being. In the past years, several LGB and/or T associations and individuals within the MENA region have been increasingly able to combat homophobia and transphobia in creative and dynamic ways and to tell their stories in the context of an increasingly transnational world (Ghoshal 2018).[3]

In this chapter, we begin by giving an overview of the legal, social, and cultural context of being trans in countries with a Muslim-majority population in the MENA region. We then complicate the victimization of trans people in the MENA region as part of the "West/East" opposition (Hélie 2012). We conclude by underscoring the importance of going beyond regional dichotomies that associate the "West" with freedom and the "East" with oppression; having a better understanding of the influence (or lack thereof) of local, national, and inter/transnational (post)colonial agendas on trans people's rights and their actual experiences; and producing possible pluralities, spaces of resistances, and subterranean discourses (Plummer 2010) of trans people and issues in this region.

3. The abbreviation "LGB and/or T" is used to differentiate between one's self-identification with a sexual orientation and one's self-identification with a gender identity because trans people might self-identify with a diversity of sexual orientations (Ryan 2020a). Following Diane Richardson (2007), we recognize that the interrelations of gender and sexuality need to be empirically examined at different levels of the social world. Thus, though we acknowledge the importance of listening to trans people and recognize that many trans people might not distinguish between classifications associated with gender identity and classifications associated with sexual orientation, we consider it important to make this distinction in theoretical-analytical terms, while also simultaneously "confronting" such a distinction with the empirical lived experiences, perceptions, and discourses of trans people themselves. Further, though our main focus within this chapter is trans people, we often refer to LGB and/or T people because of the overwhelming majority of reports agglomerating them together, independently of possible differences between them.

Trans Lives in the MENA Region: Cultural, Religious, and Legal Contexts

Trans people suffer high levels of transphobia, homophobia, discrimination, violence, and abuse in the MENA region and in other Muslim-majority countries. Although this treatment is often attributed to the socially conservative nature of Islam, a brief look into the legal, social, and cultural contexts of the MENA region shows a more ambiguous, complex, and dynamic situation. For instance, historical and anthropological accounts of trans lives have tried to show how intersex people, trans people, "effeminate" men, and/or same-sex practices were accepted in the MENA region and in Muslim-majority countries in Central Asia before the period of European colonialism and the more recent period of "Western" (post)colonialism (Alipour 2017; Fortier 2019; Massad 2007). Examples of gender-diverse people and/or individuals who engage in same-gender sexual practices while living in the MENA region include the *bacha bereesh* (beardless boys) in Iran; the *köçek* in Turkey; the *khawals* in Egypt; and the *khanith* in Oman. Members of these communities tend to be described as effeminate men or as men who adopt feminine-gender expressions (Fortier 2019; Whitaker 2016). The exception is the *mustarjil* from southern Iraq, who are described as women who adopt masculine-gender expressions and social roles, arguably out of "choice" or socioeconomic necessity (Fortier 2019; Whitaker 2016).

Moreover, though the Qur'an affirms the existence of gender differences between men and women, it also recognizes the existence of gender diversity (Altinay 2014; Haneef 2011; Zaharin and Pallotta-Chiarolli 2020). Islamic religious texts, in particular the hadith, reference people with nonnormative gender expressions, such as the *khunta*—"hermaphrodite" people, currently called "intersex" people in "Western" countries—and the *mukhannath*, or "effeminate" men.[4] Though there

4. An in-depth overview of references to gender, gender diversity, and nonnormative sexual orientation in connection with Islam is out of the scope of this article. For more information on this subject and on the experiences of Muslim LGB and/or T within Muslim-majority countries and elsewhere, see, for instance, Davies 2019; Hamzic 2016; Kugle 2014; Rahman 2014; and Zahed 2020.

are different interpretations according to different Islamic schools, the *mukhannath*, who do not have sexual desire toward women, are perceived as being accepted in social spaces where women are present (Altinay 2014; Haneef 2011; Whitaker 2016; Zaharin and Pallotta-Chiarolli 2020). Able to move between the segregated spaces of women and men, the *mukhannath* have historically played social roles as servants, matchmakers, dancers, and musicians (Altinay 2014; Fortier 2019; Haneef 2011; Whitaker 2016; Zaharin and Pallotta-Chiarolli 2020). In contrast, the hadith are said to condemn men and women who dress in clothes associated with the other gender, and the *mukhannath* who show sexual desire are also deemed unacceptable to the social order (Altinay 2014; Haneef 2011). The *khunta*—or intersex people—who are (re)assigned a binary-gender category as men or women, can be perceived as being capable of being integrated into the social and legal systems and are therefore considered nonproblematic. Intersex people who are not (re)assigned as either men or women are considered to be problematic (Haneef 2011).

Whereas medical procedures for intersex people tend to be accepted because intersexuality tends to be considered an innate condition that needs to be "corrected," gender-confirmation surgery and other medical procedures potentially used in medical gender-transition processes for trans people tend to be more controversial. Those who defend the legitimacy of gender-confirmation surgeries, mainly Shi'a jurists, tend to consider trans people to have a pathological condition that needs medical treatment to be cured, and therefore such surgical procedures are not seen as interfering in God's creation. For those who oppose gender-confirmation surgeries for trans people, mainly Sunni jurists, medical procedures used for gender-transition processes are often considered in the category of self-inflicted injuries and/or cosmetic procedures that defy God's "prescriptions" of expected (binary) gender and (hetero)sexual norms (Altinay 2014; Haneef 2011). However, advocates of critical-progressive Muslim thought tend to consider that Islam has a strong commitment to social and gender justice, religious pluralism, and the defense of human rights (Duderija 2013) and therefore opposes what they consider to be "all forms of injustices, marginalization and any form of oppression" (Zaharin and Pallotta-Chiarolli 2020, 236). Hence, feminist, queer, and progressive Muslims try to counter what they consider to be more patriarchal, homophobic, and transphobic elements of Islamic texts, in particular the hadith, for instance by questioning their reliability as sources of knowledge and jurisprudence and by considering that there are multiple, even contradictory, interpretations of Islamic laws (see, e.g., Alipour 2017; Altinay 2014; Davies 2019; Zaharin and Pallotta-Chiarolli 2020).

In the late 1980s, two important trans-related fatwas were issued in the MENA region—the first one by Ayatollah Ruhollah Khomeini in Iran in 1987 and the second one by Sheikh al-Tantawi in Egypt in 1988. Both recognized the possibility of gender-confirmation surgery for intersex and trans people "needing" to be recognized in their "real" gendered self.[5] In allowing trans people to have access to medical procedures, in particular gender-confirmation surgery, these fatwas can arguably be seen as examples of a more "tolerant" approach toward trans people in Islam. In the case of al-Tantawi's fatwa and as mentioned earlier, the acceptance of gender-confirmation surgery for intersex and trans people is based on the idea that they are born with a pathology that needs to be corrected. In this case, not only is gender-confirmation surgery not condemned, but it is also presented as the "best cure" for the affliction because it reestablishes the primacy of gender binaries (Alipour 2017, 2022; Whitaker 2016). Al-Tantawi's fatwa can be seen as an example of how the acceptance of gender-confirmation surgery for trans people by some Islamist jurists is highly medicalized. Yet Mehrdad Alipour has argued that Ayatollah Khomeini's fatwa opens up a "discursive space" in which trans and intersex people are not seen as "individuals . . . who suffer from physical or mental illness" but "should be permitted to undergo [gender-confirmation surgery] if they wish" (2022, 361). Thus, according to Alipour, Ayatollah Khomeini's fatwa dissociates mental illness from gender-confirmation surgery, considering that trans and intersex people should be allowed to choose for themselves whether to undergo gender-confirmation surgery or not, without needing "permission from specialists as a person who suffers from physical or

5. For discussions of the Ayatollah Khomeini's and Sheikh al-Tantawi's fatwas, see, for example, Alipour 2017 and Zaharin and Pallotta-Chiarolli 2020.

mental illness" (373). Significantly, Alipour considers that Ayatollah Khomeini's "fatwa does not perceive transgender and intersex people as physically or mentally ill and therefore in need of treatment" (374).

In countries where gender-confirmation surgery and gender-transition processes are legal for trans people, such as Iran and Turkey, these processes are also highly medicalized and pathologized, and trans people are considered to have an innate health problem that needs to be cured (Whitaker 2016). In these countries, to have access to legal gender recognition and to change one's name and gender marker on legal documents involve a lengthy process that entails judicial permission, medical consent, and gender-confirmation surgery. For instance, in Turkey since 1988 trans people have access to a process of legal gender recognition, whereby they can change their name and gender marker on legal documents. To do so, they need to submit an application to the court, but only under pathologizing and medicalized conditions: having a diagnosis from a team of doctors, not being married and/or getting divorced, and being eighteen years of age or older. Further, although sterilization is no longer a requirement of legal gender recognition in Turkey, many doctors have continued to require sterilization. The process of legal gender recognition is "lengthy and costly" and is subject to individual interpretations, "often, depending on the attitudes and experiences of health professionals and judges" (Ördek 2015, 65). Moreover, trans-specific health-care services—such as gender-confirmation surgeries, hormone therapies, and psychiatric services—tend to be concentrated in bigger cities, consequently excluding many trans people who are from outside of those areas and who cannot afford to travel there without the possibility of starting or completing medical and legal gender-recognition processes.

In other countries, such as the UAE and Egypt, intersex people tend to have access to medical gender procedures, whereas trans people might have access to gender-confirmation surgery as a treatment for gender dysphoria when advised by a medical commission but cannot change their name or gender markers on legal documents. In these countries, the decision to allow (or not allow) trans people to change their name is often made in a court of law, with some judges deciding in favor of trans people and others against, depending mainly on their personal position (Noralla

2022a). Yet in countries such as Egypt, Lebanon, and Kuwait, gender-confirmation surgery is increasingly difficult to obtain because the doctors performing it are considered to cause "disability" to trans people, and their licenses might be "revoked" (Noralla 2022b). Thus, trans people who can afford it end up traveling abroad to undergo gender-confirmation surgeries, but those who cannot afford to travel must access costly, illegal medical treatments, such as hormone therapy, without supervision, which might put their health at risk (Noralla 2022b, 2022c). In several other MENA countries, such as Morocco, Iraq, and Tunisia, trans people are not allowed to change their name and gender markers, and/or there are no provisions regarding legal gender recognition (Chiam et al. 2020; Ghoshal 2018; Human Rights Watch [HRW] and IraQueer 2022).

Throughout the MENA region, even where gender-transition processes are legal, countries tend not to have antidiscrimination laws that explicitly protect LGB and/or T people. In these countries, there might not be explicit (de facto) laws that criminalize trans people, but in practice (de jure) several other provisions inscribed in the penal codes are used to criminalize LGB and/or T people or people perceived as such. Moreover, although some countries of the MENA region do not criminalize nonnormative gender expression, same-sex sexual practices—sometimes referred to as "sodomy" or "sexual acts against nature"—are criminalized in several countries, such as Algeria, Lebanon, Syria, Morocco, Qatar, and Tunisia.

Laws used to criminalize LGB and/or T people or people perceived as such often associate them with practices, ideas, and values seen as a "threat" to Islam, society, and/or "traditional" notions of family. This is the case with laws related to "indecency," "public morals," offending (women's) "modesty," and "immodest" acts. Some countries, such as Jordan, Lebanon, Iran, and the UAE, have laws that criminalize the use of women's clothes by men, the use of clothes designed for the opposite sex, and/or access to women-only spaces by men.[6] In several other countries,

6. In 2022, Kuwait reversed "article 198 of the penal code," which criminalized "imitating the opposite sex," for violating people's "right to personal freedom" (Noralla 2023). Yet, according to Nora Noralla, this reversal does not necessarily mean the existence of

such as Algeria, Jordan, and the UAE, there are laws restricting freedom of association and demonstration that hinder the possibility of the development of LGB and/or T rights activism. The mismatch between legal documents and one's gender expression, owing either to the lack of a legal framework or the prohibition against changing one's name and gender markers, is also frequently used as a reason to arrest and/or harass trans people. Laws related to cybercrimes—for example, in Saudi Arabia—can also be used to criminalize LGB and/or T people. In some countries, such as Egypt, Iraq, and Jordan, security forces have also used social media to target and entrap LGB and/or T people—for instance, by creating fake accounts. Entrapment can lead to imprisonment and discriminatory measures in which LGB and/or T people, trans women in particular, are subject to "denial of food and water, family and legal representation, and medical services as well as [to] verbal, physical, and sexual assault" (HRW 2023, 4).

In Egypt, the General Directorate for Protecting Public Morality (more widely known as the "Morality Police") within the Ministry of Interior is known to extensively use online entrapment methods to track down and arrest LGB and/or T people and activists. Although it is indisputably illegal to carry out such arrests, Law No. 10 of 1961, which criminalizes sex work, has allowed the state to crackdown on LGB and/or T people. "Moral depravity," "habitual debauchery," and "violating the teachings of religion" are the most recurring and ready-set charges used against them. The Morality Police, in collusion with the media, have often delighted in creating major sex scandals, such as the raid of Bab al-Bahr bathhouse in 2014, which was initiated by a TV presenter who callously zeroed in on the people's faces, and the rainbow-flag-waving incident during a concert in 2017, including the vicious police and media campaign that was waged against LGB and/or T people and activists afterward. In the aftermath of

---

a safer space for trans people in the country. For Noralla, although Kuwait is trying to project an image of being more "liberal" than other Persian/Arab Gulf countries, it still does not recognize LGB and/or T rights and instead still subjects LGB and/or T people, in particular trans women, to violence and abuse, while increasingly limiting gender-confirmation surgery to intersex people.

the latter incident, the media incited an aggressive anti-LGBT crackdown and extensive arrests carried out by the Morality Police. Those who were arrested for raising a rainbow flag at the concert were subjected to torture and sexual harassment in detention. Several government-backed online news outlets have also consistently reported on raids on private apartments and arrests of trans individuals.

Governments in countries such as the UAE, Iran, and Saudi Arabia have also been restricting online navigation by blocking local and international websites that could be a source of information or an important space for community building, thus further limiting safe spaces for LGB and/or T people (OutRight Action International 2021). What is more, there are cases of individuals monitoring and blackmailing LGB and/or T people on social media by threating to expose them to the authorities if not paid (HRW 2023).

Violence, Discrimination, and Abuses: Trans People's Everyday Lived Experiences in the MENA Region

By criminalizing and/or not addressing the protection of LGB and/or T people, the legal frameworks of the MENA region countries allow for the existence of widespread violence committed by security forces against them as well as against those people who might be perceived as such. Thus, LGB and/or T people in the MENA region are often subject to harassment, arbitrary arrest and detention, interrogation, extortion and blackmail, torture, and other ill treatments, including sexual violence and rape. In Kuwait and the UAE, foreign people and migrants perceived as being trans have also been expelled from the country. In Egypt, Lebanon, Syria, and Tunisia, people perceived as LGB and/or T, when arrested, might be subject to "forced" anal examinations that are used as "proof" of homosexuality. In militarized countries such as Iraq (HRW and IraQueer 2022; MADRE and the International Women's Human Rights Clinic 2015), Kuwait (HRW 2012), Syria (Maydaa, Chayya, and Myrttinen 2020), and Lebanon (HRW 2019), there are reports of trans people suffering from violence, harassment, and sexual abuse committed by security forces at the checkpoints that exist throughout these countries' territories.

Trans women and "effeminate" men are often the most likely to be subjected to violence, abuse, and discrimination (Chiam et al. 2020; Girijashanker 2018; HRW 2019; Maydaa, Chayya, and Myrttinen 2020; Nasser-Eddin, Abu-Assab, and Greatrick 2018; USAID 2022). As a consequence, in countries such as Iraq and Lebanon, even cismen have been arrested "just" for looking feminine (Ghoshal 2018; HRW and IraQueer 2022; OutRight International and IraQueer 2022).[7] The more LGB and/or T people are visible or do not adhere to "accepted" gender expressions, the more likely they are to be subject to discrimination, violence, and abuse (Maydaa, Chayya, and Myrttinen 2020; USAID 2022), which "forces" many LGB and/or T people in the MENA region, as elsewhere, to keep their nonnormative sexual and gender expressions hidden and thus invisible (Marques 2020; chapter 1 in this volume). Further, the systematic violence against LGB and/or T people tends not to be treated as a hate crime and is rarely properly investigated by the police or related institutions, such as the courts. For example, in Turkey perpetrators of (extreme) violence against trans people might not be sentenced for a crime or might have their sentence attenuated due to what are considered "mitigating circumstances"—that is, actions "justified" by a need to restore the family's honor or actions owing to "unjust provocation" created by a gender panic (Westbrook and Schilt 2014) felt by the perpetrator when they "discover" that the other person is trans. The violence committed by security forces and the fear of being accused of sodomy, indecency, sex work, or other related laws used to criminalize LGB and/or T people lead many within these communities not to trust the security forces and not to report the violence committed against them.

The lack of legal protections for gender and sexual minorities, often associated with the (perceived) conservative, patriarchal, homophobic, and transphobic contexts of societies in the MENA region (e.g., Hélie 2012; HRW 2023; Muedini 2018), means that LGB and/or T people are

7. In this chapter, "cismen" are understood as men who self-identify with the gender that correlates with the socially gendered expectations of the sex they were medically assigned at birth.

often stigmatized and subjected to violence, discrimination, abuse, and hate crimes not only by state actors but also by the general population in public, private, and virtual spaces and in the different domains of social life. For instance, family members might try to pressure LGB and/or T people not to come out; LGB and/or T people might not be accepted and might be abandoned or disavowed by their families; and/or they might be victims of physical violence and/or honor killings committed by members of their families trying to "restore the family's respectability." LGB and/or T people, in particular trans people, are often discriminated against in the labor market, often having difficulties getting a job and/or in their workplaces being subject to harassment, blackmail, and sexual abuse from colleagues and their superiors (HRW 2019; Kréfa 2018). The discrimination that these individuals frequently suffer in educational settings also leads many of them to leave the education system with low qualifications, which also makes it more difficult for them to find stable employment (HRW 2019; Ördek 2015).

Health-care systems often do not provide the necessary services to LGB and/or T people, sometimes refusing to care for them and/or doing so by exploiting them (e.g., by providing services at a higher price than that paid by the general population) (HRW 2019; Maydaa, Chayya, and Myrttinen 2020; USAID 2022). Health-care staff tend to be unprepared to deal with LGB and/or T people, discriminating and mistreating them because of stigma related to their gender expression and/or sexual orientation. LGB and/or T people might also "choose" not to seek health care for fear of repercussions and "concerns about" their "privacy and safety" (USAID 2022, 92). When services for LGB and/or T people do exist, they tend to be concentrated in urban centers, so that LGB and/or T people from poor backgrounds who live in distant, rural areas have difficulty accessing quality medical services (USAID 2022). In countries such as Iraq, there is no access to gender-confirming surgery and hormonal therapy through governmental health-care institutions, so that trans people who can afford it travel to other countries, such as Iran, to undergo medical treatment (OutRight International and IraQueer 2022). Yet when they return to their own country, as previously mentioned, the mismatch between their gender expression and their legal documents as well as the limited chance to gain legal gender recognition leave these trans people vulnerable to increased violence and unable to access essential services.

LGB and/or T people, in particular trans women, tend to have difficulty accessing housing, a domain where they are also frequently subject to discrimination, harassment, blackmail, and sexual abuse from housemates and landlords (e.g., HRW 2019; Maydaa, Chayya, and Myrttinen 2020; Nasser-Eddin, Abu-Assab, and Greatrick 2018). In the Arabic-speaking countries of the MENA region, the media also tend to be seen as increasing the stigma and prejudice toward LGB and/or T people (Ghoshal 2018; Girijashanker 2018; OutRight Action International 2017). For example, reports have shown how the media often use derogatory terms to refer to LGB and/or T people and justify homophobic and transphobic remarks with religious rationales (Ghoshal 2018; Girijashanker 2018; IraQueer 2018; OutRight Action International 2017). For instance, in Egypt the media are notorious for "creating moral panic in society" (Abdel Hamid 2017, 7). Indeed, most media outlets in the country regard LGB and/or T issues as a lucrative source to increase distribution through sensationalizing events, defaming the arrested people, publishing their pictures, and vilifying them. The media coverage is known to have "demonized and indeed identified those charged with debauchery or other related crimes" and usually portrays those arrested "as a threat to the moral fabric of society" (Abdel Hamid 2017, 7). In several countries, such as Iraq, Tunisia, Bahrain, Turkey, and Syria, trans people might be denied entrance to businesses such as gyms, hotels, and cafés and/or denied services (Girijashanker 2018; HRW and IraQueer 2022; ILGA Europe 2020; Whitaker 2016).

In (post)conflict areas, such as Iraq, Libya, Syria, and Yemen, armed groups and militias add to the potential violence that many LGB and/or T people already face in their everyday lives.[8] For instance, in the case

8. Importantly, though, sexual and gender-based violence, including violence against LGB and/or T people, in (post)conflict societies needs to be perceived in a continuum, whereby it is perpetrated or condoned by governments and part of the population also during "peace" times (al-Ali 2018). This is clearly visible in the wider contexts of impunity for such violence against LGB and/or T people in countries such as Syria, Iraq, and Yemen

of Iraq, religious extremists and militias who work alongside the state—such as ʿAsaʾib ʾAhl al-Haq (Leagues of the Righteous) and Jaish al-Madhi (Madhi Army)—often target women and people with nonnormative gender expressions. In what are considered to be "weak" states, the lack of state control over the militias and the militarization of everyday life with the presence of military police and checkpoints make LGB and/or T people more vulnerable to security forces, militias, and extremist groups (Davis and Stern 2018; Ghoshal 2018; HRW 2020; IraQueer 2018; Maydaa, Chayya, and Myrttinen 2020; OutRight International and IraQueer 2022; Stern 2016). Both in Iraq and Syria, ISIS directly targeted certain sexual-orientation and gender-identity (SOGI) populations—in particular those whose gender displays appeared not to conform with gender normativities and were perceived as "effeminate" or as "homosexual"—subjecting them to "ill-treatment, torture, and death" (OutRight International 2023, 14). In Yemen, "the Houthi de facto authorities and the UAE-backed Yemeni government, committed grave human rights violations that were 'motivated by prejudice' on the basis of sexual orientation or gender identity" (OutRight International 2023, 12). In the context of an "alleged" campaign "against immorality," LGB and/or T people were detained and subjected to "rape, forced anal examinations," and other forms of "torture," such as "forced nudity," "beating of genitals," and "shaving" of "hair and eyebrows" aimed at "humiliating" trans people and "forcing them to adhere to a cisgender norm" (OutRight International 2023, 12).

These (post)conflict contexts have led many LGB and/or T people to flee their countries to perceived relatively "safer" places, such as Lebanon and Turkey, many of them with the hope of leaving the MENA region altogether (Ghoshal 2018; Maydaa, Chaya, and Myrttinen 2020). However,

(HRW 2020; HRW and IraQueer 2022; IraQueer 2018; Maydaa, Chaya, and Myrttinen 2020; OutRight International 2023). It is also worth noting that within the MENA region in general, people who do not conform to expected marriage-centered heteronormativity tend to be subject to discrimination and violence. Gender-"nonconforming" people and those perceived as "homosexual" are at higher risk of such violence and discrimination (Nasser-Eddin, Abu-Assab, and Greatrick 2018).

not only do LGB and/or T refugees face the same discrimination, violence, and abuse as national citizens, but they also face additional discrimination insecurity because they don't have the same rights as national citizens (Muedini 2018). More recently, as a consequence of governmental measures to deal with the COVID-19 health situation, the conditions of life for LGB and/or T people in general (Skinta, Sun, and Ryu 2021; USAID 2022) and for LGB and/or T refugees in particular (Maydaa, Chaya, and Myrttinen 2020) worsened considerably, with increased difficulties in accessing the labor market or the loss of their livelihoods, and there is evidence of some trans women having to resort to sex work, in which they are even more subject to violence, and having to struggle with heightened isolation (USAID 2022).

Some Light at the End of the Tunnel? LGB and/or T Activisms, Safe Spaces, and Support

Although the previous descriptions paint a particularly dark picture for LGB and/or T people, researchers have also been underscoring the importance of having an intersectional approach to understanding the lives of LGB and/or T people in the region. For instance, Charbel Maydaa, Caroline Chayya, and Henri Myrttinen (2020) argue that more privileged LGB and/or T people in Syria and Lebanon are more open about their sexual and/or gender identities as compared to those from lower sociocultural backgrounds. The authors also note that it is still possible to be out as an LGB and/or T person in some areas of Turkey and Lebanon and that "an underground diverse SOGIESC community life continues" even if "under extremely precarious circumstances" (33). According to IraQueer (n.d.), there were also safe spaces for LGB and/or T people in Baghdad in the beginning of the 2000s. In Kuwait, before the introduction of a law in 2007 stipulating the prohibition of imitating the opposite sex, trans women were said to live in relative security (HRW 2012). In Iraq and Iran, there are also reports of supportive family members who can be said to create small "bubbles" of safety for trans people (IraQueer n.d.; OutRight Action International 2016). Interestingly, OutRight Action International mentions the current existence of a diverse, "vibrant," and "safer "underground LGBTIQ community" in Saudi Arabia (2021, 61). These cases illustrate the possibility of "subterranean narratives" (Plummer 2010) in a context that appears mainly hostile to LGB and/or T people's lives.[9]

The possibility of bringing these narratives into mainstream society can also be seen by the dynamism of LGB and/or T rights organizations. From the 1990s in Turkey and Lebanon as well as particularly from the beginning of the 2000s onward in other countries of the MENA region, such as Egypt, Jordan, and Morocco, local and international governmental and nongovernmental organizations (NGOs) defending LGB and/or T rights have increasingly been established (Ghoshal 2018; Girijashanker 2018; Hélie 2012). Either virtually or physically, these organizations try to create spaces where LGB and/or T people can feel secure, at least temporarily, and where they can connect with others like themselves (Ghoshal 2018; Girijashanker 2018). Among other things, these LGB and/or T rights organizations have been working to ensure the protection of LGB and/or T people against homophobic and transphobic violence; to decriminalize same-sex conduct and to repel other legislation used to target LGB and/or T practices; to create legal and health aid for LGB and/or T people; and to promote gender equality more generally (Ghoshal; Girijashanker 2018; Limam 2017; Muedini 2018). To raise awareness for LGB and/or T people's rights, these organizations often conduct workshops and trainings with community leaders, such as imams, doctors, and local government officials, as well as with media.

The increasing visibility of LGB and/or T activism in the MENA region can also be seen in the organization of feminist and LGB and/or T art festivals, the production of theater plays, the direction of magazines, and the screening of films that address SOGI issues. For instance, since 2015 Chouf, an organization that combines advocacy for women and LGB and/or T rights, sets up an art festival in Tunis. Several artists address LGB and/or T themes, thus creating a space for dialogue with the general public and increasing the visibility of LGB and/or T issues (Girijashanker 2018; Quattrini and Triki 2019). LGB and/or T rights organizations also

9. According to Ken Plummer, subterranean narratives are "lived sexual cultures that run against the grain, where any ideas of a dominant world or a hegemonic dominance are subverted, resisted, quietly ignored, or loudly challenged" (2010, 165).

make wide use of the technologies of information by developing websites, blogs, and social media pages, where they can share antihomophobic, antitransphobic, and antidiscriminatory campaigns; raise awareness of abusive practices by state and nonstate actors; and share oral stories of LGB and/or T people and information about the legal and health issues relevant to LGB and/or T people. Despite the potential risks, some LGB and/or T people also use social media to come out, particularly if they are in exile, and to share their personal experiences with others, thus becoming a "positive" reference for them.

Local LGB and/or T organizations in the region are also networking with other activists and local and/or international organizations and establishing regional networks—such as the Arab Foundation for Freedoms and Equality, founded in 2010, and Queer MENA, founded in 2017, both based in Beirut. Together, local and international LGB and/or T rights organizations have been trying to pressure governments to be more sexual and gender inclusive (Ghoshal; Girijashanker 2018). These local LGB and/or T rights organizations tend to use international policies in dynamic and strategic ways (Ghoshal 2018; Girijashanker 2018). The example of the Civil Collective for Individual Liberties (henceforth the Collective) in Tunisia shows how the interrelations among local, international, and transnational governmental organizations and NGOs can be used to try to pressure national governments to make changes regarding the protection of LGB and/or T people.[10] In 2016, the Collective submitted a *Tunisian Shadow Report* specific to LGB and/or T people to the United Nations

10. In 2016 in Tunisia, several local and international human rights organizations—including women's and LGB and/or T rights organizations—formed the Civil Collective for Individual Liberties (Girijashanker 2018). The Collective includes LGB and/or T rights in its agenda, which aims at the abolition of Article 230 of the Tunisian Penal Code and the decriminalization of same-sex practices (Girijashanker 2018; Limam 2017). In this sense, the Collective was able to advocate for the end of forced anal testing with the National Council of the Medical Order, which subsequently "issued a statement calling for doctors to cease conducting forced anal and genital examinations" (Girijashanker 2018, 49). However, this statement does not have mandatory application, and LGB and/or T people do feel that they nevertheless still must undergo the anal examinations when they are arrested, even if it is not "forced" upon them (Girijashanker 2018).

(UN) Universal Periodic Review Session, which was cosigned by eleven civil society organizations (see HRW 2016). Whereas the report submitted by the Tunisian government to the session did not mention LGB and/or T issues, the *Shadow Report* called attention to the criminalization of same-sex practices under Article 230 of the penal code, the continuous discrimination and violence that LGB and/or T individuals are subjected to in Tunisia, the harassment and abuse that LGB and/or T people often suffer at the hands of security forces, and the lack of protections afforded to LGB and/or T individuals by the government. Several states also requested that the Tunisian government stop all forms of SOGI-based violence, recommending the repeal of Article 230 and the end of anal examinations (ILGA 2017; Limam 2017).

Despite these efforts, LGB and/or T rights activists still face several obstacles. For instance, it is often difficult for LGB and/or T people to directly participate in activism and/or for LGB and/or T activists to become visible because of social stigma and a fear of their family's reaction (Ghoshal 2018). LGB and/or T rights activists who have come out to the general public frequently face harassment in "traditional" face-to-face contexts and on social media (Ghoshal 2018). In the Persian/Arab Gulf countries, such as Bahrain, Kuwait, Oman, Qatar, Saudi Arabia, and Yemen, there is less visibility of LGB and/or T rights organizations (Ghoshal 2018). In Turkey, particularly since 2015, state actors (such as the government and local councils) and nonstate actors (such as universities) have been prohibiting pride parades and/or have requested that the police attack LGB and/or T activists when they resist these orders and organize demonstrations (ILGA Europe 2020; Muedini 2018). In Iraq, civil society organizations working with LGB and/or T rights navigate a difficult terrain, where "LGBTQ people are [perceived as] legally, religiously and socially unacceptable" (OutRight International and IraQueer 2022, 13). In this context, only a limited number of organizations are able to support LGB and/or T people. The members of one such organization, Rasan, operating in the Kurdistan region of Iraq, were arrested during a raid by the police forces in Sulaymaniyah in 2021 "based on article 401 of the [Iraqi] penal code which criminalizes 'public indecency'" (HRW and IraQueer 2022, 3). To a letter from the HRW criticizing the cycle of violence by security forces, the Kurdistan regional government responded by reinstating the Kurdistan region as a "Safe Haven," in which individual freedoms are protected and indicating that its "government does not tolerate violence against the LGBTQ community." However, it also pointed out that "championing for homosexuality," as it considered Rasan to be doing, "remains a violation of law according to the Iraqi Legislation" (HRW and IraQueer 2022, 103, 104).

In Egypt, LGB and/or T organizations cannot formally register, nor can they openly serve LGBT populations, thus preventing efforts to provide them with safe spaces as well as crucial health and legal services. Hence, organizations that do work on LGB and/or T issues must do so under the radar, without making their work known to the general public, or else face potential police harassment and arrests. In addition, in late 2017 the Egyptian Supreme Council for Media Regulation banned any coverage of LGB and/or T issues unless the coverage showed them in a negative and predatory light. Moreover, in the MENA region there is a general lack of organizations focused exclusively on trans rights (Ghoshal 2018).

From Victims to Conditioned Agents: (De)Colonizing Trans Lives and Issues

The signing of the Universal Declaration of Human Rights in 1948 marked the beginning of an international politics aimed at social justice and the well-being and development of populations. During the 1970s, "human rights began to be widely adopted as a discursive and political tool to assert individual claims against the state" (Thoreson 2017, 4). Within this context and through a series of international conferences—such as the Convention on the Elimination of all Forms of Discrimination against Women (1979), the International Conference on Population and Development in Cairo (1994), and the Beijing Platform for Action (1995)—in which different states and members of national and international organizations participated, women's rights were increasingly pushed forward into the international agenda. From the beginning of the twenty-first century onward, this international gender politics has continued—for instance, through the Women, Security, and Peace Agenda and the UN Sustainable Development Goals, 2015 to 2030—and has often been part of negotiations in processes of nation building and peace resolution in conflict-ridden areas of the "global South."

Until the early 2000s, this framework could be said to work in an ambiguous way with respect to sexual- and gender-minority populations. On the one hand, this normative framework has tended not to focus on and/or even include LGB and/or T people, leading some academics to call for a queering of the international instruments on women's rights (e.g., Davis and Stern 2018). On the other hand, the existent international human rights instruments can be said to include sexual- and gender-minority populations in a more direct manner—for example, in the right to be free from discrimination, the right to equality, and the right to privacy.[11] As such, in the MENA region some human rights organizations, in partnership with women-focused civil society organizations—such as Chouf in Tunisia and Rasan in the Kurdistan region of Iraq—also advocate for the rights of LGB and/or T people. Recommendations made by researchers and local and international NGOs working in the MENA region (e.g., HRW 2023; HRW and IraQueer 2022; Noralla 2022b) also stress countries' adherence to several international human rights treaties—such as the International Covenant on Civil and Political Rights (adopted 1966, enforced 1976) and the International Covenant on Economic, Social, and Cultural Rights (adopted 1966, enforced 1976)—to make governments accountable for the protection of minority SOGI populations. Recently, a report by OutRight International (2023) called for the inclusion of SOGI within the UN Women, Peace, and Security Agenda. Yet although some perceive this approach to be creating an opportunity to promote both the rights of women and girls and SOGI populations, there are concerns that the inclusion of minority SOGI populations in the agenda might detract from the support for women and girls (OutRight International 2023)—thus highlighting current tensions between some feminist and LGB and/or T activists in a time that is often considered to be going through a "gendered," "patriarchal backlash" (Edstrom et al. 2023).

11. See Thoreson 2017; UN Human Rights Council, "Resolution 32/2, Protection against Violence and Discrimination based on Sexual Orientation and Gender Identity," 2016.

However, since the 2000s and particularly from the 2010s on, sexual- and gender-minority populations have increasingly become part of human rights discourses in their own right (Edenborg 2019; Rahman 2019b). The protection of these populations, like that of women and girls before them, also became synonymous with the democracy, modernization, progress, and development being promoted at an international level. Within this context, in 2007 the Yogyakarta Principles established an international human rights framework in relation to sexual orientation and gender identity. In 2011, the UN Human Rights Council passed the first-ever UN resolution on sexual orientation and gender identity focused on violence and discrimination against LGB and/or T people. And in 2012, the UN made its first policy statement—"Born Free and Equal"—asserting SOGI rights as human rights, thereby legitimizing "the rights of LGBT people as a global issue" (Rahman 2019b, 15).[12] Within this context, several countries—such as the United States under Barak Obama and more recently under Joe Biden (NRT 2021) and the United Kingdom with David Cameron—adopted the "protection and promotion" (Rahman 2019b, 15) of LGBT rights as part of their foreign policies, often targeting Muslim-majority countries and/or Muslim (diaspora) communities within "Western" countries (Aizura et al. 2014; Stevens and Chaudhry 2019). In this way, LGB and/or T rights contrarily became a symbol of freedom that helped to legitimize the "war on terror," migration policies, and the "control" of other populations—as in the case of Israel's occupation of Palestine (Boellstorff et al. 2014; Mikdashi 2011; Puar 2013). However, within this context, local and international civil society organizations have also been able to conduct workshops to promote awareness and/or advocate for the protection of minority SOGI populations in the MENA region. Yet this work not only might be perceived as leading to a backlash against minority SOGI populations but also might not correspond to the (self-)perceptions and

12. The policy statement "Born to Be Free and Equal. Sexual Orientation and Gender Identity. International Human Rights Law" is available at https://www.ohchr.org/Documents/Publications/BornFreeAndEqualLowRes.pdf. A second edition of this policy statement was published in 2019 and is available at https://www.ohchr.org/Documents/Publications/Born_Free_and_Equal_WEB.pdf.

needs of LGB and/or T people in the region. An outcome of this work by outsiders involves, for instance, humanitarian staff "coaching" LGB and/or T people on "expected" nonnormative ways so that they can be considered potential candidates for "asylum" (Nasser-Eddin, Abu-Assab, and Greatrick 2018, 184).

No wonder that the human rights framework—including LGB and/or T human rights—is often subject to strong criticism. Among the critiques of it is the understanding that it legitimizes some claims, populations, and/or ways of addressing these rights, while simultaneously disregarding others, such as individuals who do not identify as LGB and/or T, because of a lack of public space for their existence (Nay 2019; Puar 2013; Rahman 2019b; Thoreson 2017).

What are considered to be the imperialistic, (post)colonial, and universalist bases of a human rights framework are also frequently criticized (Boellstorff et al. 2014; Edenborg 2019; Hélie 2012; Massad 2007; Nay 2019; Puar 2013). The human rights framework is seen as being based on "Western" political, legal, social, cultural, and historical contexts as well as on LGB and/or T people's experiences in the "global North" and thus is not ideologically neutral (Nay 2019; Rahman 2019a, 2019b; Thoreson 2017). Accordingly, the international promotion of LGB and/or T rights tends to be associated with a "linear" narrative of "progress" and "modernization" (Edenborg 2019; Nay 2019; Puar 2013; Rahman 2019b). Within this narrative, countries that uphold LGB and/or T rights—associated with secular "Western" countries—are the ones considered open, developed, and progressive, whereas countries that are perceived as being complicit with the discrimination and violence against minority SOGI people—the "religious" Muslim-majority countries—are seen as repressive, ignorant, and traditional (Altinay 2014; Edenborg 2019; Hélie 2012; Lind 2014; Massad 2007; Nay 2019; Puar 2013; Rahman 2019a).[13] That is, Muslim-majority

13. In an opposite direction and particularly in relation to trans people, Evan Towle and Lynn Morgan (2002) make a pertinent critique of the "romanticization" of (non-"Western") "third-gender" "natives" as more progressive and "accepting" of gender diversity in comparison to "Western" countries, arguing that it neglects to offer a critical approach to the possible constraints that trans people might experience in their

countries, namely MENA region countries, are often understood as homophobic and transphobic because of their compliancy with binary, patriarchal, and heteronormative norms and therefore in need to "catch up" with "Western" cultural, social, and political conditions and "ultimately [to] accept SOGI rights" (Rahman 2019b, 22). What is more, when engaging with the international human rights' framework, LGB and/or T rights organizations become susceptible to SOGI normativities conveyed by this framework (e.g., Lind 2014; Massad 2007; Puar 2013; Rahman 2019a).

In turn, states and nonstate actors (e.g., religious leaders) from the peripheries—that have (post)colonial relations with "Western" countries—might consider LGB and/or T rights as perverse, created by "imperialistic" Western states, and therefore as a menace to the sexual and gender normativities of their cultures and societies (Edenborg 2019; Massad 2007). Thus, in the context of the MENA region, where several state entities and "Western" transnational organizations are present—often with the justification of preventing and/or stopping conflict, participating in nation-building processes, and/or offering developmental aid—the perception is that there has been a backlash in relation to gender and LGB and/or T rights in the name of religious and traditional norms that often help sustain nationalist movements (Edenborg 2019; Hélie 2012; Lind 2014; Massad 2007; Rahman 2019a). Thus, it is said that in some parts of the MENA region, such as Turkey, Tunisia, the UAE, Saudi Arabia, and Egypt, "conservative" governments and religious movements "have set back women's rights, sexual freedoms, and religious diversity in recent years" (Ghoshal 2018, 13). In Egypt, the violation of the human rights of LGB and/or T individuals is further augmented "by treating non-normative gender and sexual identities pathologically" (Tahrir Institute for MENA Region Policy 2019). The Egyptian Doctors' Syndicate has classified transgenderism as a medical condition, so that to be allowed a gender-reassignment surgery, trans individuals must obtain the unanimous approval of a committee formed for this specific purpose. The committee comprises a geneticist,

particular special, social, cultural, and historical contexts. Such a romanticization can be seen, for instance, in relation to descriptions of historical and cultural acceptance of intersex people and "effeminate" men in the MENA region.

an endocrinologist, two psychiatrists, and a representative from al-Azhar Mosque, the latter of which has consistently rejected cases and since 2016 has altogether blocked the convocation of the committee to review new cases. Those who have undergone the process in Egypt have faced immense difficulty in changing the gender listed on their identity card and are rarely successful in doing so. Because the Egyptian Constitution stipulates that Islamic Sharia remains the main source of legislation, trans persons' struggles in changing their name and/or gender in official documents are unlikely to be resolved anytime soon. Despite the fatwa of 1988, which approved gender-reassignment surgery, as previously discussed, al-Azhar and the Coptic Orthodox Church refuse to provide or condone any type of support to LGB and/or T people under the assumption that such support could promote "obscenity" and "perversion."

Further, it is necessary to underscore that gender inequality as well as discrimination, violence, and abuse against LGB and/or T people are still very common in other parts of the world outside of the MENA region, even in "Western," Christian countries. For example, a recent study found that in the European Union the majority of LGB and, in particular, T people who participated in the study had suffered some kind of discrimination and/or violence (European Union Agency for Fundamental Rights 2020). In addition, from 2008 to 2022 the reported number of murdered trans people in other parts of the world—such as Brazil (1,741), Mexico (649), the United States (375), Colombia (233), Venezuela (131), India (114), and Argentina (113)—is still quite high (Trans Murder Monitoring 2023).

Importantly, it is necessary to understand LGBT and/or T experiences and SOGI rights in their spatial, material, legal, social, cultural, and historical contexts as well as in relation to their intersecting social locations but not to consider any experiences or rights as universal and/or as timeless. Particularly in the case of trans studies, there has been an emphasis on the importance of understanding "trans" as a historical and culturally contingent concept (Nay 2019; Ryan 2020b, 2020c), while also considering the transnational circulation of people, images, ideas, and knowledge that will potentially have implications for local trans experiences, expectations, knowledges, and advocacy. Toward this aim, academics (e.g., Aizura et al. 2014; Boellstorff et al. 2014; Nay 2019) have been arguing for the decolonization of trans studies, moving it beyond its Anglo-Saxon premises and focusing instead on a critical politics of solidarity and knowledge production that, among other issues, questions trans people's own role in transnational processes of trans rights aiming at social change; takes into account processes of (post)colonial violence; and pays attention not just to individuals' gender and sexual identities but also to their other social locations and the different domains of life that they move in and out of and that the individuals themselves consider meaningful. Further, there has been a move away from a portrait of trans people as "only victims" to a recognition of them as agents who not only have a voice and can tell their stories but can also participate in the decision-making processes that affect them (Boellstorff et al. 2014; Namaste 2005; Stryker [2008] 2017). It is thus important to look at SOGI populations, including trans individuals, as active agents, even if in conditioned circumstances.

Conclusion

Trans people's lives and LGB and/or T rights activism in the MENA region are conditioned by dynamic and complex processes that result from practices and normative interrelations among local, national, and inter/transnational (post)colonial agendas. Thus, trans lives in the MENA region cannot be seen simply through "Western eyes" (Mohanty 1988). Rather, as with trans people's experiences elsewhere in the world, they need to be understood as embedded within the specific spatial, legal, institutional, social, cultural, and historical contexts that frame them (Rahman 2019a).

There has been a strong politization of gender and sexuality by state and nonstate actors (Hélie 2012), visible, for instance, in the defense of what are perceived as "Western" SOGI rights. Simultaneously, there has also been a perceived backlash and "conservativism" in Muslim-majority societies, including the ones in the MENA region, which have increasingly targeted gender and sexual minorities in recent years. We caution, however, that it is necessary to recognize the heterogeneity of situations within Muslim-majority societies in general and within MENA region countries in particular. Trans people and LGB and/or T organizations in the MENA region operate in "complex realities" (Girijashanker 2018, 3). On the one hand, they suffer from widespread discrimination, violence, and abuse. On the other hand, they have shown "resilience, activism, and hard-fought legal and social progress" (Girijashanker 2018, 3).

In this sense, it is important to underscore the spatial, social, cultural, and historical specificities that frame LGBT people's experiences and activism within the different MENA region countries, their local realities, the increasing progress achieved in the recognition of LGB and/or T rights, and the heterogeneity of the MENA region countries in relation to LGB and/or T people (Girijashanker 2018; Hélie 2012; Nye 2019; Rahman 2019a, 2019b). As is the case with girls and women, the experiences of LGB and/or T people in the MENA region are heterogeneous, positioned at the intersections of several social locations, such as "ethno-religious, gendered, sexual, and racialized identities" inserted "in specific national and transnational contexts" (Rahman 2019a, 418). Consequently, it is important to take into account the possible spaces of resistances and subterranean discourses (Plummer 2010) of LGB people and particularly of T people—resistances and discourses that are visible, for instance, in the increasing number of LGB and/or T rights NGOs and in the (at least partial) adherence of several MENA countries to transnational treaties, many of which include protections for minority SOGI populations against discrimination and violence. These countries arguably may be able to put pressure on the other governments of the region to comply to the defense of the human rights of LGB and/or T people.

We conclude by again underscoring the importance of going beyond regional dichotomies that associate the "West" with freedom and the "East" with oppression; of having a better understanding of the influence (or lack thereof) of local, national, and inter/transnational (post)colonial agendas on trans people's rights and their actual experiences; and of acknowledging the possible pluralities, spaces of resistances, and subterranean discourses (Plummer 2010) on trans people and issues in the MENA region. We by no means wish to downplay the difficulties of being trans, the horrendous crimes carried out against trans individuals, or the largely uphill battle ahead to attain legal and social equality in the region. We do, however, wish to highlight the complexity of the situation and the agency of trans individuals themselves.

References

Abdel Hamid, Dalia. 2017. *The Trap: Punishing Sexual Difference in Egypt.* Cairo: Egyptian Initiative for Personal Rights. At https://eipr.org/sites/default/files/reports/pdf/the_trap-en.pdf.

Aizura, Aren Z., Trystan Cotten, Carsten/Carla Balzer/LaGata, Marcia Ochoa, and Salvador Vidal-Ortiz. 2014. Introduction to "Decolonizing the Transgender Imaginary," edited by Aren Z. Aizura, Trystan Cotten, Carsten/Carla Balzer/LaGata, Marcia Ochoa, and Salvador Vidal-Ortiz. Special issue, *TSQ: Transgender Studies Quarterly* 1, no. 3: 308–19. At https://doi.org/10.1215/23289252-2685606.

Al-Ali, Nadje. 2018. "Sexual Violence in Iraq: Challenges for Transnational Feminist Politics." *European Journal of Women's Studies* 25, no. 1: 10–27. At https://doi.org/10.1177/1350506816633723.

Alipour, Mehrdad. 2017. "Islamic Shari'a Law, Neotraditionalist Muslim Scholars and Transgender Sex-Reassignment Surgery: A Case Study of Ayatollah Khomeini's and Sheikh al-Tantawi's Fatwas." *International Journal of Transgenderism* 18, no. 1: 91–103. At https://doi.org/10.1080/15532739.2016.1250239.

———. 2022. "The Nexus between Gender-Confirming Surgery and Illness: Legal-Hermeneutical Examinations of Four Islamic Fatwas." *Journal of Middle East Women's Studies* 18, no. 3: 359–86. At https://muse.jhu.edu/article/877201.

Altinay, Rüstem Ertuğ. 2014. "Islam and Islamophobia." *TSQ: Transgender Studies Quarterly* 1, nos. 1–2: 115–18. At https://doi.org/10.1215/23289252-2399767.

Boellstorff, Tom, Mauro Cabral, Micha Cárdenas, Trystan Cotten, Eric A. Stanley, Kalaniopua Young, and Aren Z. Aizura. 2014. "Decolonizing Transgender: A Roundtable Discussion." In "Decolonizing the Transgender Imaginary," edited by Aren Z. Aizura, Trystan Cotten, Carsten/Carla Balzer/LaGata, Marcia Ochoa, and Salvador Vidal-Ortiz. Special issue, *TSQ: Transgender Studies Quarterly* 1, no. 3: 419–39. At https://doi.org/10.1215/23289252-2685669.

Chiam, Zha, Sandra Duffy, Matilda González Gil, Lara Goodwin, and Nigel Timothy Mpemba Patel. 2020. *Trans Legal Mapping Report 2019: Recognition before the Law.* Geneva: ILGA World. At https://ilga.org/downloads/ILGA_World_Trans_Legal_Mapping_Report_2019_EN.pdf.

Davies, Sharyn Graham. 2019. "Islam, Sexuality, and Gender Identity." In *Oxford Research Encyclopedias: Politics*, online ed., edited by W. R. Thompson. Oxford: Oxford Univ. Press. At https://doi.org/10.1093/acrefore/9780190228637.013.1255.

Davis, Lisa, and Jessica Stern. 2018. "WPS and LGBTI Rights." In *The Oxford Handbook of Women, Peace, and Security*, edited by Sara E. Davies and Jacqui True, 657–68. Oxford: Oxford Academic.

Duderija, Adis. 2013. "Critical-Progressive Muslim Thought: Reflections on Its Political Ramifications." *Review of Faith & International Affairs* 11, no. 3: 69–79. At https://doi.org/10.1080/15570274.2013.829987.

Edenborg, Emil. 2019. "Visibility in Global Queer Politics." In *The Oxford Handbook of Global LGBT and Sexual Diversity Politics*, edited by Michael J. Bosia, Sandra M. McEvoy, and Momin Rahman, 348–63. Oxford: Oxford Univ. Press.

Edstrom, Jerker, Ayesha Khan, Alan Greig, and Clow Skinner. 2023. "Grasping Patriarchal Backlash: A Brief for Smarter Countermoves." Countering Backlash Briefing 1, Institute of Development Studies, Brighton. At https://doi.org/10.19088/BACKLASH.2023.002.

Equaldex. n.d. "Explore the Progress of LGBTQ+ Rights across the World." At https://www.equaldex.com.

European Union Agency for Fundamental Rights. 2020. *EU-LGBTI II: A Long Way to Go for LGBTI Equality*. Luxembourg: Publication Office of the European Union. At https://fra.europa.eu/sites/default/files/fra_uploads/fra-2020-lgbti-equality_en.pdf.

Fortier, Corinne. 2019. "Sexualities: Transsexualities: Middle East, West Africa, North Africa." In *Encyclopedia of Women and Islamic Cultures Online*, edited by Suad Joseph. Leiden, Netherlands: Brill. At https://dx.doi.org/10.1163/1872-5309_ewic_COM_002185.

Ghoshal, Neela. 2018. *Audacity in Adversity: LGBT Activism in the Middle East and North Africa*. Washington, DC: Human Rights Watch. At https://www.hrw.org/sites/default/files/media_2020/07/lgbt_mena0418_web.pdf.

Girijashanker, Suraj. 2018. *Activism and Resilience: LGBTQ Progress in the Middle East and North Africa: Case Studies from Jordan, Lebanon, Morocco and Tunisia*. New York: Outright International. At https://outrightinternational.org/sites/default/files/2023-09/Activism_Resilience_MENA_EN%20%281%29.pdf.

Hamzic, Vanja. 2016. *Sexual and Gender Diversity in the Muslim World*. New York: I. B. Tauris.

Haneef, Sayed Sikandar Shah. 2011. "Sex Reassignment in Islamic Law: The Dilemma of Transsexuals." *International Journal of Business, Humanities and Technology* 1, no. 1: 1–10. At https://www.ijbhtnet.com/journals/Vol._1_No.1_July_2011/10.pdf.

Hélie, Anissa. 2012. "Risky Rights? Gender Equality and Sexual Diversity in Muslim Contexts." In *Sexuality in Muslim Contexts: Restrictions and Resistance*, edited by Anissa Hélie and Homa Hoofar, Kindle ed. New York: Zed.

Human Rights Watch (HRW). 2012. *"They Hunt Us Down for Fun": Discrimination and Police Violence against Transgender Women in Kuwait*. New York: HRW. At https://www.hrw.org/sites/default/files/reports/kuwait0112ForUpload.pdf.

———. 2016. "Submission to the United Nations Committee against Torture on Tunisia." Apr. 4. At https://www.hrw.org/news/2016/04/04/submission-united-nations-committee-against-torture-tunisia.

———. 2019. *"Don't Punish Me for Who I Am": Systematic Discrimination against Transgender Women in Lebanon*. New York: HRW. At https://www.hrw.org/sites/default/files/report_pdf/lebanon0910_pdf.pdf.

———. 2020. "Egypt: Security Forces Abuse, Torture LGBT People." *Human Rights Watch*, Oct. 1. At https://www.hrw.org/news/2020/10/01/egypt-security-forces-abuse-torture-lgbt-people.

———. 2023. *"All This Terror Because of a Photo": Digital Targeting and Its Offline Consequences for LGBT People in the Middle East and North Africa*. New York: HRW. At https://www.hrw.org/sites/default/files/media_2023/03/lgbt_mena0223web.pdf.

Human Rights Watch (HRW) and IraQueer. 2022. *"Everyone Wants Me Dead": Killings, Abductions, Torture, and Sexual Violence against LGBT People by Armed Groups in Iraq*. New York: HRW and IraQueer. At https://www.hrw.org/sites/default/files/media_2022/03/iraq_lgbt0322_web_0.pdf.

ILGA. 2017. *27th UPR Working Group Sessions: SOGIESC Recommendations*. Geneva: ILGA. At https://ilga.org/downloads/27TH_UPR_WORKING_GROUP_SESSIONS_SOGIESC_RECOMMENDATIONS.pdf.

ILGA Europe. 2020. *Annual Review of the Human Rights Situation of Lesbian, Gay, Bisexual, Trans, and Intersex People in Europe and Central Asia Covering the Period of January to December 2019*. Brussels: IGLA Europe. At https://www.ilga-europe.org/files/uploads/2022/04/annual-review-2020.pdf.

IraQueer. 2018. *Fighting for the Right to Live: The State of LGBT+ Rights in Iraq*. N.p.: IraQueer. At https://www.iraqueer.org/uploads/1/2/4/0/124034920/iraqueer___partner_baseline_study_2018.pdf.

———. n.d. *Living on the Margins: LGBT+ Stories from Iraq*. N.p.: IraQueer. At https://www.iraqueer.org/uploads/1/2/4/0/124034920/living_on_the_margins.pdf.

Kréfa, Abir. 2018. *Enquête sur les violences contre les personnes LGBTQ* (Study on violence against LGBTQ individuals). Tunis, Tunisia: Initiative Mawjoudin for Equality; Damj: Tunisian Association for Justice and Equality and Chouf. At https://sxpolitics.org/wp-content/uploads/2018/05/Rapport-Violence.pdf.

Kugle, Scott Siraj al-Haqq. 2014. *Living Out Islam: Voices of Gay, Lesbian and Transgender Muslims*. New York: New York Univ. Press.

Limam, Jinane. 2017. *Les associations LGBTQI++ en Tunisie: Emergence d'un nouveau militantisme humain*. Tunis, Tunisia: Heinrich Böll Stiftung, Afrique du Nord. At https://tn.boell.org/sites/default/files/1._etude_associations_lgbtqi_fr.pdf.

Lind, Amy. 2014. "Introduction: Development, Global Governance, and Sexual Subjectivities." In *Development, Sexual Rights and Global Governance*, edited by Amy Lind, 1–19. New York: Routledge.

MADRE and the International Women's Human Rights Clinic. 2015. *Dying to Be Free: LGBT Human Rights Violations in Iraq: In Response to the Fourth Periodic Report of the Republic of Iraq*. New York: City Univ. of New York School of Law. At https://www.iraqueer.org/uploads/1/2/4/0/124034920/iraqueer_and_outrights_action_internationals_response_to_the_united_nations_about_the_fifth_periodic_report_of_the_republic_of_iraq._-_english__1_.pdf.

Marques, Ana Cristina. 2020. "Displaying Trans (In)Visibilities." In *Trans Lives in a Globalizing World: Rights, Identities, and Politics*, edited by J. Michael Ryan, 17–33. London: Routledge.

Massad, Joseph. 2007. *Desiring Arabs*. Chicago: Univ. of Chicago Press.

Maydaa, Charbel, Caroline Chayya, and Henri Myrttinen. 2020. *Impacts of the Syrian Civil War and Displacement on SOGIESC Populations*. London: MOSAIC and Gender, Justice & Security. At https://thegenderhub.com/wp-content/uploads/2021/01/MOSAIC_Report_Online-1f443677dafb1a3e936ac0eade8236412c9f032fc4de51dc0d6387cbb67568863.pdf.

Mikdashi, Maya. 2011. "Gay Rights as Human Rights: Pinkwashing Homonation." *Jadaliyya*, Dec. 16. At https://www.jadaliyya.com/Details/24855.

Mohanty, Chandra. 1988. "Under Western Eyes: Feminist Scholarship and Colonial Discourses." In *Feminist Postcolonial Theory: A Reader*, edited by Reina Lewis and Sara Mills, 49–74. New York: Routledge.

Muedini, Fait. 2018. *LGBTI Rights in Turkey: Sexuality and the State in the Middle East*. Cambridge: Cambridge Univ. Press.

Namaste, Viviane. 2005. *Sex Change, Social Change: Reflections on Identity, Institutions, and Imperialism*. Toronto: Women's Press/Canadian Scholars' Press.

Nasser-Eddin, Nof, Nour Abu-Assab, and Aydan Greatrick. 2018. "Reconceptualising and Contextualising Sexual Rights in the MENA Region: Beyond LGBTQI Categories." *Gender & Development* 26, no. 1: 173–89. At https://doi.org/10.1080/13552074.2018.1429101.

Nay, Yv E. 2019. "The Atmosphere of Trans* Politics in the Global North and West." *TSQ: Transgender Studies Quarterly* 6, no. 1: 64–79. At https://doi.org/10.1215/23289252-7253496.

Noralla, Nora. 2022a. "Confused Judiciary & Transgender Rights: Inside the MENA Region's Case Law on Legal Gender Recognition." *Manara Magazine*, Mar. 17. At https://manaramagazine.org/2022/03/confused-judiciary-transgender-rights-inside-the-mena-regions-case-law-on-legal-gender-recognition/.

———. 2022b. "The Middle East Has an Anti-transgender Bills Problem." *The New Arab*, July 22. At https://www.newarab.com/features/middle-east-has-anti-transgender-bills-problem.

———. 2022c. "Tough Territory for Transgender People in the Middle East and the North of Africa." Tahrir Institute for Middle East Policy, Apr. 7. At https://timep.org/2022/04/07/tough-territory-for-transgender-people-in-the-middle-east-and-north-africa/.

———. 2023. "Transgender Discrimination Continues in Kuwait, despite a Court Ruling." *DAWN: Democracy for the Arab World Now*, Feb. 13. At https://dawnmena.org/transgender-discrimination-continues-in-kuwait-despite-a-court-ruling/.

NRT. 2021. "Biden Opens Major Push for LGBTIQ Rights Abroad." Feb. 7. At https://www.nrttv.com/en/News.aspx?id=26243&MapID=4.

Ördek, Kemal. 2015. "The Social Experiences of Trans People in Turkey." In *Transrespect versus Transphobia: The Social Experience of Trans and Gender-Diverse People in Colombia, India, the Philippines, Serbia, Thailand, Tonga, Turkey and Venezuela*, edited by Carsten Balzer/Carla LaGata, and Jan Simon Hutta, 62–73. Berlin: Transgender Europe. At https://transrespect.org/wp-content/uploads/2015/08/TvT-PS-Vol9-2015.pdf.

OutRight Action International. 2016. *Human Rights Report: Being Transgender in Iran*. New York: OutRight Action International. At https://outrightinternational.org/sites/default/files/2022-10/OutRightTransReport.pdf.

———. 2017. *Arab Mass Media: A Monitoring Report Looking at Sexuality and Gender Identity in Arabic Media from 2014 to 2017.* New York: OutRight Action International. Formerly at https://outrightinternational.org/sites/default/files/Eng-ArabicMedia2017-report.pdf (no longer available in English). In Arabic at https://outrightinternational.org/sites/default/files/2024-02/ATG_Arabic_Media_Guide.pdf.

———. 2021. *No Access: LGBTIQ Website Censorship in Six Countries.* New York: OutRight Action International, Citizen Lab, and OONI. At https://outrightinternational.org/sites/default/files/2022-09/NoAccess_abridged_1.pdf.

OutRight International. 2023. *LGBTQ Lives in Conflict and Crisis: A Queer Agenda for Peace, Security, and Accountability.* New York: OutRight International. At https://outrightinternational.org/sites/default/files/2023-02/LGBTQLivesConflictCrisis_0.pdf.

OutRight International and IraQueer. 2022. *"I Need to Be Free": What It Means to Be a Queer Woman in Today's Iraq.* New York: OutRight International and IraQueer. At https://outrightinternational.org/sites/default/files/2023-03/IraqReport2022_Revised_OutrightInternational_2.pdf.

Plummer, Ken. 2010. "Generational Sexualities, Subterranean Traditions, and the Hauntings of the Sexual World: Some Preliminary Remarks." *Symbolic Interaction* 33, no. 2: 163–90. At https://doi.org/10.1525/si.2010.33.2.163.

Puar, Jasbir. 2013. "Rethinking Homonationalism." *International Journal of Middle East Studies* 45, no. 2: 336–39. At https://doi.org/10.1017/S002074381300007X.

Quattrini, Silvia, and Bochra Triki. 2019. "Sexualities and LGBTQI+ Activism in Tunisia: The Example of the Feminist Movement Chouf." *LSE Blog*, Nov. 14. At https://blogs.lse.ac.uk/mec/2019/11/14/sexualities-and-lgbtqi-activism-in-tunisia-the-example-of-the-feminist-lgbt-movement-chouf/.

Rahman, Momin. 2014. *Homosexualities: Muslim Cultures and Modernity.* New York: Palgrave Macmillan.

———. 2019a. "Queer Muslim Challenges to the Internationalization of LGBT Rights: Decolonizing International Methodology through Intersectionality." In *The Oxford Handbook of Global LGBT and Sexual Diversity Politics*, edited by Michael J. Bosia, Sandra M. McEvoy, and Momin Rahman, 417–32. Oxford: Oxford Academic.

———. 2019b. "What Makes LGBT Sexualities Political? Understanding Oppression in Sociological, Historical, and Cultural Context." In *The Oxford Handbook of Global LGBT and Sexual Diversity Politics*, edited by Michael J.

Bosia, Sandra M. McEvoy, and Momin Rahman, 14–29. Oxford: Oxford Academic.

Richardson, Diane. 2007. "Patterned Fluidities: (Re)Imagining the Relationship between Gender and Sexuality." *Sociology* 41, no. 3: 457–74.

Ryan, J. Michael. 2018. "Gender Identity Laws: The Legal Status of Global Sex/Gender Identity Recognition." *LGBTQ Policy Journal* 8 (Spring): 3–16.

———. 2019. "Communicating Trans Identity: Toward an Understanding of the Selection and Significance of Gender Identity–Based Terminology." *Journal of Language and Sexuality* 8, no. 2: 221–41. At https://doi.org/10.1075/jls.19001.rya.

———. 2020a. "Born Again? (Non-)Motivations to Alter Official Sex/Gender Identity Markers on Birth Certificates." *Journal of Gender Studies* 29, no. 3: 269–81. At https://doi.org/10.1080/09589236.2019.1631148.

———. 2020b. "Expressing Identity: Toward an Understanding of How Trans Individuals Navigate the Barriers and Opportunities of Official Identity." *Journal of Gender Studies* 29, no. 3: 349–60. At https://doi.org/10.1080/09589236.2019.1570841.

———. 2020c. "Trans Lives in a Globalizing World: Rights, Identities, and Politics." In *Trans Lives in a Globalizing World: Rights, Identities, and Policies*, edited by J. Michael Ryan, 1–13. London: Routledge.

Skinta, Matthew D., Angela H. Sun, and Daniel M. Ryu. 2021. "The Impact of COVID-19 on the Lives of Sexual and Gender Minority People." In *COVID-19: Social Consequences and Cultural Adaptations*, edited by J. Michael Ryan, 230–44. London: Routledge.

Stern, Jessica. 2016. "The U.N. Security Council's Arria-Formula Meeting on Vulnerable Groups in Conflict: ISIL's Targeting of LGBTI Individuals." *University Journal of International Law and Politics* 48: 1191–98. At https://nyujilp.org/wp-content/uploads/2010/06/NYU_JILP_48_4_Stern.pdf.

Stevens, Jacqueline, and V. Varun Chaudhry. 2019. "Debating Imperial Violence and the Production of Sexualities." In *The Oxford Handbook of Global LGBT and Sexual Diversity Politics*, edited by Michael J. Bosia, Sandra M. McEvoy, and Momin Rahman, 397–416. Oxford: Oxford Academic.

Stryker, Susan. [2008] 2017. *Transgender History*. 2nd ed. Berkeley, CA: Seal Press.

Tahrir Institute for MENA Region Policy (TIMEP). 2019. "TIMEP Brief: LGBTQ Human Rights in Egypt." July 17. At https://timep.org/reports-briefings/timep-briefs/timep-brief-lgbtq-human-rights-in-egypt/.

Thoreson, Ryan R. 2017. “Thinking Queer Activism Transnationally.” *S&F Online* 14, no. 2: 1–11. At https://sfonline.barnard.edu/thinking-queer-activism-transnationally/lgbt-human-rights-in-the-age-of-human-rights/0/?print=true.

Towle, Evan B., and Lynn M. Morgan. 2002. “Romancing the Transgender Native: Rethinking the Use of the ‘Third Gender’ Concept.” *GLQ: Lesbian and Gay Studies* 8, no. 4: 469–97. At https://doi.org/10.1215/10642684-8-4-469.

Trans Murder Monitoring. 2023. “TMM Absolute Numbers (2008–Sept 2023).” At https://transrespect.org/en/map/trans-murder-monitoring/.

USAID. 2022. *LGBTQI+ Access to Formal and Informal Health Services in the MENA Region: Rapid Assessment: Final Report.* Washington, DC: United States Agency for International Development. At https://pdf.usaid.gov/pdf_docs/PA00ZDB7.pdf.

Westbrook, Laurel, and Kristen Schilt. 2014. “Doing Gender, Determining Gender: Transgender People, Gender Panics, and the Maintenance of the Sex/Gender/Sexuality System.” *Gender & Society* 28, no. 1: 32–57. At https://doi.org/10.1177/0891243213503203.

Whitaker, Brian. 2016. “Transgender Issues in the Middle East.” *Al-bab.com Blog*, Feb. 9. At https://al-bab.com/blog/2016/02/transgender-issues-middle-east.

Zaatari, Zeina. 2024. “Sexual Rights Movement(s): Problematics of Visibility.” In *Sexuality in the Middle East and North Africa: Contemporary Issues and Challenges*, edited by J. Michael Ryan and Helen Rizzo, 23–66. Syracuse, NY: Syracuse Univ. Press.

Zaharin, Aisya Aymanee M., and Maria Pallotta-Chiarolli. 2020. “Countering Islamic Conservatism on Being Transgender: Clarifying Tantawi’s and Khomeini’s Fatwas from the Progressive Muslim Standpoint.” *International Journal of Transgender Health* 21, no. 3: 235–41. At https://doi.org/10.1080/26895269.2020.1778238.

Zahed, Ludovic-Mohamed. 2020. *Homosexuality, Transidentity, and Islam: A Study of Scripture Confronting the Politics of Gender and Sexuality.* Amsterdam: Amsterdam Univ. Press.

Part Three. Sexual Health and Identity

6

An Overview of Sexual and Reproductive Health

Social Determinants and Challenges

Inas Abdelwahed

Sexual and reproductive health (SRH) is a crucial part of the health status of populations and a precondition for human development. Attention to women's health, in particular SRH, came under the spotlight during and after the International Conference on Population and Development (ICPD), which took place in Cairo in 1994. Since then, new SRH paradigms have come to be of vital importance. The ICPD Program of Action defines SRH as "a state of complete physical, mental and social well-being and not merely the absence of disease or infirmity, in all matters relating to the reproductive system and its functions and processes" (Center for Reproductive Rights and United Nations Population Fund [UNFPA] 2013, 1).

Moreover, some health scholars argue that SRH is also a socially and culturally constructed concept that is influenced by political, economic, and legal systems. As a result, perceptions of SRH differ from nation to nation (Obermeyer 1999a; Shneor, Camgöz, and Karapinar 2013). For this reason, the international definition of SRH might not always be culturally appropriate for all contexts. Hence, exploring definitions that include local cultural perspectives is crucial for designing programs to improve reproductive health outcomes (Kaddour, Hafez, and Zurayk 2005; Sadana 2002; Zurayk 2001).

Despite the remarkable global progress toward improved SRH, there are still significant gaps between high-income countries (HICs) and low/middle-income countries (LMICs) (Sippel 2014). Many LMICs still have high percentages of home deliveries without skilled birth attendees and struggle with higher rates of sexually transmitted infections (STIs), both of which are risk factors for various disabilities (Glasier et al. 2006). LMICs further lack accurate health data reports and documentation. Data on SRH diseases and births are often underreported, misreported, or unregistered.

Thus, this chapter examines a number of pressing SRH challenges in the Middle East and North Africa (MENA) region through a social and cultural lens, focusing primarily on youth and sexuality, maternal health, STIs, infertility, and men's reproductive health. Also significant to the MENA context is the number of countries that are either in active conflicts or are suffering a postconflict status. The humanitarian crises in the region have dramatically limited access to health care, including SRH care, and have made data collection and research at the national level, including the health-care field, very difficult.[1]

Social Determinants of Sexual and Reproductive Health in the MENA Region

Addressing SRH in the MENA region, with its multifaceted social, economic, cultural, political, and medical variations across the different countries, is a complex undertaking. More specifically, social determinants are any nonmedical factors that affect SRH outcomes, including interactions among political, economic, cultural, environmental, and legal influences. Social determinants also consider positions, power dynamics, and hierarchies that control access to resources.

Consequently, perceptions and determinants of SRH differ from nation to nation (Obermeyer 1999a; Shneor, Camgöz, and Karapinar 2013). However, some common challenges include but are not limited to health literacy, poor access to health services, unmet needs for family planning

1. Humanitarian settings include those both during and after natural disasters, armed conflict, and political unrest, which expose people to different types of vulnerabilities (Sphere Project 2011).

(FP), and gender inequalities. In addition, several countries in the MENA region suffer from unrest and political instability. These conditions serve as fertile grounds for humanitarian crises that aggravate the challenges of SRH morbidities, mortalities, and social inequalities. Political instability affects people's health directly and indirectly owing to the increased vulnerability to reproductive health problems and diseases.

Moreover, MENA region countries are considered LMICs, where socioeconomic status can jeopardize women's reproductive health. For instance, unequal gender-power relations and cultural barriers prevent some women from seeking antenatal care (DeJong, Bahubaishi, and Attal 2012). In addition, confining social norms around women's SRH push many women to suffer silently from reproductive health morbidities. Women may often be reluctant to seek information about sexuality in part because of the cultural norms and expectations around female virginity and chastity.

Taboos around sexuality—such as sexual health education, premarital sex, infertility, sexual dysfunctions, and so on—are considered one of the main obstacles in maintaining good reproductive health because they lead to poor SRH literacy. Studies have shown that the level of knowledge on STIs, the availability of reproductive services, the use of contraception, and safe-sex practices are generally low in the MENA region, particularly among youth and women (Barbour and Salameh 2009; Farih et al. 2014; El-Gelany and Moussa 2013; Roushdy and Sieverding 2015).

Although infertility might not be a priority for most health-care systems in the region, fertility is vital to both women's and men's psychological well-being. Infertility and assisted reproductive technologies (ARTs) are shaped and adopted differently in each country based on their needs and religious and legal codes. Notions around infertility are strongly influenced by social norms concerning masculinity and femininity as well as by religious texts. Accordingly, the region has witnessed substantial flourishing in ARTs, which has social and religious implications. A later section in this chapter is dedicated to examining infertility and ARTs, given that they offer a good example of how social and cultural contexts are key determinants of SRH in the MENA region (Inhorn 1996, 2004).

Sexual Health and Sex Education among Young People

Young people's sexual health is a topic of interest to many public-health practitioners as youth and adolescents are more likely to engage in behaviors such as alcohol and drug abuse, which increases the risk of unsafe sex. Risky behaviors put them at higher risk of contracting STIs, acquiring HIV/AIDS, having unwanted pregnancies, and being victims of sexual abuse (World Health Organization [WHO] 2014). Studies from the region indicate that health services are ill-equipped to meet youth's sexual health needs (Oraby 2013; Roudi-Fahimi 2003). In 2011, Egypt established youth-friendly clinics to provide SRH information and premarital counseling. The clinics were established in public and educational hospitals to offer information about puberty and premarital counseling. However, they did not meet youths' needs because of concerns about the quality of the services, privacy, and confidentiality (Abd El-Mawgod et al. 2020; Oraby 2013). Additional concerns were the stigma toward men and unmarried youth using the services, which has resulted in poor utilization of the services.

Moreover, the humanitarian setting in the MENA region countries has contributed to greater vulnerability of adolescents and young adults due to deficient SRH knowledge and access to information. For instance, Syrian refugee girls in Lebanon know little about puberty, FP methods, and STIs (Fahme et al. 2023). Studies have shown that poverty, economic hardship, and political unrest lead some young girls to engage in sex work, which exposes them to a greater risk of being sexual abused and contracting STIs (WHO 2002).

Sex Education and Premarital Sexual Intimacy in the MENA Region

The absence of sex education (SE) in schools and within families as well as the conservative environment in which many young people live contribute to their lack of knowledge about sexual health. Studies from Lebanon, Egypt, and Saudi Arabia show a desire among young people to have SE introduced into the school curriculum (Alsubaie 2019; El-Kak, Afifi, et al. 2001; Wahba and Roudi-Fahimi 2012), stemming from their need for access to reliable and trusted sources of information around SRH. The conservative culture of most MENA region countries is supported by religious interpretations of sacred texts that disapprove of sexual practices outside of marriage. Despite societal and religious pressures to preserve virginity and to postpone sex until marriage, different realities in the MENA region have resulted in delayed marriage and have pushed toward the presence of different marriage substitutes, such as undocumented customary marriage, which is often done in secret and may last for a limited time.

Moreover, some youth have become involved in different forms of premarital sexual intimacy and nonpenetrative sexual behaviors to explore their sexuality while aiming to keep the hymen intact (El-Kak 2013). Reviews of the region's SRH reports between 2001 and 2013 in Jordan, Egypt, Lebanon, Iran, and Tunisia showed an upward trend in premarital sexual interactions among university students (El-Kak 2013; Farahani-Khalajabadi 2015; Maatouk, Assi, and Jaspal 2023). In Saudi Arabia, around 38 percent of male high-school students experienced some sexual contact and believed that men get sexually involved before marriage (Alsubaie 2019). Young people's increasing engagement in various sexual intimacies in the absence of proper SE endangers the health of these young people. It exposes them to various diseases, unwanted pregnancies, and the spread of misconceptions and myths about sexuality. For example, female university students in Beirut who reported engaging in sexual activities and risky behaviors and who used oral contraceptive pills are less likely to use condoms (Maatouk, Assi, and Jaspal 2023). The false sense of protection gained from using oral contraception puts them at risk of acquiring STIs.

In the early 2000s, Angel Foster examined the complex association between sexuality and the conservative culture of the MENA region by interviewing female university students living in student dormitories in Tunisia. The in-depth interviews portrayed the conflicting dynamics among conservative rural traditions, students' sexual needs, and the perceived shame and stigma associated with the young women's sexual activity in the dormitories (Foster 2002). More recent studies have had similar results. Shame, guilt, and self-disrespect preoccupy many unmarried female university students in Lebanon engaging in sexual relationships (Assaad, Khalil, and Clement 2011). A survey in Egypt in 2014 echoed those findings, which are deepened by a culture of silence around intimate issues of puberty and sexuality within the family (Roushdy and Sieverding 2015).

Implementing Sex Education at Schools

The complex reality of youth living both in a region with a conservative culture but also in the new digital era with open-access sources to material on sex necessitates the presence of formal SE at schools. Despite the desire for SE from youth, parents, stakeholders, and caregivers in Saudi Arabia, Oman, Lebanon, and Egypt (Assaad, Khalil, and Clement 2011; Horanieh, Macdowall, and Wellings 2020; Riad and Forden 2021; al Zaabi et al. 2019), only two countries in the region have taken serious steps to implement SE: Lebanon and Tunisia. In the mid-1990s, Lebanon started SE in primary schools. However, the program was canceled a few years after implementation because of opposition by conservative religious parties (Assaad, Khalil, and Clement 2011). Late in 2019, Tunisia decided to provide SE in primary and secondary schools, making Tunisia the first Arab country to introduce SE to students as young as five years old (Beachum 2019). Although the program was planned to be implemented in 2021, various cultural, religious, and political factors have delayed it. Aside from the recent political instability in the Tunisian government, the content of the SE curriculum is a significant concern for parents and teachers.

Recent studies from Saudi Arabia and Oman show that parents and stakeholders support having SE at schools only if the content aligns with religious and cultural values. Saudi stakeholders and SRH providers reported that SE should focus on abstinence and harm reduction. In addition, they believed that SE is required to reduce divorce rates in Saudi Arabia. However, "harm" means more than harm to one's health, with participants in the studies viewing it as any damage to the youth's faith, reputation, and social order (Horanieh, Macdowall, and Wellings 2020).

Similarly, in a study conducted in Oman, parents reported strong support for providing SE in schools, but they also believed the content must match Islamic views to prevent premarital sex (al Zaabi et al. 2019). It is worth mentioning that views in Islamic texts and the interpretations of those texts consider sex a fundamental aspect of people's lives and encourage Muslim parents to educate their children on sexual behaviors. Hence, providing SE should not conflict with Islamic regulations. Yet although Omani parents and Saudi school teachers reported similar views on abstinence and harm reduction (Horanieh, Macdowall and Wellings 2020; al Zaabi et al. 2022), there was also a consensus on not providing their children with any information on sexual behavior. In another study conducted with Omani parents, they reported that lack of time, insufficient sexual knowledge, and taboos around sex talks are the main barriers to providing SE at home (al Zaabi et al. 2022). Most of the study's parents were aware of their children's exposure to sexual information on social media (al Zaabi et al. 2019, 2022). Following Tunisia, Egypt's minister of education has called for integrating SE into schools' curricula but only to prevent homosexuality and so-called abnormal and deviant sexual behaviors (*Egypt Independent* 2022). None of the participants in the studies mentioned here reported the importance of including the needs of the youth in the SE curricula. This may indicate that SE is approved only to achieve specific goals and agendas, such as reducing divorce rates and population growth and fighting homosexuality rather than empowering youth or providing them with quality SRH education to make informed decisions.

Seeking Sex Education through Virtual Platforms

Owing to the absence of formal sex education in schools, youth have had to find other channels, such as the internet, to seek information about sexuality (van Clief and Anemaat 2020; Wahba and Roudi-Fahimi 2012). For instance, the frequently asked questions on an Arabic-language website on emergency contraception show that there is a demand for information on contraception and how to avoid unwanted pregnancies. Most website users are registered in countries where the sociocultural fabric is highly conservative, such as Saudi Arabia, Syria, and Morocco (Foster et al. 2005). Youth in the region use Facebook groups to inquire about HIV/AIDS and share health concerns to avoid the social stigma of seeking such information in nonvirtual settings (Asiri et al. 2017). The majority of participants in Eman Asiri and colleagues' (2017) study come from Egypt, Saudi Arabia, and Libya. In 2020, the online SE platform Love Matters reported that users from the Arab region used the platform to search for topics around virginity, STIs, and pleasure content (van Clief and Anemaat 2020).

Similarly, a study conducted on nonmedical students in Egypt revealed that almost 80 percent of the students had searched online for topics related to SRH (Hassan and Masoud 2021, 1268). Students, in particular girls and young women, found confidentiality was the main advantage of accessing SRH topics online. However, having tolerant, open channels such as websites to exchange knowledge on SRH can sometimes be a double-edged sword. Many websites disseminate misconceptions, promote dangerous values such as rape culture, and spread pornographic materials. Recent studies show that many parents eagerly seek trustworthy sources for SE to provide accurate information and to educate young people about potential sexual exploitation associated with seeking sex information on the web (e.g., Gesser-Edelsburg and Arabia 2018).

Dominant social norms in the region accept sex only within the framework of marriage, but providing information even to couples who are about to get married is almost nonexistent. Iran implemented a culturally accepted premarital program on SRH and FP for university students to provide premarital counseling and sexual education to couples about to marry (Vakilian and Najmabadi 2011). Unfortunately, the program was seen as relatively inadequate because it addressed SRH only in adulthood when the reality is that knowledge about SRH and safe-sex practices must be discussed during adolescence (Mohammad et al. 2007). In addition, such programs are designed only for adults about to marry. Young people with no immediate marriage plans are excluded from them. Overall, the majority of countries in the region lack adequate premarital programs, and even when such programs are present, they are limited to laboratory tests, as in Egypt, or to premarital genetic testing, as in Bahrain and Saudi Arabia (Bamimore et al. 2015; Oraby 2013).

Maternal Mortality

Maternal mortality (MM) is one of the important indicators for countries to measure progress toward meeting the UN Sustainable Development Goals.[2] The WHO has defined the maternal mortality ratio (MMR) as

2. The declaration was signed by 189 countries in 2000, in which they committed to achieving a set of eight measurable goals (the Millennium Development Goals) to

"the annual number of female deaths from any cause related to or aggravated by pregnancy or its management (excluding accidental or incidental causes) during pregnancy and childbirth or within 42 days of termination of pregnancy, irrespective of the duration and site of the pregnancy, expressed per 100,000 live births, for a specified time period" (WHO n.d.b). The MMR is difficult to measure in most LMICs because of the limited registration system in many hospitals and the poor monitoring of deliveries, which may result in misclassification of the cause of death (Gerdts et al. 2015). Moreover, community-based studies are rare in LMICs. Hence, MM is measured only through hospital-based studies, representing women who give birth in health facilities. Home-based births are not taken into consideration. Thus, we do not have an accurate picture of how widespread MM is in the MENA LMICs.

Global and Regional Response to Maternal Mortality

It is estimated that around 287,000 women died during and following pregnancy and childbirth around the world in 2020 (WHO 2023a). Since 2000, many developed countries and HICs have made significant progress in lowering the rates of MM; however, many developing countries are still experiencing a high prevalence of MM (Graham et al. 2016; Hogan et al. 2010; El-Kak, Kabakian-Khasholian, et al. 2020; Kassebaum et al. 2014; WHO 2023a). For instance, MMR in the LMICs is estimated to be 415 maternal deaths per 100,000 live births, forty times higher than the MMR in Europe and almost sixty times higher than in Australia and New Zealand (WHO et al. 2019). This gap can be attributed in part to the humanitarian crises, political unrest, population growth, poor registration systems, and the unmet need for contraception in the LMICs. The trend might be changing, though: the MENA region had a very high MMR in

eradicate poverty, hunger, HIV/AIDS, malaria, and tuberculosis; reduce child mortality; promote gender equality and universal primary education; as well as enhance maternal and environmental health by 2015. In 2016, another seventeen measurable indicators were created (Sustainable Development Goals) to carry on the momentum of the Millennium Development Goals with more specific and culturally sensitive goals to achieve better indicators in health, environment, and gender equality by 2030 (United Nations n.d.).

1990 (115.4–147.8 deaths per 100,000 live births), but there was a remarkable decline in the MMR in 2013 (63.0–97.6 deaths per 100,000 live births) (Kassebaum et al. 2014).

Causes of Maternal Mortality

The risk factors for pregnant women vary drastically and can be medical or nonmedical. Hemorrhage, sepsis, hypertension, obstructed labor, abortion, and uterine rupture are among the most common medical causes of MM (WHO 2012). Furthermore, some noncommunicable diseases, such as diabetes and hypertension, cause several types of maternal morbidities that may result in MM. The causes of MM also vary between regions in the world. Whereas indirect causes and abortion are the primary contributors to most maternal deaths in HICs, direct causes, such as hemorrhages and hypertensive disorders, constitute the leading underlying causes of maternal deaths in the MENA region (Graham et al. 2016). Discrepancies between the LMICs and the HICs as well as differences between countries within the MENA region also exist.

For this reason, an overall regional ratio will not reflect the actual MMR of some countries. For example, estimates show that the MMR of Morocco in 2014–15 was 121 deaths per 100,000 live births, but the MMR of Kuwait was only 4 deaths per 100,000 live births in the same year (Sagynbekov 2018, 6). We must also consider that some MENA countries are in conflict, such as Syria, Palestine, Iraq, Libya, and Yemen. National representative data from those countries are therefore not available.

The Link among Maternal Mortality, Contraception, and Unwanted Pregnancies

MM risk is heightened by the number of pregnancies, the intervals between each pregnancy, and the time when women of reproductive age conceive. Risky pregnancies are higher among women younger than nineteen or older than thirty. The demographic transitions in the MENA region have resulted in more young women being of reproductive age and, hence, more women being likely to experience pregnancy and give birth. Women's role in the economy and society has also been changing, which has been linked to older age at first birth, a risk factor for MM.[3] Women with more than three children and those whose births are closely spaced are also at higher risk of MM. Hence, one strategy to reduce MM among high-risk women is to promote contraception, thereby decreasing fertility rates (Graham et al. 2016). Contraception use reduces the risk of MM by preventing short birth intervals and lowering the possibility of unwanted pregnancies, particularly in countries where abortion services are illegal.

In Jordan, women reported the need for using FP methods, but only 55 percent reported using them (Komasawa et al. 2020). The low contraception use reflects the unmet need for FP, which can be linked to the unavailability of birth-control methods as well as other various cultural and social factors. For instance, the husband's approval was the most significant factor in the Jordanian study. In Lebanon, the unmet need for FP was associated with women at low socioeconomic levels (El Khoury and Salameh 2019). Another dominant reason for the low utilization of contraception methods is the misconceptions about them. Egyptian women who did not use contraception thought that it could lead to cancer, infertility, and congenital disabilities (Eshak 2020). Moreover, the humanitarian crises across the region have led to the unavailability of contraceptive methods, disrupted health systems, sexual violence, and other situations that could lead to unwanted pregnancies (Dias Amaral and Sakellariou 2021). Hence, the unmet need for contraception contributes to the MM in the region.

In addition, studies have shown that unsafe abortion constitutes around 4.7–13.2 percent of maternal deaths globally (Say et al. 2014, e331). When safe abortion is illegal, abortions continue to take place but in septic conditions. Although the Maputo Protocol (2003) recognizes abortion as a human right, only a few countries in the MENA region, such as Sudan, Tunisia, and Algeria, have either signed or ratified the agreement, and even in those countries no application of it has been made. Other

3. Studies show that MM is higher among girls between fifteen and nineteen years old and women older than thirty (Blanc, Winfrey, and Ross 2013).

North African countries, such as Egypt, Libya, and Morocco, have neither signed nor ratified the protocol (Maffi and Tønnessen 2019). The illegality of abortion in the MENA region leads to abortion being underreported. Abortion rates are obtained only from hospitals where postabortion care is provided. Hence, it is challenging to obtain an accurate estimate of maternal deaths linked to unsafe abortions in the region.

Understanding the Social Determinants of Maternal Mortality

As mentioned earlier, SRH is a socially and culturally constructed concept. The outcomes of SRH are the result of interactions among different social, cultural, political, economic, and legal factors. The WHO's conceptual framework for the social determinants of health has identified the various interactions among the different determinants of health, which various studies have used to explain the social determinants of MM (WHO 2010).

Social and gender inequalities lead to poor access to information and health facilities. Poverty and poor access to education can limit women's access to good nutrition and appropriate health-care services (Adgoy 2018; Graham et al. 2016). The sociocultural fabric and gender inequalities can also result in more women being at risk for maternal death owing to limited decision-making power and control over resources (Adgoy 2018). Hence, maternal health and especially maternal mortality can illustrate how social and economic inequalities between and within a country's population groups contribute to MM (Graham et al. 2016).

Moreover, MM is associated with low gross domestic product per capita and the unavailability of trained nurses and midwives. For example, in a study that used data from 2012 to 2015, the highest MMR was found to be in Yemen (385 per 100,000 live births), while the lowest was reported in Kuwait (4 per 100,000 live births) (Doraiswamy et al. 2022). Moreover, most reproductive health services in the MENA region fall far short of the ideal. Not only do some services not exist, but also the quality of the services is not high, and they may not be socially accessible or affordable. In addition, the availability of trained staff and medical personnel at health facilities that can respond to maternal health emergencies is also crucial. Access to technological advances and adequate equipment highly influence the quality of the service provided. In a ten-year analysis conducted

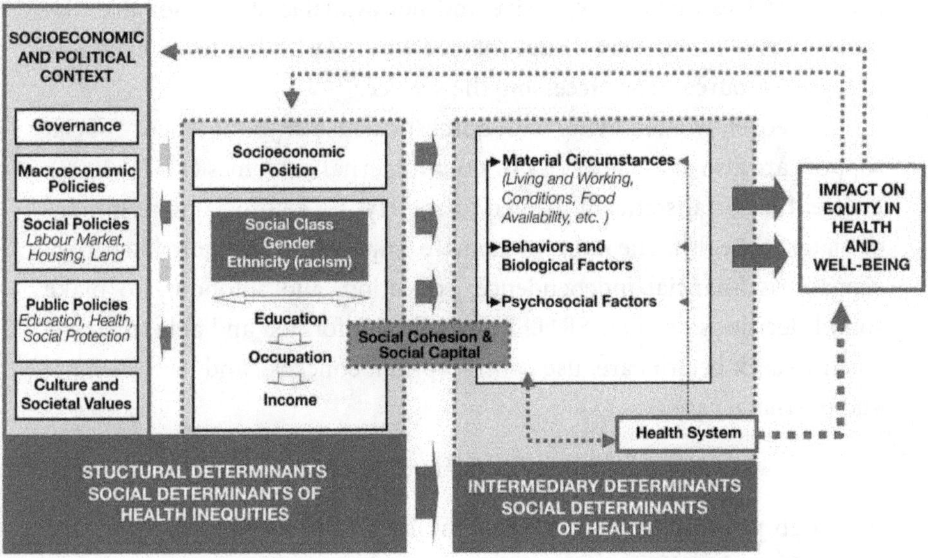

Conceptual framework of the social determinants of health. *Source*: Reproduced from WHO 2010, 6.

in a tertiary hospital in Upper Egypt, around 88 percent of the MM deaths were due to inadequate care provided at the health facility (Mohammed et al. 2020).[4]

However, addressing MM in a complex context, such as the MENA region, requires more than establishing a solid health-care system and providing equipment. Studies show that the functionality of the system—how well designed it is and how well connected it is with other social and economic dimensions—is crucial. Maternal health interventions must address the social structural determinants of MM by improving social and economic policies and using community-based approaches. Studies have shown that even when the health-care sector is well established and the provision of maternal health services exists, other factors contribute to an increase in the risk of death during pregnancy and childbirth. Maternal

4. A tertiary hospital is a hospital dedicated to a specific medical specialization—for example, a maternity hospital.

health services that are expensive and not available at a reasonable distance from home prevent disadvantaged women with low levels of education and resources from accessing the services.

Moreover, women living with domestic abuse or the absence of social support are also at a higher risk of poor maternal outcomes (WHO 2008). Hence, the social status of women in society is a key social determinant of maternal health. The more women are empowered, the more likely they can access financial independence, education, and autonomy to make sound decisions on their SRH. They will be informed and able to decide when to seek health care, use contraception, conceive, and use antenatal and postnatal care.

Maternal Mortality in Humanitarian Crises

Although projections from studies' findings and estimates indicate that the MMR in the MENA region is continuously decreasing, some countries with fragile states are still expected to have a high MMR, such as South Sudan, Yemen, Libya, Syria, and Iraq, due to the disruptions to health-care systems caused by conflict and war (Kassebaum et al. 2014; WHO et al. 2019). The political unrest and the humanitarian crises in some MENA region countries significantly weaken the health-care system, which directly affects maternal health. According to the WHO, more than 50 percent of MMs globally occur in humanitarian crisis settings (WHO n.d.a). UNFPA (2020) has reported more than 500 deaths among women and girls daily for reasons related to pregnancy in humanitarian crisis settings. Humanitarian crises and political unrest create a complex environment that threatens the safety and well-being of girls and women; it compromises the availability of basic life and health needs, including SRH services. Health-care systems that provide such services are usually disrupted or weakened, leaving many areas with no access to primary health care. In addition, the displacement that occurs as a result of the upsurge in violent conflicts leaves many refugees either in limited-resource camps or not eligible for health services as refugees in host countries. In addition, complex humanitarian crisis settings increase the rates of sexual violence, forced and child marriage, unwanted pregnancies, and unsafe abortion, all of which lead to more MM cases. Furthermore, providing medical services in areas of conflict are extremely challenging for international organizations, adding more barriers to girls and women accessing the services.

Examples of Humanitarian Crisis Challenges to SRH in Yemen and Syria

Yemen has been in active conflict since 2014 and is facing one of the most severe humanitarian crises globally, resulting in the highest MMR in the world (International Rescue Committee 2022). MM rose from 5 deaths per day in 2013 to 12 per day in 2018 (*UN News* 2019) and then to an estimated 183 deaths per day in 2020 (WHO 2023b). The active conflict in Yemen prevents SRH services, such as FP methods, and further restricts the public-health sector (Gallagher et al. 2021). In the conflict areas, it is also difficult for Yemen to receive international aid for FP methods and postpartum care. The social determinants of MM mentioned earlier remain constant even in humanitarian crises settings. Yemeni women who died during the intrapartum period were mostly likely to be found in rural areas, to be illiterate, and not to have received necessary antenatal care (Alsharif et al. 2023). Around one million women were expected to deliver in 2023, which put them at serious risk in the current situation (UNFPA 2023).

Similarly, in Syria since the onset of the civil war and the invasion of ISIS, the health-care system has faced various challenges and barriers in reducing the MMR. Hospitals and health facilities were destroyed; health-care professionals were killed, arrested, and banned from providing services; and there has been a shortage of medical equipment and supplies (Butt et al. 2022). Social inequalities such as poor access to education, residency in rural areas, and poor economic status are the main drivers of poor maternal health in Syria (Abdulrahim and Bousmah 2019).

Success Stories from the Region

Even though economic, political, cultural, and other underlying conditions challenge maternal health in the region, there are still some positive cases of addressing MM. For example, in Egypt MM has declined from 174 deaths per 100,000 live births in 1992 to 84 in 2000, 33 in 2015, and 17 in 2020 (Khalil and Roudi-Fahimi 2004; Sagynbekov 2018; WHO et al. 2023). Tunisia has also been strikingly successful, with its MMR declining remarkably from 131 per 100,000 live births in 1990 to 62 in 2015. The same pattern can be observed in Jordan, with MMR showing a significant reduction from 110 deaths per 100,000 live births in 1990 to 58 in 2015 (Sagynbekov 2018).

The significant decline in Egypt can be attributed in part to the initiative led by the Ministry of Health and the Healthy Mother–Healthy Child program implemented by John Snow, Inc. The initiative focused on shifting from home deliveries to hospital deliveries by building the capacity of health-care facilities and medical personnel. The Ministry of Health has also improved the quality of the registration system and data documentation and has further promoted contraception use in Upper Egypt, the country's poorest region (Egyptian Ministry of Health and Population, El-Zanaty and Associates, and ICF International 2015). In Tunisia, deaths related to induced abortions have declined considerably, from 2.3 percent in 1999 to 0.6 percent in 2006, which is the result of the Tunisian law that legalizes medical abortions (Farhat et al. 2012, 167).

Maternal Mortality and Cesarean Deliveries

Aside from the factors described so far, cesarean deliveries are a further risk factor for MM because they are associated with severe maternal morbidities, such as dense adhesions, uterine rupture, and severe bleeding (Souza et al. 2010). In a Tunisian study, around 35 percent of maternal deaths were after C-section deliveries (Farhat et al. 2012, 168). A national Jordanian study also observed the same trend, where 35.5 percent of maternal deaths were associated with C-section deliveries (Amarin et al. 2010, 154). As for Egypt, there is a significant increase in the rate of C-section deliveries compared to the rate of regular deliveries, most notably in the private sector. The proportion of C-sections increased from 32.4 percent to 61.8 percent of the total institution-based deliveries between 2005 and 2014 (al-Rifai 2017, 420), a fourfold increase in the rate of C-section deliveries compared to regular deliveries.[5] Thus, there is a significant urgency for shifting the

5. The percentage of births by C-section were not mentioned in the Jordon and Tunisia studies for the same period. Both studies focused on MM and its predisposing factors.

attention toward eliminating barriers to regular deliveries, particularly for economically and socially disadvantaged mothers. This could be achieved by implementing recent WHO recommendations for interventions, such as providing women with adequate information on C-section deliveries in antenatal care clinics and implementing a hospital-based, structured monitoring/auditing system that provides a mandatory second opinion from senior doctors when a C-section is requested (WHO 2018).

Social Determinants of Infertility in the MENA Region

Infertility is defined as the inability to conceive after at least one year of repetitive sexual intercourse without using contraceptive methods (Hassanin, Abd-El-Raheem, and Shahin 2010). Primary infertility is when a man or a woman is unable to produce one live birth, whereas secondary infertility is defined as the inability to produce an additional live birth (Mascarenhas et al. 2012). In a global study based on secondary data obtained from 277 demographic health surveys using a unified algorithm to measure infertility, it was found that 48.5 million couples around the world are infertile (Mascarenhas et al. 2012). It is probable that the number of infertile couples is considerably higher than this, given that the health survey reached only ever-married women, ignoring unmarried women and men. Global estimates on infertility are not rigorously accurate in LMICs due to the limited number of population-based surveys conducted on infertility, disparities in defining the period needed for diagnosing infertility, and the lack of consistency on how to reach the target population (Rutstein and Shah 2004). For instance, omitting women who use contraception will result in underestimating the actual prevalence of infertility. Moreover, studies that ignore men's infertility and depend solely on estimates obtained from infertile women will also result in biased estimates.

Causes of Infertility

Infertility can be attributed to either female or male factors. In other cases, it is due to unknown causes or to a combination of male and female factors. Etiological causes for infertility vary drastically. They can be categorized into preventable causes—which constitute the majority—and unpreventable causes. Some cases of infertility are idiopathic, which means they cannot be traced back to a specific cause. *Unpreventable causes* of infertility, responsible for only 5 percent of the cases, are attributed mainly to hormonal disturbances, immunological conditions, genetic disorders, and anatomical dysfunctions (Boonmongkon 2002, 281). *Preventable causes* are responsible for around 85 percent of the cases of infertility. They are mainly conditions related to cases of neglected STIs and other reproductive tract infections and inflammatory diseases. For instance, pelvic inflammatory disease can result in fibrosis, adhesions, and severe permanent damage to the fallopian tubes, eventually resulting in infertility (Brunham, Gottlieb, and Paavonen 2015).[6]

In addition, unsafe abortion is the underlying cause of 2 percent of infertility cases, contributing to around 20–30 percent of complicated STI cases (Sharma, Mittal, and Aggarwal 2009, 79). Moreover, septic obstetric and unhygienic practices are significant contributors to infertility. Such practices include unsafe abortion, septic dilation, curettage, insertion of an intrauterine device, and putting herbs and chemicals into the vagina (Sharma, Mittal, and Aggarwal 2009). Unhygienic obstetric interventions eventually lead to reproductive tract infections, resulting in pelvic inflammatory disease and infertility afterward. Malpractice during delivery and in postabortion care in the MENA region is common and plays an essential role in women's life experiences and experiences with medical regimes. Different studies from the region report such malpractice—namely, perineal shaving, the use of manual vacuums, and unnecessary episiotomies (vaginal cuts) to facilitate delivery—and their impact on women's reproductive health (Dabash et al. 2010; Kabakian-Khasholian et al. 2000). For instance, discussions with Egyptian women on obstetric practices reveal recurring vaginal examinations prior to delivery with no medical justification, especially when maternal health care is given in a teaching hospital. Invasive interventions, sutures, and the insertion of foreign bodies into the reproductive tract were also reported (El-Nemer, Downe, and Small 2006). Such practices render women susceptible to

6. Pelvic inflammatory disease is infection-induced inflammation of the female upper reproductive tract; it is usually a complication of neglected and untreated STIs.

postdischarge reproductive tract infections, particularly in health units with poor infection-control standards.

Reasons for male infertility are different from those for female infertility. Environmental agents such as pollutants, exposure to toxins, and heat were found to be associated with male infertility. A case-control study conducted in Lebanon to assess the association between male infertility and exposure to the civil war found that exposure to reproductive toxicants and war-related psychological stresses was 1.57 times higher among infertile men (Kobeissi et al. 2008, 343). Smoking, prevalent among men in the MENA region, also ranked among the highest risk factors for male infertility (Agarwal, Makker, and Sharma 2008).

The Sociocultural Aspect of Infertility

In most of the communities in the region, raising children is associated with social, economic, and even political power and security (Greil, McQuillan, and Slauson-Blevins 2011). For instance, in a region suffering from poverty, meager social security, and medical services, children are a valuable asset to the family's welfare because they inherit family businesses/possessions and take care of aging parents (Dyer 2007). Furthermore, political dynamics vigorously promote pronatalism among communities, especially those of ethnic minorities who aspire to achieve increased political representation (Inhorn 2012). In addition, in such a patriarchal region, bearing numerous children is seen as safeguarding a woman from divorce. It secures a higher status for her and preserves her right to inheritance, especially if most of her children are boys (Inhorn 1996). Although infertility might not be seen as a pathological deficiency, it has become part of the medical domain, whereby medical and pharmaceutical industries compete in developing solutions for it.

Gender and Infertility

Research on infertility in the region has revealed that infertility is gendered. Medical and social anthropologists argue that illnesses are best understood through their cultural context. Although responsibility for infertility is held by both men and women, infertility and ARTs research has historically focused on female infertility, while ignoring male infertility medically and socially (Inhorn and Patrizio 2015). However, addressing infertility from a social perspective sheds light on its underlying determinants, including different social norms, gender roles, and cultural standards; for example, medical research on infertility often focuses on women who seek medical help. Hence, the unit of analysis is mainly a woman who perceives herself as unhealthy for being incapable of fulfilling the social expectation of becoming a mother.

Despite the diversity that countries in the MENA region show regarding language, customs, economic conditions, and political regimes, they share a broad spectrum of cultural norms and social ideologies that identify an infertile woman as a "diseased woman." This identification is supported by some communities' consideration of motherhood as the only social role for women. Despite the region's relatively high prevalence of male infertility, infertility in general—among other reproductive responsibilities—is still seen as a "female problem." Hence, male infertility is rarely addressed. In some conservative cultures, male infertility contradicts the notion of masculinity and is mistakenly linked to impotence. Consequently, research on fertility is biased and suggests underreported male infertility rates (Agarwal, Makker, and Sharma 2008). Scholars believe the prevalence of male infertility in the MENA region to be substantially higher than reported (Inhorn 2012; Kobeissi et al. 2008). However, this problem is not unique to the region. It reflects the lack of research on male infertility on a global level (Forste 2002).

Ethnographic research from the region has also documented how infertile women are stigmatized. In rural Egypt, infertile women are called "Um Ghayeb" (Mother of the Unborn). This form of address links motherhood directly to a woman's social identity. Given that every woman has to be a mother, the childless woman is "the mother of the absent." Therefore, all the blame for the absence of children is put on women. This apportionment of blame may also justify and normalize polygamy and accept harmful rituals to "heal" infertile women as a strategy to conceal male infertility (Agarwal, Makker, and Sharma 2008). *Kabsa*—or *mushahara*, as it is also known—is a classic example of such a ritual and is viewed as the leading cause of female infertility in rural Egypt and Sudan (Inhorn 1994). *Kabsa* means that the infertile woman's reproductive system is "bound," so she needs to go through certain rituals to overcome this boundedness. The rituals usually involve the sharing of blood and other bodily fluids, animals, defloration, and time spent in cemeteries. Men's involvement in the rituals of *kabsa* is minimal, limited mainly to providing blood or other bodily fluids. Women predominantly carry out the rituals for the "afflicted" woman (Inhorn 1994). This ritual symbolizes the dichotomy around infertility in patriarchal societies. The burden of infertility is carried by women, whereby they are responsible for finding solutions for their infertility, and men's involvement is minimal in this journey of healing.

The psychological impact and anxiety associated with infertility are also gendered. Male infertility is seen as a challenge to masculinity. For instance, Marcia Inhorn (2004) reveals how infertile Egyptian men link fertility to manhood, which leads them to perceive themselves as less masculine. Some of them even describe themselves as not being men in reference to their inability to procreate. The social structure of pronatal societies pressures men into having children, in particular sons, to preserve their family titles for the future (Inhorn 1996; Obermeyer 1999b). While male infertility contradicts men's masculine identity, female infertility marginalizes infertile women. A study conducted in Tehran revealed common themes of ostracism, loss of social status and dignity, domestic violence, and marital instability (Hasanpoor-Azghdy et al. 2015). An infertile woman is seen as a bad omen, so she is excluded from social events and gatherings.

Assisted Reproductive Technologies

As mentioned earlier, in the MENA region the sociocultural norms around family size, motherhood, and parenthood have resulted in perceiving infertility as a disease. In the past decade, the medical field has witnessed a remarkable expansion in the delivery of ARTs since the International Federation of Fertility highlighted their importance (Inhorn and Patrizio 2015). ARTs, including in vitro fertilization (IVF), were designed to treat men's infertility and women's fallopian tube obstructive infertility. Despite the expansions in IVF services, they are still inaccessible to large segments of the region's population owing to social, cultural, and economic barriers (Serour 2008b).

Although more than forty-five years have elapsed since the first successful IVF in 1978, the development and growth of IVF clinics in MENA did not happen until the mid-2000s (Inhorn and Patrizio 2015). This slow adoption of IVF in the region is tied to disparities between the countries in the region. Several countries could not access IVF developments because of political unrest and social inequalities. For instance, regional or civil wars between 2003 and 2012 in Yemen, Syria, and Iraq disrupted the health-care systems, causing people to seek medical services elsewhere to solve their infertility (Inhorn and Patrizio 2015), which reflects an unmet need for IVF clinics in some regions. In addition, the cost of such technologies is considerably high, particularly bearing in mind the poor health-care settings and the low-economic status of most countries of the region. This unmet need for IVF applies especially to areas where fertility is highly desired, such as rural areas.

As elsewhere, in the MENA region ARTs are not provided by governments or covered by medical insurance. They are regulated by the private sector (Serour 2008b). However, because of the immense psychological burden of infertility in the region, some countries—for example, the Persian/Arab Gulf countries—have offered ARTs at a subsidized cost (Serour 2008b). Egypt is a leading provider of IVF clinics in the region. Its first IVF clinic was established in 1986 (Inhorn 2012). Despite the flourishing of ARTs in Egypt, however, there are only a few clinics in Cairo that provide IVF at a subsidized cost (Inhorn 2009; Serour 2008b). Iran shows a slightly similar pattern, where the government has started paying attention to infertility and shifted the priority toward providing ARTs even to neighboring countries (Sadeghi 2015). Hence, access to ARTs highlights what should be a crucial concept in public health: the ethical principle of justice and providing health care for all.

On the one hand, health-care services should be accessible to all without excluding any social class, race, or age group. On the other hand, because of limited financial resources and the costly medical procedures of ARTs, some countries have to prioritize and focus their expenditures on more pressing health problems that constitute a more significant burden on their economies (Inhorn and Patrizio 2015; Serour 2008b). However, resource allocation in health usually sounds unethical, primarily when the medical service is restricted to those who can pay. Accordingly, when ARTs are restricted to the upper class in low-resource countries, it may indicate that there is no interest in treating poor people who are experiencing infertility.

Not only financial aspects but also other social and religious factors control the access to ARTs in the MENA region. The cultural and religious context of the region is highly complex. Thus, various forces and ideologies interfere with allowing ARTs care to infertile couples. Current interpretations of religious teachings are a good example. The three prominent religions of the region—Judaism, Christianity, and Islam—maintain a negative attitude toward involving science in procreation (Serour 2008b). Although surrogacy is allowed in Judaism, sperm donation is forbidden for Jews. In Christianity, diverse opinions exist regarding ARTs. Whereas some sects allow ARTs, others tend to oppose gamete donation but allow ARTs for married couples (Serour 2008a). Islamic Sharia has shown differing opinions as well. In general, ARTs are recommended in Sharia within a specific framework, especially when a third person is involved. Sharia also strongly advocates for IVF to be limited to married couples and accordingly disapproves of the use of a dead husband's or wife's gametes. In addition, surrogacy is a heated topic of debate in Islam. It was allowed by the Islamic Fikh Council of Mecca in 1984. However, after al-Azhar Mosque rejected it, the Islamic Fikh Council reversed its decision (Serour 2008a). Whereas Sunni authorities strongly forbid surrogacy, some Shi'a authorities allow it, along with all forms of third-party donation, including sperm donation and oocyte donation (Clarke 2015).

Nonetheless, scrutiny of how religious authorities handle infertility reveals an apparent contradiction. On the one hand, religious texts strongly praise procreation. On the other hand, authorities restrict access to treatments for problems that cause infertility. When the medical guidelines and bylaws that regulate ARTs are based on religious virtue, barriers to access ARTs can be created. Such barriers might have minimal influence in the West, where medical guidelines are secularized. However, religious authorities are often considered the main reference in the MENA region even for nonreligious issues.

In addition, different forms of social inequalities in accessing ARTs go beyond the financial and the religious. For instance, most clinics impose age restrictions on women who request ARTS but not on men (Peterson 2005). Restricting ARTs only to younger women might sound logical, given that women after menopause cannot produce ova. However, a potential solution for this could be egg freezing. However, this option is available only to women with fatal medical conditions and sometimes isn't offered even to them (Abdelwehab and Samy 2017). So-called social oocyte cryopreservation (SOC), or "egg freezing," allows women with no medical condition that threatens their fertility to bear children when their fertility decreases. Although SOC is legalized in Islam, there is a socio-moral debate about it. Some argue that SOC is against human nature as it leads to older women having children, with a significant age gap between mother and child. Such children would therefore be more likely to become orphans early in their lives (Weber-Guskar 2018). However, some might find that SOC provides women with solutions and a higher degree of autonomy to plan their lives freely without the pressure of reaching thirty-five but still being childless. The reality is slowly changing. The United Arab Emirates, for example, has allowed women older than thirty-five to preserve their ova after obtaining the Ministry of Health's approval (Inhorn 2016; Zaman 2017). There are some health concerns about providing IVF for older women because the risk of the procedure might be slightly higher. However, there is no evidence or longitudinal study on births following IVF and SOC together (Weber-Guskar 2018).

The MENA region's sociocultural context does not accept any unconventional form of family that contradicts heteronormativity. Accordingly, a valid marriage between a man and a woman is a prerequisite for providing ART services. This also applies to a widowed woman who wants to conceive with her husband's preserved sperm because, according to religious teachings, their marriage ceased to exist with the husband's death. Discussing ARTs in the MENA region will inevitably lead us to look at the unique use of ARTs in the context of the Palestinian-Israeli conflict. The usage of ARTs in Israel is considered the highest in the world because Israel allows different types of ARTs for Israeli citizens with almost no restrictions. However, in this context ARTs can also refer more to the practice of smuggling sperm as a tool of resistance and rebellion against the Israeli occupation of Palestine.

Male Palestinian prisoners are not allowed conjugal visits (Vertommen 2017), so their sperm is smuggled out of Israeli jails, usually in candy boxes, chocolate bars, or packs of wafers, and their wives use that smuggled sperm to get pregnant. The practice became famous and common after a private ARTs clinic in Ramallah decided to support the Palestinian community by providing this service to the wives of the prisoners who had to be detained for life. Sperm smuggling became socially accepted given that in most cases written approval from the families of both partners is obtained before the procedure is conducted, which is necessary to avoid the shame and dishonor that wives might face when becoming pregnant while their husbands are in jail (Vertommen 2017). Such practices present an example of how ARTs are used to rebel against an Israeli biopolitics that oppresses Palestinians by controlling their fertility and show how conservative communities might become more open to accepting new forms of ARTs to overcome settler-colonial goals (Vertommen 2017).

Reproductive Health of Men: A Neglected Reality

The ICPD shed light on the role of men in reproductive health and how to enhance men's involvement in the SRH of women. The general discourse of the ICPD was perceived as progressive at that time (mid-1990s) in that issues of women's autonomy over their bodies, abandonment of female genital mutilation, and ending gender-based violence were given high priority. The local context in the MENA region, characterized as it is by patriarchy, did not readily embrace the ICPD's progressive tone (El-Dawla 1999). Carla Obermeyer (1999a) found a lack of culturally/politically appropriate terms or definitions in the region for what the ICPD recommended. Accordingly, how the MENA region responded to the ICPD's agenda on men's SRH was also shaped by patriarchy.

There is still no clear definition of what comprises reproductive health for men, in part because reproductive health has become synonymous with FP, maternal health, and other women's health issues (Inhorn 2006). Public-health initiatives in the region focus on men's involvement in FP as a supportive role to women rather than design "men-centered" health programs. Stereotypes around masculinity have also shaped men's perception of their roles and responsibilities regarding SRH (Inhorn and Wentzell 2011). For instance, studies usually focus on health issues that affect men's masculine identity, such as infertility, impotence, and sexual dysfunction. Little to no attention is given to STIs among men, knowledge on how to have good SRH, or men's views about and experiences with parenthood.

Moreover, addressing men in research on STIs and HIV/AIDS in the region is usually associated with blaming men for spreading STIs to their sexual partners. Such research neglects that men are also victims of the infection and disregards more significant inequalities and structural violence (Basu 1996). Speaking of STIs among men brings out an important example of inequality in addressing STIs among sexual minorities, such as gay men and men who have sex with men. Gay men and men who have sex with men not only carry the stigma of being responsible for transmitting STIs to their sexual partners but are also denied access to different health services by health-care workers. The deep-rooted societal and religious stigma around sexual minorities has contributed to systematic discrimination against them in health care (see also chapters 4 and 7 in this volume). Lack of knowledge and men's misperceptions regarding their role in SRH and FP suggest that attention given to SRH is women centered. For example, men in Egypt and Jordan reported a relatively high level of knowledge of women's methods of FP, such as IUDs, oral contraceptive pills, and long-acting injections (Egyptian Ministry of Health and Population, El-Zanaty and Associates, and ICF International 2015; Hamdan-Mansour et al. 2016). However, condoms and vasectomies were the two least frequently mentioned methods of FP in the Jordan survey (Hamdan-Mansour et al. 2016). Calls for involving men in FP were rationalized by the fact that men are traditionally the decision makers in the family. Hence, including men would be associated with better health outcomes in terms of higher usage of FP methods. However, promoting male contraceptive methods was not the core of the initiatives, nor were men the leading target group of these initiatives (Greene et al. 2006). Promoting female contraceptive methods, giving feminine names to infertility clinics, and targeting only women in health campaigns will continue to negatively affect men's SRH (Basu 1996). Furthermore, traditional patriarchal assumptions about women's exclusive responsibility for childbearing have resulted in downplaying men's role in the process.

Conclusion

The MENA region has a significant young-adult population, political unrest, humanitarian crises, and a complex sociocultural fabric that dictates various traditions and norms. Health outcomes, particularly SRH, are products of the interactions among social, cultural, and religious values and customs. Political unrest and economic hardships also shape the environment around access to SRH services because access is usually unequal among different societal groups because of war, poverty, social class, gender, and other factors. SRH in this region is focused on women's reproductive health. Women's sexuality is approached through a patriarchal lens, which limits women's SRH in pregnancy and motherhood. Women in most of the MENA region are still seen as subordinate second-class citizens incapable of being responsible for their own SRH decisions.

More attention should also be given to the SRH of men, marginalized populations, minorities, and youth. In addition, addressing SRH in conservative communities requires strong political will. Governments must effectively collaborate with civil society and the private sector to ensure comprehensive as well as culturally and gender-sensitive SRH services for all. Moreover, SRH services should be designed considering the region's recent dynamic resulting from political conflicts, wars, and humanitarian crises. Finally, it is essential to acknowledge the immense impact of the revolution in information technologies, which has led to remarkable sociocultural changes that have manifested in new relationship trends and sexual behaviors among youth.

References

Abd El-Mawgod, Mohamed M., Shimaa A. Elghazally, Heba M. Mohammed, Mariam Roshdy Elkayat, and Doaa M. M. Osman. 2020. "Views and Attitudes of University Students in Upper Egypt towards Youth Health Centers." *Journal of the Egyptian Public Health Association* 95, no. 1: art. 24.

At https://doi.org/10.1186/s42506-020-00046-x. PMID: 32990875; PMCID: PMC7524945.

Abdelwehab, Samar, and Mahmoud Samy. 2017. "Obstacles Facing Oocyte Cryopreservation in the Middle East." *Obstetrics & Gynecology International Journal* 7, no. 2: art. 00238. At https://doi.org/10.15406/ogij.2017.07.00238.

Abdulrahim, Sawsan, and Marwân-al-Qays Bousmah. 2019. "Regional Inequalities in Maternal and Neonatal Health Services in Iraq and Syria from 2000 to 2011." *International Journal of Health Services* 49, no. 3: 623–41.

Adgoy, E. Teages. 2018. "Key Social Determinants of Maternal Health among African Countries: A Documentary Review." *MOJ Public Health* 7, no. 3: 140–44.

Agarwal, Ashok, Kartikeya Makker, and Rakesh Sharma. 2008. "Clinical Relevance of Oxidative Stress in Male Factor Infertility: An Update." *American Journal of Reproductive Immunology* 59, no. 1: 2–11.

Alsharif, Afaf, Faisal Ahmed, Abdullah M. Almatary, and Mohamed A. Badheeb. 2023. "Maternal Mortality over a Seven-Year Period of Conflict at Jiblah Referral Hospital in Ibb City, Yemen: A Retrospective Observational Study." *Cureus* 15, no. 6: art. e41044. At https://doi.org10.7759/cureus.41044.

Alsubaie, Ali Saad R. 2019. "Exploring Sexual Behaviour and Associated Factors among Adolescents in Saudi Arabia: A Call to End Ignorance." *Journal of Epidemiology and Global Health* 9, no. 1: 76–80. At https://doi.org/10.2991/jegh.k.181210.001.

Amarin, Zouhair, Yousef Khader, Abdelhakeem Okour, Hashim Jaddou, and Raeda al-Qutob. 2010. "National Maternal Mortality Ratio for Jordan, 2007–2008." *International Journal of Gynecology & Obstetrics* 111, no. 2: 152–56.

Asiri, Eman, Mohamed Khalifa, Syed-Abdul Shabir, Md Nassif Hossain, Usman Iqbal, and Mowafa Househ. 2017. "Sharing Sensitive Health Information through Social Media in the Arab World." *International Journal for Quality in Health Care* 29, no. 1: 68–74.

Assaad, Yammine, Iman Khalil, and Pierre Clement. 2011. "Sex Education in Lebanon and France." In *ESERA 2011 Conference: Science Learning and Citizenship*, edited by Andrée Tiberghien and Pierre Clément, 157–62. Lyon, France: ESERA.

Bamimore, Mary Aderayo, Ahmed Zaid, Yajnavalka Banerjee, Ahmad al-Sarraf, Marianne Abifadel, Nabil G. Seidah, Khalid al-Waili, et al. 2015. "Familial Hypercholesterolemia Mutations in the Middle Eastern and North African

Region: A Need for a National Registry." *Journal of Clinical Lipidology* 9, no. 2: 187–94.

Barbour, Bernadette, and Pascale Salameh. 2009. "Consanguinity in Lebanon: Prevalence, Distribution, and Determinants." *Journal of Biosocial Science* 41, no. 4: 505–17.

Basu, AlakaMalwade. 1996. "ICPD: What about Men's Rights and Women's Responsibilities?" *Health Transition Review* 6, no. 2: 225–27.

Beachum, Lateshia. 2019. "Tunisia Launches a State-Sponsored Sex-Education Program, a Rarity in the Arab World." *Washington Post*, Dec. 19. At https://www.washingtonpost.com/world/2019/12/05/tunisia-launches-state-sponsored-sex-education-program-rarity-arab-world/.

Blanc, Ann K., William Winfrey, and John Ross. 2013. "New Findings for Maternal Mortality Age Patterns: Aggregated Results for 38 Countries." *PLOS ONE* 8, no. 4: art. e59864. At https://journals.plos.org/plosone/article?id=10.1371/journal.pone.0059864.

Boonmongkon, Pimpawun. 2002. "Family Networks and Support to Infertile People." In *Current Practices and Controversies in Assisted Reproduction*, report of a meeting on "Medical, Ethical and Social Aspects of Assisted Reproduction" held at WHO headquarters in Geneva, Switzerland, September 17–21, 2001, edited by Effy Vayena, Patrick J. Rowe, and P. David Griffin, 281–86. Geneva: World Health Organization. At https://iris.who.int/bitstream/handle/10665/42576/9241590300.pdf?sequence=1.

Brunham, Robert C., Sami L. Gottlieb, and Jorma Paavonen. 2015. "Pelvic Inflammatory Disease." *New England Journal of Medicine* 372, no. 21: 2039–48.

Butt, Malaika Saeed, Zoaib Habib Tharwani, Muhammad Muzzamil, and Hania Mansoor Rafi. 2022. "Maternal Mortality and Its Prominence in the Syrian Arab Republic: Challenges, Efforts, and Recommendations." *Annals of Medicine and Surgery* 82: art. 104584. At https://doi.org/10.1016/j.amsu.2022.104584. PMID: 36124216; PMCID: PMC9482119.

Center for Reproductive Rights (CRR) and the United Nations Population Fund (UNFPA). 2013. *ICPD and Human Rights: 20 Years of Advancing Reproductive Rights through UN Treaty Bodies and Legal Reform*. New York: CRR. At https://www.unfpa.org/publications/icpd-and-human-rights.

Clarke, Morgan. 2015. "Islamic Bioethics in Transnational Perspective." In *Assisted Reproductive Technologies in the Third Phase: Global Encounters and Emerging Moral Worlds*, edited by Kate Hampshire and Bob Simpson, 30–45. New York: Berghahn.

Dabash, Rasha, Mohamed Cherine Ramadan, Emad Darwish, Nevine Hassanein, Jennifer Blum, and Beverly Winikoff. 2010. "A Randomized Controlled Trial of 400-μg Sublingual Misoprostol versus Manual Vacuum Aspiration for the Treatment of Incomplete Abortion in Two Egyptian Hospitals." *International Journal of Gynecology & Obstetrics* 111, no. 2: 131–35.

El-Dawla, Aida Seif. 1999. "The Political and Legal Struggle over Female Genital Mutilation in Egypt: Five Years since the ICPD." *Reproductive Health Matters* 7, no. 13: 128–36.

DeJong, Jocelyn, Najiaand Bahubaishi, and Bothaina Attal. 2012. "Effects of Reproductive Morbidity on Women's Lives and Costs of Accessing Treatment in Yemen." *Reproductive Health Matters* 20, no. 40: 129–38.

Dias Amaral, Bianca, and Dikaios Sakellariou. 2021. "Maternal Health in Crisis: A Scoping Review of Barriers and Facilitators to Safe Abortion Care in Humanitarian Crises." *Frontiers in Global Women's Health* 2: art. 699121. At https://doi.org/10.3389/fgwh.2021.699121.

Doraiswamy, Sathyanarayanan, Sohaila Cheema, Patrick Maisonneuve, Anupama Jithesh, and Ravinder Mamtani. 2022. "Maternal Mortality in the Middle East and North Africa Region—How Could Countries Move towards Obstetric Transition Stage 5?" *BMC Pregnancy and Childbirth* 22: art. 552. At https://doi.org/10.1186/s12884-022-04886-7.

Dyer, Silke J. 2007. "The Value of Children in African Countries: Insights from Studies on Infertility." *Journal of Psychosomatic Obstetrics & Gynecology* 28, no. 2: 69–77.

Egyptian Ministry of Health and Population, El-Zanaty and Associates, and ICF International. 2015. *Egypt Demographic and Health Survey 2014*. Cairo: Egyptian Ministry of Health and Population; Rockville, MD: ICF International. At https://dhsprogram.com/pubs/pdf/fr302/fr302.pdf.

Egypt Independent. 2022. "Egypt to Integrate Sexual Education into the Basic Curricula." Sept. 17. At https://www.egyptindependent.com/egypt-to-integrate-sexual-education-into-the-basic-curricula/.

Eshak, Ehab. 2020. "Myths about Modern and Traditional Contraceptives Held by Women in Minia, Upper Egypt." *Eastern Mediterranean Health Journal* 26, no. 4: 417–25.

Fahme, Sasha Abdallah, L'Emira Lama El Ayoubi, Jocelyn DeJong, and Maia Sieverding. 2023. "Sexual and Reproductive Health Knowledge among Adolescent Syrian Refugee Girls Displaced in Lebanon: The Role of Schooling and Parental Communication." *PLOS Global Public Health* 3, no. 1: art. e0001437. At https://doi.org/10.1371/journal.pgph.0001437.

Farahani-Khalajabadi, Farideh. 2015. "Unmet Needs of Adolescent and Young People's Sexual and Reproductive Health in Iran." *Journal of Reproduction & Infertility* 16, no. 3: 121–22.

Farhat, Essia Ben, Mohamed Chaouch, Hela Chelli, Mohamed F. Gara, Noureddine Boukraa, Mounira Garbouj, Mongi Hamrouni, et al. 2012. "Reduced Maternal Mortality in Tunisia and Voluntary Commitment to Gender-Related Concerns." *International Journal of Gynecology & Obstetrics* 116, no. 2: 165–68.

Farih, Manal, Khalid Khan, Della Freeth, and Catherine Meads. 2014. "Protocol Study: Sexual and Reproductive Health Knowledge, Information-Seeking Behavior and Attitudes among Saudi Women: A Questionnaire Survey of University Students." *Reproductive Health* 11: art. 34. At https://doi.org/10.1186/1742-4755-11-34.

Forste, Renata. 2002. "Where Are All the Men? A Conceptual Analysis of the Role of Men in Family Formation." *Journal of Family Issues* 23, no. 5: 579–600.

Foster, Angel. 2002. "Young Women's Sexuality in Tunisia: The Health Consequences of Misinformation among University Students." In *Everyday Life in the Muslim Middle East*, 2nd ed., edited by Donna Lee Owen and Evelyn A. Early, 98–110. Bloomington: Indiana Univ. Press.

Foster, Angel M., Lisa Wynn, Aida Rouhana, Chelsea Polis, and James Trussell. 2005. "Reproductive Health, the Arab World and the Internet: Usage Patterns of an Arabic-Language Emergency Contraception Web Site." *Contraception* 72, no. 2: 130–37.

Gallagher, Meghan C., Catherine N. Morris, Aisha Fatima, Rebekah W. Daniel, Abdikani Hirsi Shire, and Bibiche Malilo Matala Sangwa. 2021. "Immediate Postpartum Long-Acting Reversible Contraception: A Comparison across Six Humanitarian Country Contexts." *Frontiers in Global Women's Health* 2: art. 613338. At https://doi.org/10.3389/fgwh.2021.613338.

El-Gelany, Saad, and Ola Moussa. 2013. "Reproductive Health Awareness among Educated Young Women in Egypt." *International Journal of Gynecology & Obstetrics* 120, no. 1: 23–26.

Gerdts, Caitlin, Ozge Tunçalp, Heidi Johnston, and Bela Ganatra. 2015. "Measuring Abortion-Related Mortality: Challenges and Opportunities." *Reproductive Health* 12: art. 87. At https://doi.org/10.1186/s12978-015-0064-1.

Gesser-Edelsburg, Anat, and Munawar Abed Elhadi Arabia. 2018. "Discourse on Exposure to Pornography Content Online between Arab Adolescents and Parents: Qualitative Study on Its Impact on Sexual Education and Behavior." *Journal of Medical Internet Research* 20, no. 10: art. e11667. At https://www.jmir.org/2018/10/e11667/.

Glasier, Anna, A. Metin Gülmezoglu, George P. Schmid, Claudia Garcia Moreno, and Paul F. A. Van Look. 2006. "Sexual and Reproductive Health: A Matter of Life and Death." *The Lancet* 368, no. 9547: 1595–607.

Graham, Wendy, Susannah Woodd, Peter Byass, Veronique Filippi, Giorgia Gon, Sandra Virgo, Doris Chou, et al. 2016. "Diversity and Divergence: The Dynamic Burden of Poor Maternal Health." *The Lancet* 388, no. 10056: 2164–75.

Greene, Margaret E., Manisha Mehta, Julie Pulerwitz, Deirdre Wulf, Akinrinola Bankole, and Susheela Singh. 2006. "Involving Men in Reproductive Health: Contributions to Development." Background paper commissioned by the United Nations Development Project for the report *Public Choices, Private Decisions: Sexual and Reproductive Health and the Millennium Development Goals*, edited by Stan Bernstein, with Charlotte Juul Hansen. New York: United Nations Millennium Project. At https://knowledgecommons.popcouncil.org/cgi/viewcontent.cgi?article=1608&context=departments_sbsr-hiv.

Greil, Arthur, Julia McQuillan, and Kathleen Slauson-Blevins. 2011. "The Social Construction of Infertility." *Sociology Compass* 5, no. 8: 736–46.

Hamdan-Mansour, A. M., A. O. Malkawi, T. Sato, S. H. Hamaideh, and S. I. Hanouneh. 2016. "Men's Perceptions of and Participation in Family Planning in Aqaba and Ma'an Governorates, Jordan." *Eastern Mediterranean Health Journal* 22, no. 2: 124–32. At https://doi.org/10.26719/2016.22.2.124.

Hasanpoor-Azghdy, Syedeh Batool, Masoumeh Simbar, and Abouali Vedadhir. 2015. "The Social Consequences of Infertility among Iranian Women: A Qualitative Study." *International Journal of Fertility & Sterility* 8, no. 4: 409–20. At https://doi.org/10.22074/ijfs.2015.4181.

Hassan, Sherine, and Omar Masoud. 2021. "Online Health Information Seeking and Health Literacy among Non-medical College Students: Gender Differences." *Journal of Public Health* 29: 1267–73.

Hassanin, Ibrahim, Taher Abd-El-Raheem, and Ahmed Y. Shahin. 2010. "Primary Infertility and Health-Related Quality of Life in Upper Egypt." *International Journal of Gynecology & Obstetrics* 110, no. 2: 118–21.

Hogan, Margaret C., Kyle J. Foreman, Mohsen Naghavi, Stephanie Y. Ahn, Mengru Wang, Susanna M. Makela, Alan D. Lopez, et al. 2010. "Maternal Mortality for 181 Countries, 1980–2008: A Systematic Analysis of Progress towards Millennium Development Goal 5." *The Lancet* 375, no. 9726: 1609–23.

Horanieh, Nour, Wendy Macdowall, and Kaye Wellings. 2020. "Abstinence versus Harm Reduction Approaches to Sexual Health Education: Views of Key Stakeholders in Saudi Arabia." *Sex Education* 20, no. 4: 425–40.

Inhorn, Marcia C. 1994. "Kabsa (aka Mushāhara) and Threatened Fertility in Egypt." *Social Science & Medicine* 39, no. 4: 487–505.

———. 1996. *Infertility and Patriarchy: The Cultural Politics of Gender and Family Life in Egypt.* Philadelphia: Univ. of Pennsylvania Press.

———. 2004. "Middle Eastern Masculinities in the Age of New Reproductive Technologies: Male Infertility and Stigma in Egypt and Lebanon." *Medical Anthropology Quarterly* 18, no. 2: 162–82.

———. 2006. "Defining Women's Health: A Dozen Messages from More than 150 Ethnographies." *Medical Anthropology Quarterly* 20, no. 3: 345–78.

———. 2009. "Right to Assisted Reproductive Technology: Overcoming Infertility in Low-Resource Countries." *International Journal of Gynecology & Obstetrics* 106, no. 2: 172–74.

———. 2012. *Local Babies, Global Science: Gender, Religion and In Vitro Fertilization in Egypt.* New York: Routledge.

———. 2016. "Cosmopolitan Conceptions in Global Dubai? The Emiratization of IVF and Its Consequences." *Reproductive Biomedicine & Society Online* 2: 24–31. At https://www.sciencedirect.com/science/article/pii/S2405661816300053.

Inhorn, Marcia C., and Pasquale Patrizio. 2015. "Infertility around the Globe: New Thinking on Gender, Reproductive Technologies and Global Movements in the 21st Century." *Human Reproduction Update* 21, no. 4: 411–26.

Inhorn, Marcia C., and Emily A. Wentzell. 2011. "Embodying Emergent Masculinities: Men Engaging with Reproductive and Sexual Health Technologies in the Middle East and Mexico." *American Ethnologist* 38, no. 4: 801–15.

International Rescue Committee. 2022. "Crisis in Yemen: Protracted Conflict Pushes Yemenis Deeper into Need." Jan. 12. At https://www.rescue.org/article/crisis-yemen-protracted-conflict-pushes-yemenis-deeper-need.

Jaspal, Rusi. 2024. "Islam and Homosexuality: Identity, Threat, and Sexual Well-Being among Muslim Gay Men." In *Sexuality in the Middle East and North*

Africa: Contemporary Issues and Challenges, edited by J. Michael Ryan and Helen Rizzo, 137–60. Syracuse, NY: Syracuse Univ. Press.

Jaspal, Rusi, Ismaël Maatouk, and Moubadda Assi. 2024. "Identity, Mental Health, and Coping among Sexual Minorities in the Middle East and North Africa: The Case of Lebanon." In *Sexuality in the Middle East and North Africa: Contemporary Issues and Challenges*, edited by J. Michael Ryan and Helen Rizzo, 236–58. Syracuse, NY: Syracuse Univ. Press.

Kabakian-Khasholian, Tamar, Oona Campbell, Mona Shediac-Rizkallah, and Françoise Ghorayeb. 2000. "Women's Experiences of Maternity Care: Satisfaction or Passivity?" *Social Science & Medicine* 51, no. 1: 103–13.

Kaddour, Afamia, Raghda Hafez, and Huda Zurayk. 2005. "Women's Perceptions of Reproductive Health in Three Communities around Beirut, Lebanon." *Reproductive Health Matters* 13, no. 925: 34–42.

El-Kak, Faysal. 2013. "Sexuality and Sexual Health: Constructs and Expressions in the Extended Middle East and North Africa." *Vaccine* 31 (Supplement 6): G45–G50. At https://doi.org/10.1016/j.vaccine.2012.10.120.

El-Kak, Faysal, Rema Soweida Afifi, Carol Taljeh, Mayada Kanj, and Mona C. Shediac-Rizkallah. 2001. "High School Students in Postwar Lebanon: Attitudes, Information Sources and Perceived Needs Related to Sexual and Reproductive Health." *Journal of Adolescent Health* 29, no. 3: 153–55.

El-Kak, Faysal, Tamar Kabakian-Khasholian, Walid Ammar, and Anwar Nassar. 2020. "A Review of Maternal Mortality Trends in Lebanon, 2010–2018." *International Journal of Gynecology & Obstetrics* 148, no. 1: 14–20.

Kassebaum, Nicholas J., Amelia Bertozzi-Villa, Megan S. Coggeshall, Katya A. Shackelford, Caitlyn Steiner, Kyle R. Heuton, Diego Gonzalez-Medina, et al. 2014. "Global, Regional, and National Levels and Causes of Maternal Mortality during 1990–2013: A Systematic Analysis for the Global Burden of Disease Study 2013." *The Lancet* 384, no. 9947: 980–1004.

Khalil, Karima, and Farzaneh Roudi-Fahimi. 2004. *Making Motherhood Safer in Egypt*. Washington, DC: MENA Policy Briefs, Population Reference Bureau.

El Khoury, Ghada, and Pascale Salameh. 2019. "Assessment of the Awareness and Usages of Family Planning Methods in the Lebanese Community." *BMJ Sexual & Reproductive Health* 45, no. 4: 269–74.

Kobeissi, Loulou, Marcia C. Inhorn, Antoine B. Hannoun, Najwa Hammoud, Johnny Awwad, and Antoine A. Abu-Musa. 2008. "Civil War and Male Infertility in Lebanon." *Fertility and Sterility* 90, no. 2: 340–45.

Komasawa, Makiko, Motoyuki Yuasa, Yoshihisa Shirayama, Miho Sato, Yutaka Komasawa, and Malak Alouri. 2020. "Demand for Family Planning Satisfied with Modern Methods and Its Associated Factors among Married Women of Reproductive Age in Rural Jordan: A Cross-Sectional Study." *PLOS ONE* 15, no. 3: art. e0230421. At https://doi.org/10.1371/journal.pone.0230421.

Maatouk, Ismael, Moubadda Assi, and Rusi Jaspal. 2023. "Predicting Sexual Risk and Sexual Health Screening in a Sample of University Students in Lebanon: A Cross-Sectional Study." *Journal of American College Health* 71, no. 2: 593–99. At https://doi.org/10.1080/07448481.2021.1899188.

Maffi, Irene, and Liv Tønnessen. 2019. "The Limits of the Law: Abortion in the Middle East and North Africa." *Health and Human Rights Journal* 21, no. 2: 1–6.

Mascarenhas, Maya N., Seth R. Flaxman, Ties Boerma, Sheryl Vanderpoel, and Gretchen A. Stevens. 2012. "National, Regional, and Global Trends in Infertility Prevalence since 1990: A Systematic Analysis of 277 Health Surveys." *PLOS Medicine* 9, no. 12: art. e1001356. At https://doi.org/10.1371/journal.pmed.1001356.

Mohammad, Kazem, Farideh Khalaj Abadi Farahani, Mohammad Reza Mohammadi, Siamak Alikhani, Mohammad Zare, Fahimeh Ramezani Tehrani, Ali Ramezankhani, et al. 2007. "Sexual Risk-Taking Behaviors among Boys Aged 15–18 Years in Tehran." *Journal of Adolescent Health* 41, no. 4: 407–14.

Mohammed, Mo'men M., Saad El Gelany, Ahmed Rida Eladwy, Essam Ibrahium Ali, Mohamed T. Gadelrab, Emad M. Ibrahim, Eissa M. Khalifa, et al. 2020. "A Ten Year Analysis of Maternal Deaths in a Tertiary Hospital Using the Three Delays Model." *BMC Pregnancy and Childbirth* 20: art. 585. At https://doi.org/10.1186/s12884-020-03262-7.

El-Nemer, Amina, Soo Downe, and Neil Small. 2006. "'She Would Help Me from the Heart': An Ethnography of Egyptian Women in Labor." *Social Science & Medicine* 62, no. 1: 81–92.

Obermeyer, Carla Makhlouf. 1999a. "The Cultural Context of Reproductive Health: Implications for Monitoring the Cairo Agenda." *International Family Planning Perspectives* 25 (Supplement): S50–S52, S55. At https://doi.org/10.2307/2991872.

———. 1999b. "Fairness and Fertility: The Meaning of Son Preference in Morocco." In *Dynamics of Values in Fertility Change*, edited by Richard Leete, 275–92. Oxford: Oxford Univ. Press.

Oraby, Doaa M. 2013. "Sexual and Reproductive Health among Young People in Egypt: The Role and Contribution of Youth-Friendly Services." *Sex Education* 13, no. 4: 470–77.

Peterson, Madelyn M. 2005. "Assisted Reproductive Technologies and Equity of Access Issues." *Journal of Medical Ethics* 31, no. 5: 280–85.

Riad, Germeen, and Carie L. Forden. 2021. "'If We Didn't Talk, We Would Be Like Ostriches Burying Our Heads in the Sand': Attitudes toward Sexuality, Gender, and Sex Education among Child Protection Social Workers in Egypt." *Children and Youth Services Review* 129: art. 106205. At https://doi.org/10.1016/j.childyouth.2021.106205.

Al-Rifai, Rami H. 2017. "Trend of Caesarean Deliveries in Egypt and Its Associated Factors: Evidence from National Surveys, 2005–2014." *BMC Pregnancy and Childbirth* 17, no. 1: 417–30.

Roudi-Fahimi, Farzaneh. 2003. *Women's Reproductive Health in the Middle East and North Africa*. Washington, DC: MENA Policy Briefs, Population Reference Bureau.

Roushdy, Rania, and Maia Sieverding. 2015. *Panel Survey of Young People in Egypt (SYPE) 2014: Generating Evidence for Policy, Programs, and Research*. Cairo: Population Council. At https://doi.org/10.31899/pgy9.1070.

Rutstein, Shea Oscar, and Iqbal H. Shah. 2004. *Infecundity, Infertility, and Childlessness in Developing Countries*. DHS Comparative Reports no. 9. Geneva: World Health Organization.

Sadana, Ritu. 2002. "Definition and Measurement of Reproductive Health." *Bulletin of the World Health Organization* 80, no. 5: 407–9.

Sadeghi, Mohammad Reza. 2015. "Access to Infertility Services in Middle East" (editorial). *Journal of Reproduction & Infertility* 16, no. 4: 179.

Sagynbekov, Ken. 2018. *Childhood and Maternal Health in the Middle East and North Africa*. Santa Monica, CA: Milken Institute. At https://assets1b.milkeninstitute.org/assets/Publication/ResearchReport/PDF/Childhood-and-Maternal-Health-in-MENA.pdf.

Say, Lale, Doris Chou, Alison Gemmill, Özge Tunçalp, Ann-Beth Moller, Jane Daniels, A. Metin Gülmezoglu, et al. 2014. "Global Causes of Maternal Death: A WHO Systematic Analysis." *The Lancet Global Health* 2, no. 6: e323–e333.

Serour, Gamal I. 2008a. "Islamic Perspectives in Human Reproduction." *Reproductive BioMedicine Online* 17 (Supplement 3): 34–38. At https://doi.org/10.1016/S1472-6483(10)60328-8.

———. 2008b. "Medical and Socio-cultural Aspects of Infertility in the Middle East." *ESHRE Monographs* 2008, no. 1: 34–41. At https://doi.org/10.1093/humrep/den143.

Sharma, S., S. Mittal, and P. Aggarwal. 2009. "Management of Infertility in Low Resource Countries." *BJOG: An International Journal of Obstetrics & Gynecology* 116, no. S1: 77–83.

Shneor, Rotem, Selin Metin Camgöz, and Pinar Bayhan Karapinar. 2013. "The Interaction between Culture and Sex in the Formation of Entrepreneurial Intentions." *Entrepreneurship & Regional Development* 25, nos. 9–10: 781–803.

Sippel, Serra. 2014. "ICPD beyond 2014: Moving beyond Missed Opportunities and Compromises in the Fulfilment of Sexual and Reproductive Health and Rights." *Global Public Health* 9, no. 6: 620–30.

Souza, Joao P., A. M. Gülmezoglu, Pisake Lumbiganon, Malinee Laopaiboon, Guillermo Carroli, Bukola Fawole, and P. Ruyan. 2010. "Caesarean Section without Medical Indications Is Associated with an Increased Risk of Adverse Short-Term Maternal Outcomes: The 2004–2008 WHO Global Survey on Maternal and Perinatal Health." *BMC Medicine* 8: art. 71. At https://doi.org/10.1186/1741-7015-8-71.

Sphere Project. 2011. *The Sphere Project: Humanitarian Charter and Minimum Standards in Humanitarian Response.* Northampton, UK: Belmont Press/Sphere Project. At https://www.cpcnetwork.org/wp-content/uploads/2014/06/Measuring-Violence-Against-Children-in-Humanitarian-Settings-FINAL-REPORT.pdf.

United Nations. n.d. "Department of Economic and Social Affairs: Sustainable Development: The 17 Goals." At https://sdgs.un.org/goals.

United Nations Population Fund (UNFPA). 2020. "Minimum Initial Service Package (MISP) for SRH in Crisis Situations." Nov. At https://www.unfpa.org/resources/minimum-initial-service-package-misp-srh-crisis-situations.

———. 2023. *UNFPA Response in Yemen Situation Report #1: January–March 2023.* New York: UNFPA. At https://www.unfpa.org/sites/default/files/resource-pdf/UNFPA%20Yemen%20-%20Situation%20Report%20-%20Jan%20-%20Mar%202023.pdf.

UN News. 2019. "Yemen: Maternal and Newborn Health 'on the Brink of Total Collapse,' UNICEF Alerts." June 14. At https://news.un.org/en/story/2019/06/1040531.

Vakilian, Katayon, and Khadijeh Mirzaei Najmabadi. 2011. "Reproductive Health in Iran: International Conference on Population and Development Goals." *Oman Medical Journal* 26, no. 2: 143–47.

van Clief, Lindsay, and Elianne Anemaat. 2020. "Good Sex Matters: Pleasure as a Driver of Online Sex Education for Young People." *Gates Open Research* 3: art. 1480. At https://doi.org/10.12688/gatesopenres.13003.2.

Vertommen, Sigrid. 2017. "Babies from behind Bars: Stratified Assisted Reproduction in Palestine/Israel." In *Assisted Reproduction across Borders: Feminist Perspectives on Normalizations, Disruptions and Transmissions*, edited by Merete Lie and Nina Lykke, 225–36. New York: Routledge.

Wahba, Mamdouh, and Farzaneh Roudi-Fahimi. 2012. *The Need for Reproductive Health Education in Schools in Egypt*. Washington, DC: MENA Policy Briefs, Population Reference Bureau. At https://www.prb.org/wp-content/uploads/2021/02/10102012-reproductivehealth-education-egypt.pdf.

Weber-Guskar, Eva. 2018. "Debating Social Egg Freezing: Arguments from Phases of Life." *Medicine, Health Care and Philosophy* 21, no. 3: 325–33.

World Health Organization (WHO). 2002. *World Report on Violence and Health*. Geneva: WHO. At https://apps.who.int/iris/bitstream/handle/10665/42495/9241545615_eng.pdf?sequence=1.

———. 2008. *Building the Knowledge Base on the Social Determinants of Health: Review of Seven Countries in the Eastern Mediterranean Region*. Geneva: WHO. At https://iris.who.int/bitstream/handle/10665/119880/dsa939.pdf?sequence=1.

———. 2010. *A Conceptual Framework for Action on the Social Determinants of Health*. Geneva: WHO. At https://apps.who.int/iris/handle/10665/44489.

———. 2012. *The WHO Application of ICD-10 to Deaths during Pregnancy, Childbirth and the Puerperium: ICD-MM*. Geneva: WHO. At https://apps.who.int/iris/bitstream/handle/10665/70929/9789241548458_eng.pdf?sequence=1.

———. 2014. *Health for the World's Adolescents: A Second Chance in the Second Decade*. Geneva: WHO. At https://iris.who.int/bitstream/handle/10665/112750/WHO_FWC_MCA_14.05_eng.pdf?sequence=1.

———. 2018. *WHO Recommendations: Non-clinical Interventions to Reduce Unnecessary Caesarean Sections*. Geneva: WHO. At https://apps.who.int/iris/bitstream/handle/10665/275377/9789241550338-eng.pdf.

———. 2023a. "Maternal Mortality." *World Health Organization Newsroom*, Feb. 22. At https://www.who.int/news-room/fact-sheets/detail/maternal-mortality.

———. 2023b. "WHO Advocacy to Empower Female Health Workers in Yemen." *WHO in Yemen News*, Mar. 28. At https://www.emro.who.int/yemen/news/who-advocacy-to-empower-female-health-workers-in-yemen.html.

———. n.d.a. "Children in Humanitarian Settings." At https://www.who.int/teams/maternal-newborn-child-adolescent-health-and-ageing/child-health/children-in-humanitarian-settings#:~:text=Approximately%2050%25%20of%20maternal%2C%20newborn,even%20experience%20neglect%20and%20maltreatment.

———. n.d.b. "Maternal Mortality Ratio (per 100,000 Live Births)." At https://www.who.int/data/gho/indicator-metadata-registry/imr-details/26.

World Health Organization (WHO), United Nations Children's Fund (UNICEF), United Nations Population Fund (UNFPA), World Bank Group, and the United Nations Department of Economic and Social Affairs Population Division. 2019. *Trends in Maternal Mortality: 2000–2017 (Executive Summary).* Geneva: WHO. At https://www.unfpa.org/sites/default/files/resource-pdf/Maternal_mortality_exec_summary.pdf.

———. 2023. *Trends in Maternal Mortality: 2000 to 2020 (Executive Summary).* Geneva: WHO. At https://iris.who.int/bitstream/handle/10665/372247/9789240069251-eng.pdf?sequence=1.

Al Zaabi, Omar, Margaret Heffernan, Eleanor Holroyd, and Mervyn Jackson. 2019. "Islamic Parents' Attitudes and Beliefs towards School-Based Sexual and Reproductive Health Education Programmes in Oman." *Sex Education* 19, no. 5: 534–50.

———. 2022. "Parent–Adolescent Communication about Sexual and Reproductive Health Including HIV and STIs in Oman." *Sex Education* 22, no. 5: 611–27.

Zaman, Samihah. 2017. "Egg and Sperm Freezing Growing among Unmarried in UAE." *Gulf News*, July 30. At https://gulfnews.com/uae/health/egg-and-sperm-freezing-growing-among-unmarried-in-uae-1.2066583.

Zurayk, Huda. 2001. "The Meaning of Reproductive Health for Developing Countries: The Case of the Middle East." *Gender & Development* 9, no. 2: 22–27.

7

Identity, Mental Health, and Coping among Sexual Minorities in the Middle East and North Africa

The Case of Lebanon

Rusi Jaspal, Ismaël Maatouk,
and Moubadda Assi

In contrast to the significant advances that have been made in relation to the rights and well-being of sexual minorities in many Western societies, countries in the Middle East and North Africa (MENA) can be hostile and even dangerous environments for sexual minorities. Even in the more liberal countries in the MENA region, such as Lebanon and Jordan, sexual minorities may face stigma, harassment, and persecution. In addition to their state-sanctioned stigmatization, they are socialized within social, cultural, and religious contexts in which the family is central to identity, and, thus, family honor is of utmost importance (Kazarian 2005; Maatouk and Jaspal 2022), and contravention of the coercive norm of compulsory heterosexuality may be seen as a threat to family honor. Socialization within a cultural context in which one's sexual orientation is constructed as being morally flawed can lead sexual minorities to internalize these beliefs at a psychological level, to conceal their identity from others as a self-protection strategy, and, in some cases, to pass themselves off as heterosexual. According to dominant theories from social psychology, stigma at multiple levels (i.e., institutional, communal, and social) can result in threats to social and psychological well-being and precipitate modifications to one's sense of identity. However, data concerning the lives, identities, and well-being of sexual minorities specifically in MENA are scarce. Through the lens of minority stress theory (Meyer 2003) and identity process theory (Jaspal and Breakwell 2014), this chapter focuses on the interactions of identity, mental health, and coping among sexual minorities in MENA, with a particular focus on Lebanon. More specifically, the ways in which sexual minorities construct and protect their sense of identity in the face of social psychological stressors are examined.

MENA Region: Social, Cultural, Religious, and Political Aspects

The MENA region covers a wide geographical area stretching from Morocco to Iran and encompasses many distinct social, cultural, religious, and political identities. The region includes low-, medium- and high-income countries. Countries in MENA have distinct political systems, ranging from multiparty democracies to absolute monarchies. It is thus difficult to generalize about the region. Various countries in the MENA have faced significant political and economic instability and demographic changes, which have undoubtedly had a negative effect on the psychological well-being of the general population (Jaspal, Assi, and Maatouk 2020). This psychological stress has been further accentuated by the increasing economic problems with which local populations have been confronted. Indeed, in Lebanon, devaluation of the local currency and the collapse of the banking system have led to significant job insecurity, poverty, and uncertainty about the future. The outbreak of COVID-19 in Lebanon and across the region in March 2020 and the lockdown measures that followed it resulted in further detriment to the economy and, indeed, to psychological well-being (Maatouk, Assi, and Jaspal 2022a).

Countries within the MENA region vary in their treatment of sexual minorities. For instance, several countries utilize sodomy laws or constitutional interpretation to arrest, imprison, and persecute gay and bisexual men (Simmons 2010). Egypt serves as a case in point: despite the absence of laws forbidding homosexuality in Egypt, sixty men were detained on the Queen Boat in 2001 for homosexual acts (Awwad 2010). Other countries, such as Sudan, Saudi Arabia, Yemen, Qatar, Kuwait, and Iran, do have legislation prohibiting homosexuality (Ungar 2002). There have been numerous reports of neighbors disappearing, friends being arrested, and accusations of homosexuality being leveled against individuals, which can lead people to fear for their safety. In these societies, (suspected) sexual minorities may be rejected, ostracized, and harassed (Simmons 2010). Only one country in the MENA region, Jordan, has decriminalized same-sex behavior. However, sexual minorities remain marginalized in Jordanian society, and there are claims that government institutions still persecute sexual minorities and the organizations that support them (Movahedi 2017).

The main focus of this chapter is Lebanon. When compared to other MENA countries, Lebanon is widely considered to be relatively tolerant of sexual minorities. Its capital city, Beirut, is one of the most socially progressive cities in the region, with a vibrant gay community as well as gay bars, clubs, and community centers. Although geographically and culturally located in the Middle East, Lebanon has had significant European influences and retains a relatively strong cultural connection with Europe, in particular France.

Having been a French protectorate, Lebanon gained its independence from the French Republic in 1943. Between 1943 and 1975, Lebanon was one of a small minority of democratic states in the MENA region and espoused a tolerant stance on religious and cultural diversity. However, in 1975 the Lebanese Civil War, a bloody and protracted sectarian conflict, began. It, in turn, led to the collapse of the Lebanese government, and by 1990 more than a million Lebanese citizens had been uprooted from their homes and ninety thousand had lost their lives (Labaki and Abou Rjeily 1994). The Lebanese Civil War radically changed the demographic profile of Lebanon, although the country is still home to various religious communities, including Christian Maronites, Greek Catholics, Greek Orthodox, Sunni and Shiʿa Muslims, and Druze. Moreover, the Civil War weakened both the political and economic structures of Lebanon and led to a fragmentation of Lebanese national identity. Citizens came to see themselves first and foremost as members of their respective religious groups, which were in turn entwined with political interests. The content of Lebanese national identity continues to be debated, and its precariousness is regularly demonstrated in the face of geopolitical events in the MENA region.

Religion is a powerful identity in most MENA societies, including in Lebanon. Although Islam is by far the most prominent religion in the region, it is practiced differently in the region's various countries. Furthermore, several MENA countries have significant Christian and other religious minorities. Religion is widely rated as being an important identity by citizens in MENA countries, and the social representations associated with religion often guide people's sense making and worldview (e.g., Hoffman 2020). Religious attitudes toward homosexuality are generally negative, and homosexuality is often constructed as being contrary to Abrahamic religious doctrine (Kugle 2009). However, it must be noted that societal attitudes toward homosexuality are complex: in some MENA societies, same-sex desire (especially male bisexuality) is silently tolerated, and labels such as *gay* and *bisexual* are not routinely used due to their association with Western societies (Maatouk and Jaspal 2020).

Religious discourse has been widely drawn upon to substantiate the negative stance on homosexuality in Lebanese society. This is true of all religious groups in Lebanon, which, despite their political differences, have generally converged in their opposition to sexual minorities in the country. Like many MENA countries, Lebanon has a problematic track record on sexual-minority rights. According to Article 534 of the Lebanese Penal Code of 1943, sexual relations that "contradict the law of nature" are prohibited by law, and those found guilty of this offense (which can include homosexual relations) may face up to a year in prison (Human Rights Watch 2018; Makarem 2011). Although this law has occasionally been used to harass, persecute, and sometimes prosecute sexual minorities, it is not widely enforced, and several senior Lebanese lawmakers have indeed disputed the law and the degrading investigative practices (e.g., anal examinations) it facilitates.

Social Representations of Homosexuality

Social representations of homosexuality in MENA countries are generally very negative (Roscoe and Murray 1997). In addition to religious institutions, dominant channels of societal information, such as Lebanese television and the media, contribute to the stigmatization of sexual minorities. In their analysis of Lebanese television shows, series, and interviews, Aya

Touma Sawaya and Antoine Beayno (2021) found that sexual minorities were generally subjected to prejudice and hostility and were represented as a vulnerable group, which might fuel prejudice and homonegativity in the general population. Moreover, in their cross-national study of newspaper representations of homosexuality, Amy Adamczyk, Chunrye Kim, and Margaret Schmuhl (2018) found that in Lebanese periodical articles, same-sex relations and desire were often associated with other stigmatized issues, such as drug addiction and sex parties. It is easy to see how this discursive "coupling" of stigmatized issues might promote a social representation that homosexuality is immoral and socially detrimental.

Indeed, public-opinion research shows this to be the case. A study conducted in 2013 revealed that 80 percent of the Lebanese respondents did not believe that homosexuality was acceptable (Horowitz et al. 2013, 22). Sahar Obeid and colleagues (2020) conducted an attitudinal survey of four hundred heterosexual individuals in Lebanon and found that almost a third of the sample had highly homophobic attitudes. Demographic factors, such as higher income and level of education, and knowing someone who is gay were associated with lower homophobia. In view of the negative social representations of homosexuality in Lebanese society, many sexual-minority individuals conceal their sexuality from others, which in turn may decrease the general likelihood of knowing someone who is gay.

Yet despite the social, religious, and political constraints on open expressions of sexual-minority identities, many do find ways of enacting their sexual identities (see also Jaspal 2014). Beirut has a relatively vibrant LGBT community, and there are venues where sexual minorities can meet, socialize, and derive social support from one another. Moreover, online gay social networking sites and apps are pervasively used among sexual minorities. Many take advantage of these opportunities for interpersonal engagement and social support. However, not everyone has the level of self-acceptance that might lead to engagement with these spaces; some sexual minorities struggle to assimilate and accommodate their sexuality into their identities and refuse to engage with others who share their sexual orientation. They may fear involuntary disclosure of their sexuality. More generally, it must be noted that Beirut is by no means representative of the whole of Lebanon or, indeed, of MENA, which is generally intolerant of homosexuality and devoid of a "gay culture" in a Western sense.

Dominant social representations of homosexuality also shape the nature and quality of service provision, including health care. While trying to accommodate homosexuality into their identity, sexual minorities may seek mental health care. Negative experiences in a health-care context may result in long-term maladaptive coping (e.g., Jolley and Jaspal 2020). Studies have yielded conflicting findings. For instance, in their study of 141 health-care providers in Lebanon, Hady Naal and colleagues (2020) found that the vast majority of health-care participants exhibited positive attitudes and behaviors toward sexual minorities and that mental health professionals were especially likely to reject the social representation that homosexuality constitutes a mental disorder. In contrast, Hasan Abdessamad and Omar Fattal (2014) reported that only half of the health-care practitioners surveyed in their study on Lebanon were willing to address the medical needs of sexual minorities, highlighting a deep-rooted stigma toward this community in their sample. Moreover, there was a widespread social representation that homosexuality was a disease requiring reparative therapy.

In a similar vein, Sarah Abboud and colleagues (2020) conducted a content analysis of interviews with thirteen sexual-minority individuals and community-based organizations and found that there was widespread anticipation of discrimination in relation to health care. The authors argue that there is a need for affirmative health-care educational and training programs with respect to sexual minorities and that effective collaboration between community-based organizations and health-care institutions is required to improve both access to health care for sexual minorities and effective delivery of health care to this population.

In view of widespread societal stigma toward sexual minorities in Lebanon, they may face social and psychological challenges in relation to their sexual orientation. Some empirical studies of gay and bisexual men in Lebanon provide important insight into the lived experiences of sexual minorities. Indeed, key work in this area is summarized in this chapter. It is noteworthy that there has generally been less focus on the lived experiences, identities, and well-being of other sexual-minority groups, such as lesbians and bisexual men and women (see also chapter 5 in this volume for an overview of trans identity in the MENA region).

Stressors and Identity Processes

Social psychology has much to offer the study of social representation, identity, and well-being among sexual minorities in Lebanon. Minority stress theory (Meyer 2003) has become an important theoretical framework for examining the impact of "stressors" associated with one's minority identity. Stressors include events, situations, and widespread societal perceptions that can lead to psychological stress. Despite the considerable diversity that characterizes sexual minorities, experiences of stigma, prejudice, and discrimination are remarkably common, although they may be manifested to varying degrees. It is thus argued in minority stress theory that sexual minorities face stress that is unique to them and additive (over and above the habitual stressors that people in the general population face); chronic because it is rooted in long-standing and relatively stable social and cultural structures; and socially based because it arises from social processes, institutions, and representations rather than from individual characteristics. The theory identifies three processes of minority stress: external events and conditions that cause stress; the expectation of such events and conditions and the vigilance that this expectation can create in the minority individual; and the internalization of the general stigma directed toward sexual minorities.

According to minority stress theory, the interaction between identity and stress is key to understanding well-being in sexual minorities. More specifically, it is hypothesized that stress because of one's sexual-minority status has a greater psychological impact in individuals with a stronger commitment to their sexual-minority (i.e., gay, lesbian, or bisexual) identity. Identity process theory (Breakwell 2015; Jaspal 2018; Jaspal and Breakwell 2014) enables us to examine the impact of stressors, such as stigmatizing social representations, homonegativity, and victimization, on the construction, operation, and management of identity. (The theory is outlined in detail in chapter 4 of this volume.)

Unlike westernized societies, where independence and detachment from the nuclear family may be sought at an early age, Lebanon is regarded as a collectivist society in which family and cultural norms prevail. With family ranking very highly as a primary social institution, young people in Lebanon may feel compelled to conform to dominant norms that satisfy family expectations. Otherwise, they may experience the pressure of stigma and rejection. Therefore, both the construction and expression of identity among homosexuals in Lebanon can be subjected to a hefty negotiation that may delay or inhibit sexual identity expression. Acceptance by one's family is thus likely to be central to the construction of a positive sense of identity that is characterized by self-esteem, self-efficacy, continuity, and positive distinctiveness (Maatouk and Jaspal 2022).

Recent developments in identity process theory have focused on the concept of identity resilience (Breakwell, Fino, and Jaspal 2022; Breakwell and Jaspal 2022; Jaspal and Breakwell 2022). "Identity resilience" refers to the extent to which the individual perceives their identity to be characterized by feelings of self-esteem, self-efficacy, continuity, and positive distinctiveness. This is essentially a trait in that individuals will develop a general sense of their overall level of the four prime identity principles based on many factors, including their past experiences, personality traits, and social context. As a trait, identity resilience has been found to affect the extent to which one experiences identity threat, with higher identity resilience being related to lower identity threat (Lopes and Jaspal 2022). The trait also influences the adoption of more effective coping strategies (Jaspal, Assi, and Maatouk 2022). Put simply, a person with high baseline identity resilience may be less susceptible to identity threat when exposed to a hazard to identity (that is, a stressor). They may be more resistant to stressors with the potential to induce identity threat and have greater access to varied and effective coping strategies, potentially extinguishing the hazard before it becomes a fully-fledged threat to identity. In the next section, a significant stressor associated with gay identity is discussed: internalized homonegativity.

Internalized Homonegativity

Identity process theory posits that assimilation-accommodation and evaluation are key processes of identity construction. In view of the negative social representations of homosexuality that permeate Lebanese society, sexual minorities may have limited scope for appending positive value to their sexuality and may in fact internalize the negative social representations they encounter. It has been found that internalized homonegativity among Lebanese sexual minorities is associated with higher religiosity, parental rejection, and vigilance as well as with a lower sense of belonging to the LGBT community (Michli and El Jamil 2022). Given the importance of the family in the collectivist society of Lebanon, parental stigma toward one's sexual orientation may lead one to internalize this stigma. Furthermore, as outlined earlier in this chapter, religion does appear to constitute a major source of negative social representations of homosexuality (Schuck and Liddle 2001). This may present something of a dilemma: religion is a powerful force in Lebanese society and a primary component of identity, but it is clearly also a source of identity threat with regard to sexuality.

Although there is limited research in the MENA region concerning lesbians and bisexual men and women, it has been found elsewhere that bisexual men may be at greater risk of internalized homonegativity than gay men (Feinstein and Dyar 2017; Maatouk and Jaspal 2022). More specifically, bisexual men may face marginalization from both heterosexuals and gay men, who may negate their bisexual identity and expect them to adopt either a heteronormative or a gay lifestyle (Dodge et al. 2016). In view of these social pressures, it could be hypothesized both that bisexual men internalize the stigma that they encounter in relation to their sexual orientation and that they are less likely to disclose their bisexuality to other people.

Minority stress theory suggests that exposure to distal and proximal stressors, such as internalized homonegativity, may result in poor mental health outcomes. In other societies, internalized homonegativity has been shown to be associated with a variety of poor mental health outcomes, including depression, anxiety, insecure attachment styles, substance-use disorders, self-harm, and suicidal ideation (Frost and Meyer 2009; Jaspal, Lopes, and Rehman 2021). In Lebanon, there is evidence that sexual minorities, including gay and bisexual men, face greater psychological distress (Assi, Maatouk, and Jaspal 2020), more disordered eating patterns (Naamani and El Jamil 2021), and higher rates of depression

(Wagner, Ghosh-Dastidar, et al. 2019) than heterosexuals. Conversely, self-acceptance and outness have been found to be related to better mental health outcomes (Michli and El Jamil 2022; Wagner, Ghosh-Dastidar, et al. 2019). As research has shown, when one accepts one's identity and expresses a willingness to disclose it to others, one is more likely to access both positive social representations and social support (Jaspal and Breakwell 2014).

A study of mental health based on data from two hundred gay and bisexual men in Lebanon in 2022 found that bisexual men were more likely than gay men to be expected by their family to have a heterosexual marriage and that bisexual men reported lower overall levels of "outness" than gay men (Maatouk and Jaspal 2022). In other words, they had disclosed their sexual identity to fewer people, and even if they had disclosed it, it was acknowledged infrequently. Furthermore, those who reported being expected by their family to have a heterosexual marriage also exhibited higher internalized homonegativity and lower outness than those who did not face this family expectation. The study concludes that being bisexual was also associated with increased likelihood of exhibiting internalized homonegativity. Religiosity was related to increased internalized homonegativity, on the one hand, but attending a place of worship was associated with decreased depression and anxiety, on the other. These findings reveal an important pattern—namely, that dominant-group memberships (such as in one's religion and ethnicity) are facilitators of effective coping in the face of psychological stressors, but that, overall, sexual minorities have decreased access to these group memberships. Furthermore, under close scrutiny it appears that some subgroups of sexual minorities (i.e., bisexual men) are at disproportionately high risk of poor well-being outcomes. As a negative self-schema, internalized homonegativity is associated with poor mental health (Herek and McLemore 2007).

Mental Health

The World Health Organization aptly defines mental health as "a state of well-being in which an individual realizes his or her own abilities, can cope with the normal stresses of life, can work productively and is able to make a contribution to his or her community" (2013, 38). Thus, mental health is not just the absence of disorders, such as depression, anxiety, and psychological distress. To promote good mental health, it is important to identify possible indicators of poor mental health (such as psychological distress), the risk factors for developing poor mental health (such as chronic identity threat), and, indeed, protective factors (such as sense of community).

As an indicator of poor mental health, psychological distress is defined as an "unpleasant emotional experience of a psychological (i.e., cognitive, behavioral, emotional) and/or social nature that interferes with an individual's ability to effectively cope with a given situation" (Sellick and Edwardson 2007, 535). It can be transient or chronic. According to identity process theory, psychological distress can arise in response to identity threat, especially when the threat is severe, unresolved, and chronic (Jaspal 2018). Indeed, in various studies, identity threat and psychological distress are positively correlated (e.g., Assi, Maatouk, and Jaspal 2020; Breakwell and Jaspal 2022; Jaspal, Lopes, et al. 2021). Psychological distress can have significant implications for both physical and psychological health (Ozbay et al. 2007). When psychological distress arises in response to specific events, the key to stable mental health is for the individual to possess the social and psychological resources to overcome this negative psychological experience. In the absence of such resources, psychological distress can become chronic and adversely affect the individual's long-term mental health.

There are observed sex differences in relation to psychological distress. Previous research conducted in Lebanon generally suggests that women report higher and more severe psychological distress than men (Ayyash-Abdo and Alamuddin 2007; Barbour, Saadeh, and Salameh 2012). However, Taha Itani, Florian Fischer, and Janet Junqing Chu found a 70 percent prevalence of exposure to community violence in Lebanese young adults (both men and women) that was also associated with psychological distress (2018, 262). These findings suggest that within sexual-minority groups, lesbian and bisexual women may be especially susceptible to psychological distress. The multitude of stressors prevalent in the Lebanese context, such as communal tensions, violence, war, and, more recently, the COVID-19 pandemic (and its negative sequelae), is likely to affect the entire population.

There is cross-cultural evidence that sexual minorities are more susceptible to depressive symptomatology (including psychological distress) due, in part, to stressors associated with their sexual-minority status (e.g., Assi, Maatouk, and Jaspal 2020; Jaspal, Lopes, and Rehman 2019; Rehman, Lopes, and Jaspal 2020). In Lebanon, Lilla Orr and colleagues found that a third of their gay and bisexual male survey respondents reported previous experiences of discrimination or violence due to their sexual-minority status and that low socioeconomic status was a significant correlate of such experiences (2019, 10268). Furthermore, in their qualitative interview study Glenn Wagner, Frances Aunon, and colleagues (2013) found that Lebanese gay and bisexual men face identity struggles in relation to their sexuality due to both perceived stigma from others and internal conflict in relation to their sexuality and religion.

In addition, in their survey of 226 young gay and bisexual men in Beirut, Glenn Wagner, Bonnie Ghosh-Dastidar, and colleagues reported that almost two-thirds of their participants had experienced discrimination in the past year (2019, 513). They conducted a hierarchical multiple-regression model to predict major depression, with structural stressors (employment and legal status), sexual-minority-related stressors (discrimination, discomfort with sexual identity), and social support as predictors, and they controlled for basic sociodemographic characteristics (age, any university education, relationship status). Discomfort with one's sexuality emerged as the only statistically significant predictor of major depression. In their interview study with thirty-one gay and bisexual men in Beirut, Wagner, Aunon, and colleagues (2013) found that most of these men struggled to assimilate and accommodate their sexuality within their sense of identity due to perceived stigma and in particular to the perceived immorality of homosexuality, which they regarded as being at odds with their religion. The stigma that they faced entailed verbal harassment, ridicule, and mistreatment by significant others, including friends and family. These experiences may undermine feelings of self-esteem, continuity, and, due to perceived identity incompatibility, psychological coherence. Dominant coping strategies included social avoidance and limiting interactions with others to protect identity from actual and anticipated stigma.

Just before the COVID-19 outbreak, we conducted a survey study of 209 students in Lebanon (Assi, Maatouk, and Jaspal 2020). Our sample included gay, bisexual, and lesbian participants and heterosexual participants (as a comparator group). Sexual minorities scored lower on religiosity but higher on psychological distress and were more likely to report self-harm than heterosexual participants, all of which could be attributed, as minority stress theory would predict, to the cumulative effects of psychological stressors associated not only with sexuality but also with the social, political, and economic stressors prevalent in Lebanese society. In their cross-sectional survey of 129 Lebanese gay men, Mohamad Naamani and Fatimah El Jamil (2021) found, when controlling for demographic variables, that self-objectification and shame proneness were positively associated with disordered eating. This suggests that negative social representations of homosexuality (even among sexual minorities themselves) may contribute to poor mental health.

There is also evidence that sexual minorities who are migrants from within the MENA region may experience significant challenges in assimilating and accommodating their sexual orientation in their identity. A qualitative interview study of twenty-five gay Iranian men who had settled in the United Kingdom described the social and psychological challenges associated with being gay in Iran, such as the perception that being gay was entirely incompatible with being Muslim and that being gay represented a flaw in one's identity (Jaspal 2014). Interviewees generally reported concealing their sexual orientation from others for fear of rejection, persecution, and even prosecution. Overall, interviewees described severe, unresolved, and chronic identity threat.

Sexual minorities who are also migrants tend to face additional psychosocial stressors, such as violence and discrimination. Orr and colleagues (2019) found that gay and bisexual men born outside of Lebanon (most of whom are Syrian migrants) were much more likely than Lebanese-born gay and bisexual men to report at least one type of discrimination or violence, which was associated with having a lower socioeconomic status. Similarly, another comparative study of Lebanese-born and migrant gay and bisexual men in Lebanon found that migrant gay and bisexual men reported higher stigma in health-care and employment settings than their Lebanese-born counterparts (Maatouk, Assi, and Jaspal 2022b). In view of the risks to psychological well-being in sexual minorities in general, it is important to examine the coping resources that may or may not be available to migrant sexual minorities.

Coping, Social Support, and Activism

Dominant social psychological theories—such as minority stress theory, the social cure perspective, and, indeed, identity process theory—highlight the significance of group memberships and social support as predictors of coping effectively with psychological stress (Jetten, Haslam, and Alexander 2012; Lyons 1996; Meyer 2003).

Activism is an important dimension of coping for sexual minorities, and it is noteworthy that LGBT activism has grown considerably in Lebanon (Nagle 2018). Since 2006, sexual-minority groups in Lebanon have organized awareness- and visibility-raising events, such as the International Day against Homophobia, Biphobia, Intersexism, and Transphobia, or IDAHOBIT (see also chapter 1 in this volume). However, both Muslim and Christian religious leaders in Lebanon have repeatedly opposed LGBT pride events. For instance, the government canceled Lebanon's Pride Week commemorating the IDAHOT 2017 on the grounds that the program might lead to unrest and violence. It did not issue a public statement regarding cancellation but rather resorted to coercion and threatening language. For instance, the protection of organizers and venue owners was not guaranteed in the event of unrest and violence, which clearly undermined the long-standing notion of LGBT pride events as a "safe space" for sexual minorities in which their identities and diversity more generally can be celebrated. All of the major faith groups in Lebanon opposed the pride events. Religious factions in Lebanon converged in their condemnation of homosexuality, creating a precarious social context for sexual minorities struggling to construct and manage their identities.

Helem is one of the most prominent LGBT organizations in Lebanon.[1] It is a significant nongovernmental, nonprofit organization established in 2004 to advocate for the visibility and rights of sexual minorities in the region and against discrimination on social, cultural, and legal grounds. The organization has made a significant contribution to positive social change in Lebanon. For instance, it has helped secure the release of LGBT people following unreasonable arrest and has proactively challenged homonegativity in the media by hosting continuous workshops and roundtable events for Lebanese and international news agencies (Makarem 2011). Another organization, Mosaic, offers a holistic program to improve the health and well-being of sexual minorities in Lebanon and in the broader MENA region. Through its national presence in Lebanon and its regional networks in the MENA region, Mosaic strategically aims to encourage the peaceful coexistence of groups in society. Unfortunately, Helem, Mosaic, and other organizations have not yet succeeded in securing political and religious support to overturn Article 534 of the Lebanese Penal Code, which can be used to criminalize same-sex sexual behavior.

Help seeking (including accessing these support organizations) is influenced by many factors. First, it must be noted that although there is a high prevalence of psychological disorders in Lebanon, such as anxiety and mood disorders, formal help seeking for these disorders has been found to be relatively low even in the general population (Karam, Mneimneh, Dimassi, et al. 2008; Karam, Mneimneh, Karam, et al. 2006). For instance, in his cross-sectional survey of Lebanese college students, Hussein Wehbe (2011) found that self-stigma was associated with less favorable attitudes toward psychological counseling. Self-stigma may also preclude social engagement with other people. There is limited research into coping styles among men and women in Lebanon, but patriarchal norms emphasizing male dominance may generally make help seeking and social engagement (as coping strategies) especially difficult for men (Karam, Karam, et al. 2019).

In societies with widespread negative social representations of sexual minorities, such as Lebanese society (Obeid et al. 2020), sexual-minority

1. "Helem" stands for Himaya Lubnaniya lil Mithliyeen wal Mithliyat (Lebanese Protection for Gays and Lesbians) and means "dream."

individuals may focus on aspects of identity other than their sexuality and draw on religious coping in response to stressors associated with these other aspects of identity (such as job insecurity, COVID-19, and so on). They may need to keep their religion and sexuality separate in their identity in order to continue to protect psychological coherence. Indeed, religion is a key source of identity and belonging in Lebanon and the MENA region more generally. Yet religion and homosexuality do seem to be at odds in the eyes of many.

In our recent work, we have examined coping styles in sexual minorities (Jaspal, Assi, and Maatouk 2022). Our data indicate that religiosity is positively associated with identity resilience, which in turn suggests that feeling identified with a religious group enables individuals to derive greater feelings of self-esteem, self-efficacy, positive distinctiveness, and continuity. As predicted in identity process theory, identity resilience is in turn associated with the use of more effective and sustainable coping styles—namely, social engagement and, thus, rethinking/planning. In addition to its positive relationship with identity resilience, religiosity is associated with effective coping styles through ethnic identification. In other words, feeling identified with one's religious group is associated with feeling identified with one's ethnic group, and it is likely that having several meaningful group memberships available to one enables one to cope with psychological distress in a more effective and sustainable manner. A key finding from this research is that sexual minorities are more susceptible to psychological distress but less identified with religiosity, which appears to function as a key facilitator of effective coping in Lebanese society. Sexual minorities may therefore be less able to access effective and sustainable coping strategies and are more susceptible to unsustainable coping, namely concealment and pretense. The implications of the widespread social representation that religion and homosexuality are at odds may thus have broader ramifications for identity and well-being in sexual minorities in Lebanon.

Conclusions

In this chapter, empirical research into identity and well-being in sexual minorities in the MENA region (with a focus on Lebanon) has been discussed.

It is shown that sexual minorities in the region face multifaceted stressors, such as stigma on the basis of their sexual identity and internalized homonegativity. In many countries, negative social representations of sexual minorities are embedded in key societal institutions, such as the law, the media, and health care. Exposure to these stressors may result in threats to identity among sexual minorities; in particular, self-esteem and psychological coherence may be especially susceptible to threat. In societies characterized by political and economic instability, such as Lebanese society, stressors—both those specific to sexual minorities and those experienced in the general population—and resultant threats to identity may be accentuated, leading to poor well-being outcomes. In view of economic and religious instability, enforced migration has occurred across the entire region, and migrants who are sexual minorities appear to face greater inequalities than the general population and even than Lebanese-born sexual minorities. In the MENA region, religiosity and self-identification with religious (and ethnic) groups appear to constitute key sources of social support and thus reflect a prime coping strategy. Yet sexual minorities may have decreased access to these support networks, potentially leading to a reliance on alternative, less adaptive forms of coping. The implications for mental health and well-being may be significant, especially as countries in the MENA region continue to face social, political, and economic challenges because of both geopolitical instability and the COVID-19 crisis. We hope that this chapter will stimulate further research into identity and well-being in sexual minorities in the region, which should inform policy and practice there.

References

Abboud, Sarah, Hady Naal, Amanda Chahine, Samy Taha, Omar Harfouch, and Hossam Mahmoud. 2020. "'It's Mainly the Fear of Getting Hurt': Experiences of LGBT Individuals with the Healthcare System in Lebanon." *Annals of LGBTQ Public and Population Health* 1, no. 3: 165–85. At https://connect.springerpub.com/content/sgrlgbtq/1/3/165.

Abdessamad, Hasan M., and Omar Fattal. 2014. "Lebanese Medical Association for Sexual Health: Advancing Lesbian, Gay, Bisexual, and Transgender Health in Lebanon." *LGBT Health* 1, no. 2: 79–81. At https://doi.org/10.1089/lgbt.2013.0039.

Adamczyk, Amy, Chunrye Kim, and Margaret Schmuhl. 2018. "Newspaper Presentations of Homosexuality across Nations: Examining Differences by Religion, Economic Development, and Democracy." *Sociological Perspectives* 61, no. 3: 399–425. At https://doi.org/10.1177/0731121417724563.

Assi, Moubadda, Ismael Maatouk, and Rusi Jaspal. 2020. "Psychological Distress and Self-Harm in a Religiously Diverse Sample of University Students in Lebanon." *Mental Health, Religion & Culture* 23, no. 7: 591–605. At https://doi.org/10.1080/13674676.2020.1788524.

Awwad, Julian. 2010. "The Postcolonial Predicament of Gay Rights in the Queen Boat Affair." *Communication and Critical/Cultural Studies* 7, no. 3: 318–36. At https://doi.org/10.1080/14791420.2010.504598.

Ayyash-Abdo, Huda, and Rayane Alamuddin. 2007. "Predictors of Subjective Well-Being among College Youth in Lebanon." *Journal of Social Psychology* 147, no. 3: 265–84. At https://doi.org/10.3200/SOCP.147.3.265-284.

Barbour, Bernadette, Nina Saadeh, and Pascale R. Salameh. 2012. "Psychological Distress in Lebanese Young Adults: Constructing the Screening Tool 'BDS-22.'" *International Journal of Culture and Mental Health* 5, no. 2: 94–108. At https://doi.org/10.1080/17542863.2011.563043.

Breakwell, Glynis M. 2015. *Coping with Threatened Identities*. London: Psychology Press.

Breakwell, Glynis M., Emanuele Fino, and Rusi Jaspal. 2022. "The Identity Resilience Index: Development and Validation in Two UK Samples." *Identity* 22, no. 2: 166–82.

Breakwell, Glynis M., and Rusi Jaspal. 2022. "Coming Out, Distress and Identity Threat in Gay Men in the United Kingdom." *Sexuality Research & Social Policy* 19, no. 3: 1166–77.

Dodge, Brian, Debby Herbenick, M. Reuel Friedman, Vanessa Schick, Tsung-Chieh (Jane) Fu, Wendy Bostwick, Elizabeth Bartelt, et al. 2016. "Attitudes toward Bisexual Men and Women among a Nationally Representative Probability Sample of Adults in the United States." *PLOS ONE* 11, no. 10: art. e0164430. At https://doi.org/10.1371/journal.pone.0164430.

Feinstein, Brian A., and Christina Dyar. 2017. "Bisexuality, Minority Stress, and Health." *Current Sexual Health Reports* 9, no. 1: 42–49. At https://doi.org/10.1007/s11930-017-0096-3.

Frost, David M., and Ilan H. Meyer. 2009. "Internalized Homophobia and Relationship Quality among Lesbians, Gay Men, and Bisexuals." *Journal of Counseling Psychology* 56, no. 1: 97–109. At https://doi.org/10.1037/a0012844.

Herek, Gregory M., and Kevin A. McLemore. 2007. "Sexual Orientation and Mental Health." *Annual Review of Clinical Psychology* 3: 353–75. At https://doi.org/10.1146/annurev.clinpsy.3.022806.091510.

Hoffman, Michael. 2020. "Religion, Sectarianism, and Democracy: Theory and Evidence from Lebanon." *Political Behavior* 42, no. 4: 1169–200. At https://doi.org/10.1007/s11109-019-09538-9.

Horowitz, Juliana M., Katie Simmons, Jacob Poushter, Aaron Ponce, Cathy Barker, and Kat Devlin. 2013. *The Global Divide on Homosexuality.* Washington, DC: Pew Research Center.

Human Rights Watch. 2018. *World Report, Country: Lebanon.* New York: Human Rights Watch. At https://www.hrw.org/world-report/2018/country-chapters/lebanon.

Itani, Taha, Florian Fischer, and Janet Junqing Chu. 2018. "The Lifetime Prevalence of Exposure to Community Violence among Lebanese University Students: Association with Behavioural and Mental Health Correlates." *International Journal of Adolescence and Youth* 23, no. 2: 259–67. At https://doi.org/10.1080/02673843.2017.1337585.

Jaspal, Rusi. 2014. "Sexuality, Migration and Identity among Gay Iranian Migrants to the UK." In *Queering Religion, Religious Queers*, edited by Yvette Taylor and Ria Snowdon, 44–60. London: Routledge.

———. 2018. *Enhancing Sexual Health, Self-Identity and Wellbeing among Men Who Have Sex with Men: A Guide for Practitioners.* London: Jessica Kingsley.

———. 2024. "Islam and Homosexuality: Identity, Threat, and Sexual Well-Being among Muslim Gay Men." In *Sexuality in the Middle East and North Africa: Contemporary Issues and Challenges*, edited by J. Michael Ryan and Helen Rizzo, 137–60. Syracuse, NY: Syracuse Univ. Press.

Jaspal, Rusi, Moubadda Assi, and Ismael Maatouk. 2020. "The Potential Impact of the COVID-19 Pandemic on Mental Health Outcomes in Societies with Economic and Political Instability: The Case of Lebanon." *Mental Health Review Journal* 25, no. 3: 215–19. At https://doi.org/10.1108/MHRJ-05-2020-0027.

———. 2022. "Coping Styles in Heterosexual and Non-heterosexual Students in Lebanon: A Cross-Sectional Study." *International Journal of Social Psychology* 37, no. 1: 33–66.

Jaspal, Rusi, and Glynis M. Breakwell. 2014. *Identity Process Theory: Identity, Social Action and Social Change.* Cambridge: Cambridge Univ. Press.

———. 2022. "Identity Resilience, Social Support and Internalized Homonegativity in Gay Men." *Psychology & Sexuality* 13, no. 5: 1270–87.

Jaspal, Rusi, Barbara Lopes, and Zaqia Rehman. 2021. "A Structural Equation Model for Predicting Depressive Symptomatology in Black, Asian and Minority Ethnic Lesbian, Gay and Bisexual People in the UK." *Psychology & Sexuality* 12, no. 3: 217–34. At https://doi.org/10.1080/19419899.2019.1690560.

Jaspal, Rusi, Barbara Lopes, Liam Wignall, and Claire Bloxsom. 2021. "Predicting Sexual Risk Behaviour in British and European Union University Students in the United Kingdom." *American Journal of Sexuality Education* 16, no. 1: 140–59. At https://doi.org/10.1080/15546128.2020.1869129.

Jetten, Jolanda, Catherine Haslam, and S. Haslam Alexander, eds. 2012. *The Social Cure: Identity, Health and Well-Being.* London: Psychology Press.

Jolley, Daniel, and Rusi Jaspal. 2020. "Discrimination, HIV Conspiracy Theories and Pre-exposure Prophylaxis Acceptability in Gay Men." *Sexual Health* 17, no. 6: 525–33.

Karam, E. G., G. E. Karam, C. Farhat, L. Itani, J. Fayyad, A. N. Karam, Z. Mneimneh, et al. 2019. "Determinants of Treatment of Mental Disorders in Lebanon: Barriers to Treatment and Changing Patterns of Service Use." *Epidemiology and Psychiatric Sciences* 28, no. 6: 655–61. At https://doi.org/10.1017/S2045796018000422.

Karam, Elie G., Zeina N. Mneimneh, Hani Dimassi, John A. Fayyad, Aimee N. Karam, Soumana C. Nasser, Somnath Chatterji, et al. 2008. "Lifetime Prevalence of Mental Disorders in Lebanon: First Onset, Treatment, and Exposure to War." *PLOS Medicine* 5, no. 4: art. e61. At https://doi.org/10.1371/journal.pmed.0050061.

Karam, Elie G., Zeina N. Mneimneh, Aimee N. Karam, John A. Fayyad, Soumana C. Nasser, Somnath Chatterji, and Ronald C. Kessler. 2006. "Prevalence and Treatment of Mental Disorders in Lebanon: A National Epidemiological Survey." *The Lancet* 367, no. 9515: 1000–1006. At https://doi.org/10.1016/S0140-6736(06)68427-4.

Kazarian, Shahe S. 2005. "Family Functioning, Cultural Orientation, and Psychological Well-Being among University Students in Lebanon." *Journal of Social Psychology* 145, no. 2: 141–54. At https://doi.org/10.3200/SOCP.145.2.141-154.

Kugle, Scott Siraj al-Haqq. 2009. *Homosexuality in Islam: Critical Reflection on Gay, Lesbian, and Transgender Muslims.* Oxford: Oneworld.

Labaki, Boutros, and Khalil Abou Rjeily, eds. 1994. *Bilan des guerres du Liban: 1975–1990.* Paris: L'Harmattan.

Lopes, Barbara, and Rusi Jaspal. 2022. "Identity Processes and Psychological Wellbeing upon Recall of a Significant 'Coming Out' Experience in Lesbian,

Gay and Bisexual People." *Journal of Homosexuality* 71, no. 1: 207–31. At https://doi.org/10.1080/00918369.2022.2111536.

Lyons, Evanthia. 1996. "Coping with Social Change: Processes of Social Memory in the Reconstruction of Identities." In *Changing European Identities: Socio-psychological Analyses of Social Change*, edited by Glynis M. Breakwell and Evanthia Lyons, 31–40. Oxford: Butterworth-Heinemann.

Maatouk, Ismael, Moubadda Assi, and Rusi Jaspal. 2022a. "Self-Harm and Suicidal Ideation during the COVID-19 Outbreak in Lebanon: A Preliminary Study." *Journal of Health Research* 36, no. 4: 705–13. At https://www.emerald.com/insight/content/doi/10.1108/JHR-01-2021-0029/full/html.

———. 2022b. "Sexual Health among HIV-Negative Gay and Bisexual Men in Lebanon: A Comparison between Native and Immigrant/Refugee Communities." *Journal of Refugee Studies* 35, no. 1: 675–85. At https://doi.org/10.1093/jrs/feab079.

Maatouk, Ismael, and Rusi Jaspal. 2020. "Religion, Male Bisexuality and Sexual Health in Lebanon." In *Bisexuality, Religion, and Spirituality: Critical Perspectives*, edited by Andrew Kam-Tuk Yip and Alex Toft, 137–55. London: Routledge.

———. 2022. "Internalized Sexual Orientation Stigma and Mental Health in a Religiously Diverse Sample of Gay and Bisexual Men in Lebanon." *Journal of Homosexuality* 70, no. 8: 1441–60. At https://doi.org/10.1080/00918369.2022.2030617.

Makarem, Ghassan. 2011. "The Story of HELEM." *Journal of Middle East Women's Studies* 7, no. 3: 98–112.

Marques, Ana Cristina, Salma Talaat, and J. Michael Ryan. 2024. "The (Im)Possibilities of Being Trans in the MENA Region." In *Sexuality in the Middle East and North Africa: Contemporary Issues and Challenges*, edited by J. Michael Ryan and Helen Rizzo, 161–94. Syracuse, NY: Syracuse Univ. Press.

Meyer, Ilan H. 2003. "Prejudice, Social Stress, and Mental Health in Lesbian, Gay and Bisexual Populations: Conceptual Issues and Research Evidence." *Psychological Bulletin* 129: 674–97. At https://doi.org/10.1037/0033-2909.129.5.674.

Michli, Sara, and Fatimah El Jamil. 2022. "Internalized Homonegativity and the Challenges of Having Same-Sex Desires in the Lebanese Context: A Study Examining Risk and Protective Factors." *Journal of Homosexuality* 69, no. 1: 75–100. At https://doi.org/10.1080/00918369.2020.1809893.

Movahedi, M. J. 2017. "Gay-Bashing in Jordan—by the Government." *Human Rights Watch*, Aug. 30. At https://www.hrw.org/news/2017/08/30/gay-bashing-jordan-government.

Naal, Hady, Sarah Abboud, Omar Harfoush, and Hossam Mahmoud. 2020. "Examining the Attitudes and Behaviors of Health-Care Providers toward LGBT Patients in Lebanon." *Journal of Homosexuality* 67, no. 13: 1902–19. At https://doi.org/10.1080/00918369.2019.1616431.

Naamani, Mohamad, and Fatimah El Jamil. 2021. "Correlates of Disordered Eating among Gay Men in Lebanon." *Eating Behaviors* 40: art. 101477. At https://doi.org/10.1016/j.eatbeh.2021.101477.

Nagle, John. 2018. "Crafting Radical Opposition or Reproducing Homonormativity? Consociationalism and LGBT Rights Activism in Lebanon." *Journal of Human Rights* 17, no. 1: 75–88. At https://doi.org/10.1080/14754835.2016.1246956.

Obeid, Sahar, Chadia Haddad, Wael Salame, Nelly Kheir, and Souheil Hallit. 2020. "Correlates of Homophobic Attitudes in Lebanon: Results of a Cross-Sectional Study." *Journal of Homosexuality* 67, no. 6: 844–62. At https://doi.org/10.1080/00918369.2018.1557954.

Orr, Lilla, Fatma M. Shebl, Robert Heimer, Kaveh Khoshnood, Russell Barbour, Danielle Khouri, Elie Aaraj, et al. 2019. "Violence and Discrimination against Men Who Have Sex with Men in Lebanon: The Role of International Displacement and Migration." *Journal of Interpersonal Violence* 36, nos. 21–22: 10267–84. At https://doi.org/10.1177/0886260519884684.

Ozbay, Fatih, Douglas C. Johnson, Eleni Dimoulas, C. A. Morgan III, Dennis Charney, and Steven Southwick. 2007. "Social Support and Resilience to Stress: From Neurobiology to Clinical Practice." *Psychiatry* (Edgmont) 4, no. 5: 35–40.

Rehman, Zaqia, Barbara Lopes, and Rusi Jaspal. 2020. "Predicting Self-Harm in an Ethnically Diverse Sample of Lesbian, Gay and Bisexual People in the United Kingdom." *International Journal of Social Psychiatry* 66, no. 4: 349–60. At https://doi.org/10.1177/0020764020908889.

Roscoe, Will, and Stephen O. Murray, eds. 1997. *Islamic Homosexualities: Culture, History and Literature*. New York: New York Univ. Press.

Sawaya, Aya Touma, and Antoine Beayno. 2021. "The Representation of LGBTQ+ Individuals on Television in Lebanon" (letter to the editor). *Journal of Gay & Lesbian Mental Health* 25, no. 2: 128–31. At https://doi.org/10.1080/19359705.2020.1843584.

Schuck, Kelly D., and Becky J. Liddle. 2001. "Religious Conflicts Experienced by Lesbian, Gay, and Bisexual Individuals." *Journal of Gay and Lesbian Psychotherapy* 5, no. 2: 63–82. At https://doi.org/10.1300/J236v05n02_07.

Sellick, Scott M., and Alan D. Edwardson. 2007. "Screening New Cancer Patients for Psychological Distress Using the Hospital Anxiety and Depression Scale." *Psycho-Oncology* 16: 534–42. At https://doi.org/10.1002/pon.1085.

Simmons, Heather. 2010. "Dying for Love: Homosexuality in the Middle East." *Human Rights and Human Welfare* 10, no. 1: 160–72. At https://digitalcommons.du.edu/hrhw/vol10/iss1/30.

Ungar, Mark. 2002. "State Violence and LGBT Rights." In *Violence and Politics: Globalization's Paradox*, edited by Kenton Worcester, Sally Avery Bermanzohn, and Mark Ungar, 48–66. New York: Routledge.

Wagner, Glenn J., Frances M. Aunon, Rachel L. Kaplan, Rita Karam, Danielle Khouri, Johnny Tohme, and Jacques Mokhbat. 2013. "Sexual Stigma, Psychological Well-Being and Social Engagement among Men Who Have Sex with Men in Beirut, Lebanon." *Culture, Health & Sexuality* 15, no. 5: 570–82. At https://doi.org/10.1080/13691058.2013.775345.

Wagner, Glenn J., Bonnie Ghosh-Dastidar, Cynthia El Khoury, Carol Abi Ghanem, Eli Balan, Susan Kegeles, Matt G. Mutchler, et al. 2019. "Major Depression among Young Men Who Have Sex with Men in Beirut, and Its Association with Structural and Sexual Minority–Related Stressors, and Social Support." *Sexuality Research and Social Policy* 16, no. 4: 513–20. At https://doi.org/10.1007/s13178-018-0352-y.

Wehbe, Hussein. 2011. "Predictors of Attitudes toward Psychological Counseling among Lebanese College Students." *Graduate Student Journal of Psychology* 13: 25–29.

World Health Organization (WHO). 2010. *A Conceptual Framework for Action on the Social Determinants of Health*. Geneva: WHO.

———. 2013. *Mental Health Action Plan 2013–2020*. Geneva: WHO Document Production Services. At https://www.who.int/publications/i/item/9789241506021.

Zaatari, Zeina. 2024. "Sexual Rights Movement(s): Problematics of Visibility." In *Sexuality in the Middle East and North Africa: Contemporary Issues and Challenges*, edited by J. Michael Ryan and Helen Rizzo, 23–66. Syracuse, NY: Syracuse Univ. Press.

Rethinking Sexuality in the Middle East and North Africa

Helen Rizzo and J. Michael Ryan

In this volume, the chapters provide regional perspectives on some of the important institutions, movements, and issues related to sexuality(-ies) in the Middle East and North Africa (MENA) region, such as sexuality and the law, sexual rights movements, Islam and homosexuality, sexual and reproductive health, sexualities and the internet, and homonationalism. They highlight the diversity across the MENA region in terms of the legal status of sexuality, the lived realities of sexual minorities, the influence of religion and technology, and activist engagement with and political resistance to issues of sexual equality. The chapters also demonstrate the importance of taking an intersectional approach when discussing the institutions and issues focused on. Understanding sexuality in the MENA region is not complete without recognizing its intersections with religious status, social class, age, gender, race, ethnicity, language, family status, and access to technology, among many other factors. Although there is some general sense of a homogenous approach, we want the readers of this volume to conclude that the MENA region is not monolithic and that the cultures and societies in this region are not unchanging and static, especially when it comes to sexuality.

One of the enduring popular images of the MENA region is that its societies and cultures are among the most oppressive, if not the most oppressive, in relation to sexuality. Most scholarship available to date unfortunately confirms this perception. That said, although there are still enduring signs of sexual oppression in the region, there are also signs that sexual equality has become an increasingly important issue to many in region, not simply to women and sexual minorities.

We have argued elsewhere that "classic patriarchy and the ideal of the patriarchal gender contract is becoming less and less a reality in the MENA region due to social changes that have taken place, particularly since the 1960s" (Ryan and Rizzo 2020, 237). As patriarchy breaks down, so too, one can assume, will ideals and instantiations supporting sexual inequality. Other factors, including increased urbanization, modernization, and the spread of access to technology, are also poised to increase greater acceptance for or, at a minimum, tolerance of varying sexual practices and ideologies. As women gain increasing autonomy, and as same-sex marriages fail to destroy modern society, there are promising signs that sexual equality is on the rise, if ever so slowly, even in what is arguably the most sexually oppressive region of the world today.

The Future of Sexualities in the MENA Region

The future of how sexualities are understood, recognized, and able to be lived in the MENA region is uncertain at best, precarious at worst. On the one hand, although the region has seen advances in gender equality and an entrenched battle against the oppressive forces of patriarchy (Ryan and Rizzo 2020), advances in sexual equality have occurred more slowly and in many instances taken a step backward. On the other hand, although the region arguably had a more monolithic approach to sexualities in previous eras, recent decades have seen an increasing diversity in responses to issues of sexuality. The future of sexualities in the region will depend on a number of factors, including local and global politics, the spread and use of technology, continued activism, advances in scholarship, military intervention, and increased contact with and knowledge of the lived experiences of others.

Benjamin Barber examines in his now classic work *Jihad vs. McWorld* (1995) the impact of the struggle between globalization and corporate control of the political process (McWorld), on the one hand, and traditional values in the form of extreme nationalism and/or religious orthodoxy, on the other. Barber's work is an attempt to instantiate the more theoretical debates of homogenization and heterogenization. Although he argues for the power of small, democratic, local institutions to wage battle, he ultimately seems to argue that McWorld has the better chance to win "the struggle." Achieving this success might seem daunting in the realm of many aspects of everyday life, but if we apply this model to the realm of sexual equality, then the situation in the MENA region perhaps looks brighter. There are widespread indicators that "McWorld" is moving increasingly in the direction of greater sexual equality—for example, in issues related to empowering women (Elliott 2008); recognizing legal unions between two people in love, regardless of their medically assigned sex at birth (Lee and Mutz 2019); and allowing individuals to legally and safely identify as the gender of their choice (Ryan 2018). That said, the forces of "jihad" have responded with an intensified battle against these advances (for example, Brunei briefly relegalized the stoning of people caught engaging in same-sex activities [Tan 2019], and there has been a recent resurgence in the crackdown on gays in Egypt [Ghoshal 2018b]). The battle between "jihad" and McWorld will no doubt continue in the realm of sexual equality for the foreseeable future.

The global clash for sexual equality is already playing out in a number of international arenas. MENA state-level opposition to LGBTQ+ rights on the international stage has often come through the states' participation in the Organisation of Islamic Cooperation (OIC). The OIC is the second-largest intergovernmental organization in the world (after the United Nations), representing fifty-seven states and more than 1.8 billion people. It claims to be "the collective voice of the Muslim world" and "endeavors to safeguard and protect the interests of the Muslim world in the spirit of promoting international peace and harmony among various people of the world."[1] Unfortunately, the "various people of the world" alluded to clearly do not include LGBTQ+ individuals because the OIC has been at the forefront of opposing LGBTQ+ rights and protections at the international level (Blitt 2016). For example, in 2012 the United Nations Human Rights Council held its first meeting on discrimination based on sexual orientation and gender identity. During the meeting, Pakistan, speaking

1. From the OIC website at https://www.oic-oci.org/.

on behalf of the OIC, stated, "Licentious behaviour promoted under the so-called concept of sexual orientation is against the fundamental teachings of various religions, including Islam. From this perspective, legitimizing homosexuality and other personal sexual behaviors in the name of sexual orientation is unacceptable" (clip included in Solash 2012). In another example, in 2016 Egypt submitted a letter to the United Nations General Assembly on behalf of the OIC to block the involvement of eleven LGBTQ+ organizations in an upcoming high-level meeting on ending HIV/AIDS.

The expanding availability of the internet is another area likely to affect the future of sexualities in the region. For example, Internet World Stats (2022) found that as of July 2022 internet penetration in the Middle East was at 79.7 percent, well above the global average of 68.6 percent. That said, there was considerable variation among countries in the region, with the highest internet penetration level in Bahrain (100 percent) and the lowest level in Yemen (27 percent). The importance of the internet in spreading "counter" ideologies is most clearly demonstrated by the number of countries that block certain websites and the dominant role social media played in the revolutions of the Arab Spring. Research has also shown the particular importance of the internet in accessing information on sexuality (Denney and Tewksbury 2017), including on issues related to sexual health (Freeman et al. 2018), the identity formation of LGBTQ+ individuals (Ryan 2013, 2019), and activism in response to sexual violence (Linder et al. 2016; Rizzo, Price, and Meyer 2012). As internet access continues to spread, it seems likely that so, too, will its impact on sexualities.

The continued role of activists will also play a significant role in the future of sexualities in the region (see the Human Rights Watch report *Audacity in Adversity* [Ghoshal 2018a] for an overview of the triumphs and adversities faced by activists in the region). A number of organizations in the region are productively engaged in sexual activism, including Helem, the Arab Foundation for Freedoms and Equality, the Coalition for Sexual and Bodily Rights in Muslim Societies, the Egyptian Initiative for Personal Rights, and the Baghdad Women's Association. These groups and many others have been at the forefront of pushing for greater sexual equality in the region. Even more encouraging is that recent years, especially since the Arab Spring, have seen an increase in not only the number of organizations committed to sexual equality but also the number of activists and everyday individuals taking part in those organizations.

Another important factor in the move toward greater sexual equality will be the growing amount of scholarship dedicated to the issue. Until recently, there has been a relative dearth of academic scholarship that critically examines sexual issues in the region. This trend has started to change, and we are now seeing the beginnings of an explosion of interest and critically minded research beginning to appear. For example, the International Men and Gender Equality Survey, completed in 2017, was the largest survey in the MENA region to explore issues of masculinity, including those related to sexuality (El Feki, Heilman, and Barker 2017). This kind of innovative scholarship is allowing researchers access to data that were never available before and prompting innovative research possibilities to better explore the actual state of sexualities in the region. As scholarship continues to increase, so too will what we know about sexualities in the region, and as what we know about sexualities in the region increases, we can anticipate that so too will activism related to greater sexual equality, as will the backlashes to it.

One of the key potentials for scholarship is to help better explore exactly how sexuality is understood in the region. Serena Tolino has argued that "in the Middle East two representations of homosexuality currently coexist: one representation, which is more traditional, approaches homosexuality as an issue of homosexual acts, while the other defines homosexuality as a sexual identity that stresses emotional components" (2014, 86). One could broaden Tolino's argument to add how homosexuality is understood merely as attraction (even without behavior or identity) and, more generally, to include how sexuality is understood in a more general sense. Is it perceived as based on behaviors? Attractions? Identities? Some combination thereof? Answers to these fundamental questions will be necessary to better understand what sexuality means to those living in the region, how it is experienced in everyday life, why there is such opposition to its varied forms, and what can be done to bring greater equality around various sexuality-related issues.

The MENA region's position in the larger global economic and political structure will also be a key factor in deciding the fate of sexualities in the region. International actors, most notably the United States, have often overlooked gross human rights violations related to sexuality even as they have cited such violations as cause for invasion. For example, the United States has maintained close ties with Saudi Arabia despite that country's blatant oppression of many forms of gender and sexual expressions. Yet at the same time it cites the alleged oppression of women and female sexuality as one of several competing rationales to invade several countries in the region, including Iraq and Afghanistan. Few would argue that it is not the control of global energy reserves that has been the primary factor in both overlooking and overblowing particular issues. It will thus be interesting to see how the international community changes its stance to human rights in general and to sexual rights in particular in the region once the region is no longer a leading source of global energy.

Concluding Thoughts

Country-level signals concerning sexual equality have been mixed. For example, a survey released by the Arab Barometer research network in 2019 revealed that most people in the region supported the right of a woman to become prime minister or president (cited in Dale et al. 2019). Simultaneously, the majority of those surveyed, including women, felt that men should have the final say on all domestic matters. As Aseel Alayli of Arab Barometer noted, "Opinions regarding women's rights and the[ir] roles in society are progressing unevenly in the Middle East and North Africa. There is little agreement that women should play equal roles in public and private life" (qtd. in Reuters 2019). Acceptance of homosexuality has also progressed unevenly. One survey found that acceptance varied between a low of 5 percent in Palestinian territories to a "high" of 26 percent in Algeria (Statista 2020). It is also noteworthy that in most MENA countries honor killings were seen as more acceptable than homosexuality.

Barber's (1995) image of "jihad versus McWorld" is a useful one for understanding how the future of sexuality will play out in the MENA region. As the world becomes increasingly interconnected, will the forces of McWorld, those associated with greater sexual equality, win out? Or will those associated with a firm, determined commitment to traditional roles, values, practices, and attitudes be the victor? Or, as is arguably happening with other global issues, will there be some compromised, blended situation resulting from the conflict between the two? Our hope is for greater sexual equality. The future reality has yet to be written.

In sum, we hope that we have provided useful reviews of the literature on important topics from a regional perspective for scholars in the field of women's, gender, and sexuality studies in the MENA region. We also hope that we have provided important insights on social change in the MENA region based on an intersectional perspective from diverse societies for undergraduate and graduate students as well as for interested lay readers. We hope this work will provide a solid foundation for those who will do further in-depth research on the ever-changing dynamics of sexuality in the contemporary Middle East and North Africa.

References

Barber, Benjamin. 1995. *Jihad vs. McWorld: How Globalism and Tribalism Are Reshaping the World.* New York: Times Books.

Blitt, Robert C. 2016. "Equality and Nondiscrimination through the Eyes of an International Religious Organization: The Organization of Islamic Cooperation's (OIC) Response to Women's Rights." *Wisconsin International Law Journal* 34, no. 4: 755–822.

Dale, Becky, Irene de la Torre Arenas, Clara Guibourg, and Tom de Castella. 2019. "The Arab World in Seven Charts: Are Arabs Turning Their Backs on Religion?" *BBC News*, June 24. At https://www.bbc.com/news/world-middle-east-48703377.

Denney, Andrew S., and Richard Tewksbury. 2017. "ICTs and Sexuality." In *Handbook of Technology, Crime, and Justice*, edited by M. R. McGuire and Thomas J. Holt, 113–33. London: Routledge.

Elliott, Catherine M., ed. 2008. *Global Empowerment of Women: Responses to Globalization and Politicized Religion.* London: Routledge.

El Feki, Shereen, Brian Heilman, and Gary Barker, eds. 2017. *Understanding Masculinities: Results from the International Men and Gender Equality Survey (IMAGES)—Middle East and North Africa.* Cairo: United Nations Women; Washington, DC: Promundo-US.

Freeman, Georgia, Lucy Watchirs Smith, Anna McNulty, and Basil Donovan. 2018. "Sexual Health and Students: The Pathways Travelled by Those with Sexual Health Concerns." *Sexual Health* 15, no. 1: 76–78.

Ghoshal, Neela. 2018a. *Audacity in Adversity: LGBT Activism in the Middle East and North Africa*. Washington, DC: Human Rights Watch. At https://www.hrw.org/sites/default/files/media_2020/07/lgbt_mena0418_web.pdf.

———. 2018b. "More Arrests in Egypt's LGBT Crackdown, but No International Outcry." *Human Rights Watch*, Jan. 22. At https://www.hrw.org/news/2018/01/22/more-arrests-egypts-lgbt-crackdown-no-international-outcry.

Internet World Stats. 2022. "Internet Usage in the Middle East" (table). At https://www.internetworldstats.com/stats5.htm.

Lee, Hye-Yon, and Diana C. Mutz. 2019. "Changing Attitudes toward Same-Sex Marriage: A Three-Wave Panel Study." *Political Behavior* 41, no. 3: 701–22.

Linder, Chris, Jess S. Myers, Colleen Riggle, and Marvette Lacy. 2016. "From Margins to Mainstream: Social Media as a Tool for Campus Sexual Violence Activism." *Journal of Diversity in Higher Education* 9, no. 3: 231–44.

Reuters. 2019. "Middle East Survey Sees Patchy Progress in Views on Women's and LGBT Rights." *VOA News*, June 25. At https://www.voanews.com/middle-east/middle-east-survey-sees-patchy-progress-views-womens-and-lgbt-rights.

Rizzo, Helen, Anne M. Price, and Katherine Meyer. 2012. "Anti–Sexual Harassment Campaign in Egypt." *Mobilization* 17, no. 4: 457–75.

Ryan, J. Michael. 2013. *Improving Survey Measurement Questions for Sexual Minorities and the Trans Population: Toward an Understanding of the Socially Constructed Nature of the Trans Life Course*. Ann Arbor, MI: ProQuest.

———. 2018. "Gender Identity Laws: The Legal Status of Global Sex/Gender Identity Recognition." *LGBTQ Policy Journal* 8, no. 1: 3–16.

———. 2019. "Communicating Trans Identity: Toward an Understanding of the Selection and Significance of Gender Identity–Based Terminology." *Journal of Language and Sexuality* 8, no. 2: 221–41.

Ryan, J. Michael, and Helen Rizzo. 2020. "Rethinking Gender in the Contemporary Middle East and North Africa." In *Gender in the Middle East and North Africa: Contemporary Issues and Challenges*, edited by J. Michael Ryan and Helen Rizzo, 235–38. Boulder, CO: Lynne-Rienner.

Solash, Richard. 2012. "Historic UN Session on Gay Rights Marked by Arab Walkout." Radio Free Europe/Radio Liberty, Mar. 7. At https://www.rferl.org/a/arab_states_leave_un_gay-rights_debate/24508579.html.

Statista. 2020. "Share of Arab Respondents Who Believe Homosexuality Is Acceptable across the Middle East and North Africa (MENA) as of 2019." Graph, Statista Research Department, Aug. 26. At https://www.statista.com/statistics/1019666/mena-arab-respondents-on-homosexuality/.

Tan, Yvette. 2019. "Brunei Implements Stoning to Death under Anti-LGBT Laws." *BBC News*, Apr. 3. At https://www.bbc.com/news/world-asia-47769964.

Tolino, Serena. 2014. "Homosexuality in the Middle East: An Analysis of Dominant and Competitive Discourses." *Deportate, esule, profughe (DEP)* 25: 72–91.

Contributor Biographies

Index

Contributor Biographies

Inas Abdelwahed is a physician, public-health professional, and Kofi Annan Global Health Leadership fellow. She has a master's degree in public health from the American University of Beirut. She has ten years of practical experience in public health in the MENA region. She has worked in the public and private sectors as well as with international nongovernmental organizations. Inas has worked closely with different United Nations (UN) agencies, such as the UN Human Rights Council and the UN Program on HIV and AIDS, as well as with the World Health Organization. She has experience in managing projects, designing training curricula, and conducting research projects. She is experienced in the fields of sexual and reproductive health, HIV/AIDS, mental health, and health in humanitarian crises. She has currently shifted to the field of digital health, in particular the quality assurance and patient safety of telehealth services and chronic-disease management. In addition, Inas has research experience in both quantitative and qualitative methodologies, systematic reviews, content analysis, and research ethics.

Moubadda Assi is a technical officer for emerging infectious diseases at the World Health Organization Country Office in Lebanon. He previously supported different humanitarian and health emergencies in the eastern Mediterranean region, including Syria, Yemen, and Lebanon. He maintained his involvement in academic research and developed a particular interest in identity construction and social representations among sexual minorities during his previous role as technical officer at the national AIDS Program in Lebanon.

Maryam Hisham Fouad is adjunct faculty of sociology at the American University in Cairo, where she has been teaching since the fall of 2020. She holds a bachelor of arts degree in political science with a specialization in international relations and a minor in history from the American University in Cairo, where she graduated with honors in 2017. In 2020, she earned her master of arts degree in sociology and anthropology from the same institution, graduating with highest honors. Her research interests lie in gender issues in Egypt and the Middle East, which she incorporates into her teaching of several sociology courses as well as her work with marginalized groups in the development sector.

Gilly Hartal is a senior lecturer in the Gender Studies Program at Bar-Ilan University. Her research and teaching interests include geographies of sexualities and gender, queer theory, qualitative methodologies, and, specifically, the production of spatial belonging through discourses of inclusion and exclusion along national, ethnic, gendered, class, and sexual trajectories. She has published in journals such as *Urban Studies*, *Environment and Planning C: Politics and Space*, the *Journal of Homosexuality*, *Social and Cultural Geography*, *Gender, Place & Culture*, *Sexualities*, and the *Journal of Rural Studies*.

Rusi Jaspal is pro vice chancellor (research and knowledge exchange) and professor of psychology at the University of Brighton in the United Kingdom. He is the author or editor of six books and has produced hundreds of peer-reviewed journal articles and book chapters, many of which focus on aspects of identity and psychological well-being.

Ismaël Maatouk is a dermatologist from Beirut, Lebanon. His main field of research concerns sexually transmitted infections (STIs) and HIV and their key populations, with ten years of experience in this field. He worked in Beirut in private practice, in the National AIDS Program at the Ministry of Health, and in the World Health Organization (WHO) Country Office on several HIV and STIs activities, including capacity building, Pre-Exposure Prophylaxis implementation, HIV self-test implementation, maintenance and enhancement, and program review. In 2022, he joined the Global HIV, Hepatitis, and STIs Programs in WHO headquarters as an STIs cross-cutting technical officer.

Ana Cristina Marques earned her PhD in sociology from ISCTE–University Institute of Lisbon. She has worked as a lecturer and a researcher in Portugal, the United Kingdom, and the Kurdistan region of Iraq. She is currently the research coordinator for the project Conditions of Women in Iraq being conducted for the Centre française de recherches sur l'Irak. Her research interests include gender, family, intimacy, and personal lives.

Orna Sasson-Levy is professor in the Department of Sociology and Anthropology as well as in the Program of Gender Studies at Bar-Ilan University and serves as Bar-Ilan's diversity and gender-equity commissioner. Her research and teaching interests include feminist theory, militarism and gender, Israeli ethnicities, and new social movements. She has published numerous articles in major refereed journals, including *Gender & Society*, the *Sociological Quarterly*, and the *British Journal of Sociology*, and she has authored four books.

Salma Talaat is a Cairo-based lawyer and currently works at a renowned regional law firm, where she provides corporate and commercial legal services to clients in various sectors. She is a dual-degree graduate after pursuing and obtaining a political science degree from the American University in Cairo simultaneously with a bachelor of laws from Cairo University. Ms. Talaat has also published and coauthored publications in the fields of law, political science, and development.

Grant Walsh-Haines is a former faculty member of the Political Science Department at South Texas College. He was also an adjunct in the Gender and Women's Studies Program at the University of Wyoming for more than ten years. Now unaffiliated, Grant works in editing and publishing roles on projects that promote national and global understanding of difference.

Zeina Zaatari is director of the Arab American Cultural Center as well as adjunct faculty in anthropology and faculty fellow in the Honors College at the University of Illinois at Chicago. She is the author of "Sarah Hegazy and the Struggle for Freedom" (2020), and her recent publications include two coedited books: *Routledge Handbook on Women of the Middle East* (with Suad Joseph, 2023) and *The Politics of Engaged Gender Research in the Arab Region: Feminist Fieldwork and Knowledge Production* (with Suad Joseph and Lena Meari, 2022). Zeina is associate editor for the Middle East and Africa for the *Encyclopedia of Women and Islamic Cultures*. She is a cofounder and elected board member of the Women Human Rights Defenders–MENA Coalition as well as president-elect of the board of the Association for Middle East Women's Studies (2024–26).

Index

J. Michael Ryan is professor-researcher (*docente-investigador*) at Pontificia Universidad Católica del Perú. After receiving his PhD in sociology from the University of Maryland, he has held academic positions at leading universities across five continents. Before returning to academia, Dr. Ryan worked as a research methodologist at the National Center for Health Statistics (which is part of the Centers for Disease Control and Prevention) in Washington, DC, where he led multiple projects aimed at improving national statistical survey methodology. Dr. Ryan is coauthor (with George Ritzer) of *The McDonaldization of Society*, 11th ed. (forthcoming), and the highly successful textbook *Introduction to Sociology*, 6th ed. (2023). He is also the author (with Serena Nanda) of *COVID-19: Social Inequalities and Human Possibilities* (2022). Dr. Ryan has edited multiple volumes, including *Gender in the Middle East and North Africa: Contemporary Issues and Challenges* (with Helen Rizzo, 2020).

Helen Rizzo is associate professor of sociology in the Sociology, Egyptology, and Anthropology Department at the American University in Cairo (AUC), and she received her PhD in sociology from The Ohio State University in 2000. She is also the academic director of the Tomorrow's Leaders Gender Scholars undergraduate scholarship program and director of the Cynthia Nelson Institute for Gender and Women's Studies at AUC. She has numerous publications on women's rights in Kuwait. Her book *Islam, Democracy and the Status of Women: The Case of Kuwait* was published in 2005, and she is the coeditor (with J. Michael Ryan) of *Gender in the Middle East and North Africa: Contemporary Issues and Challenges* (2020). Her more recent projects focus on activism against public sexual violence in Egypt, including issues of masculinities.

Printed in the USA
CPSIA information can be obtained
at www.ICGtesting.com
CBHW020518170924
14319CB00004B/4

9 780815 604907